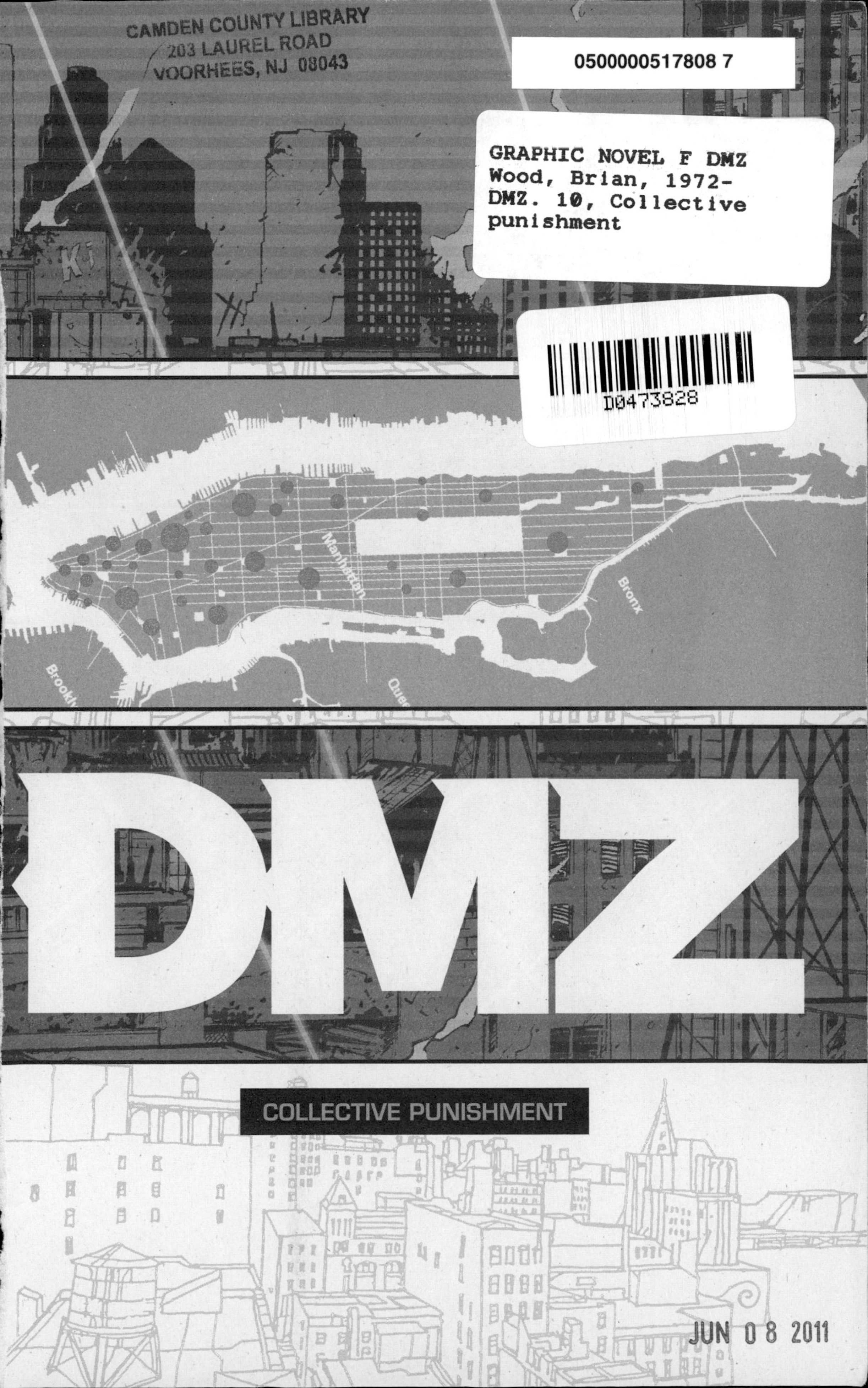
Manhattan
Bronx
DMZ
COLLECTIVE PUNISHMENT

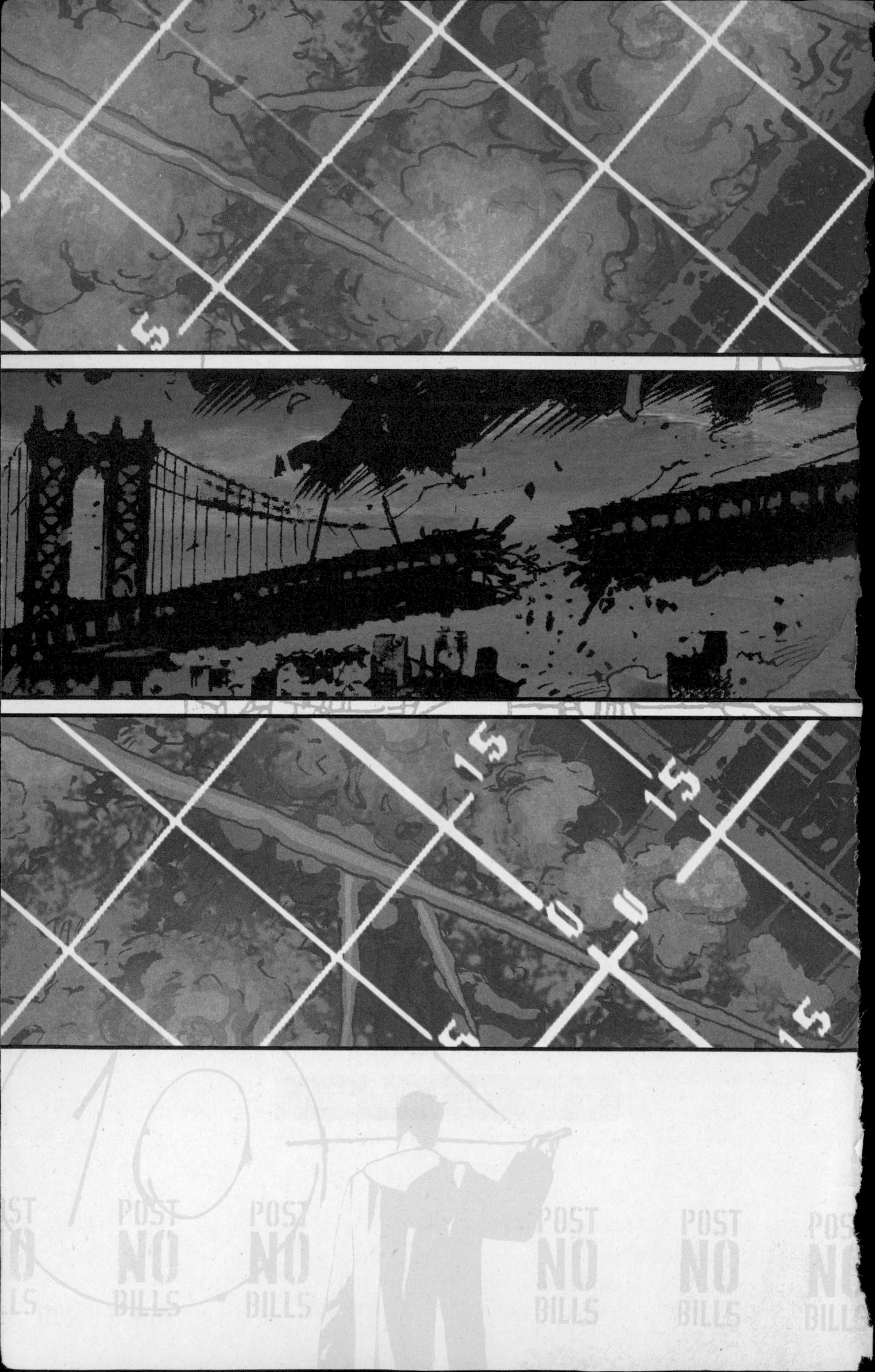
POST NO BILLS
POST NO BILLS
POST NO BILLS
POST NO BILLS

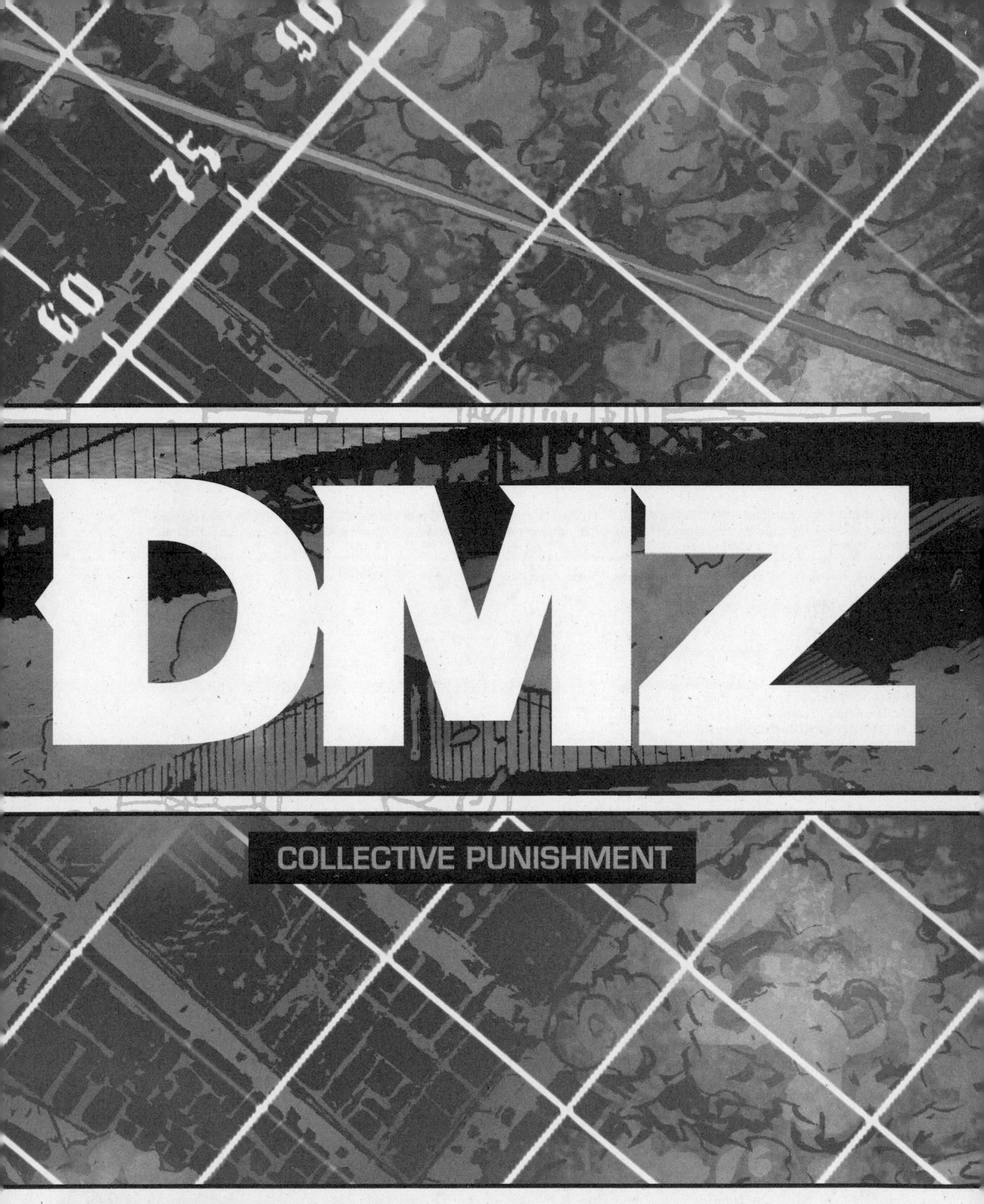

DMZ

COLLECTIVE PUNISHMENT

BRIAN WOOD WRITER

ANDREA MUTTI *FIVE HOURS UNDER FIRE* **NATHAN FOX** *GHOST PROTECTOR*
CLIFF CHIANG *AMINA, MOTHER OF ONE* **DANIJEL ZEZELJ** *A DECADE ON THE WALL*
DAVID LAPHAM *MATTY'S WAR*
ARTISTS

JEROMY COX COLORIST **JARED K. FLETCHER** LETTERER

COVER BY **BRIAN WOOD**

ORIGINAL SERIES COVERS BY **JOHN PAUL LEON**
DMZ CREATED BY **BRIAN WOOD** AND **RICCARDO BURCHIELLI**

Karen Berger SVP-Executive Editor **Will Dennis** Editor-original series **Mark Doyle** Associate Editor-original series
Bob Harras Group Editor-Collected Editions **Robbin Brosterman** Design Director-Books

DC COMICS

Diane Nelson President **Dan DiDio** and **Jim Lee** Co-Publishers **Geoff Johns** Chief Creative Officer **Patrick Caldon** EVP-Finance and Administration
John Rood EVP-Sales, Marketing and Business Development **Amy Genkins** SVP-Business and Legal Affairs **Steve Rotterdam** SVP-Sales and Marketing
John Cunningham VP-Marketing **Terri Cunningham** VP-Managing Editor **Alison Gill** VP-Manufacturing **David Hyde** VP-Publicity
Sue Pohja VP-Book Trade Sales **Alysse Soll** VP-Advertising and Custom Publishing **Bob Wayne** VP-Sales **Mark Chiarello** Art Director

Logo and front cover designed by Brian Wood
Publication design by Robbie Biederman

SUSTAINABLE FORESTRY INITIATIVE
www.sfiprogram.org
Certified Fiber Sourcing
www.sfiprogram.org
Fiber used in this product line meets the
sourcing requirements of the SFI program.
www.sfiprogram.org SGS-SFICOC-0130

DMZ: COLLECTIVE PUNISHMENT

DC Comics, 1700 Broadway, New York, NY 10019. A Warner Bros. Entertainment Company. Printed in USA. First Printing. ISBN: 978-1-4012-3150-7

Library of Congress Cataloging-in-Publication Data

Wood, Brian, 1972-
DMZ. Collective punishment / writer, Brian Wood ; pencils, Andrea
Mutti.
    p. cm. -- (DMZ ; v. 10)
"Originally published in single magazine form as DMZ #55-59."
ISBN 978-1-4012-3150-7 (softcover)
1. Militia movements--United States--Comic books, strips, etc. 2.
Graphic novels. I. Mutti, Andrea, 1973- II. Title. III. Title:
Collective punishment.
PN6727.W59D556 2011
741.5'973--dc22
                    2011008935

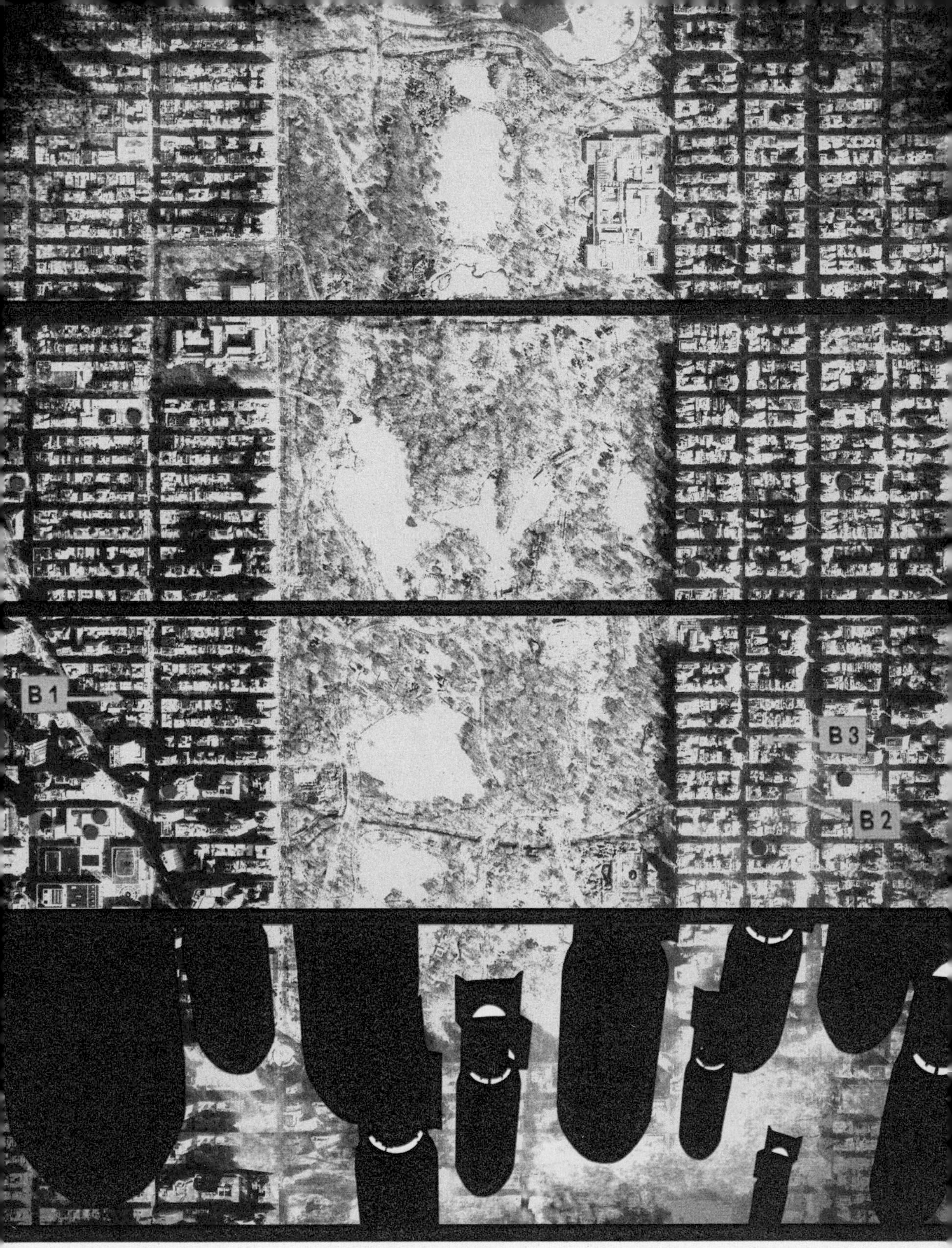
B1
B3
B2

FIVE HOURS UNDER FIRE

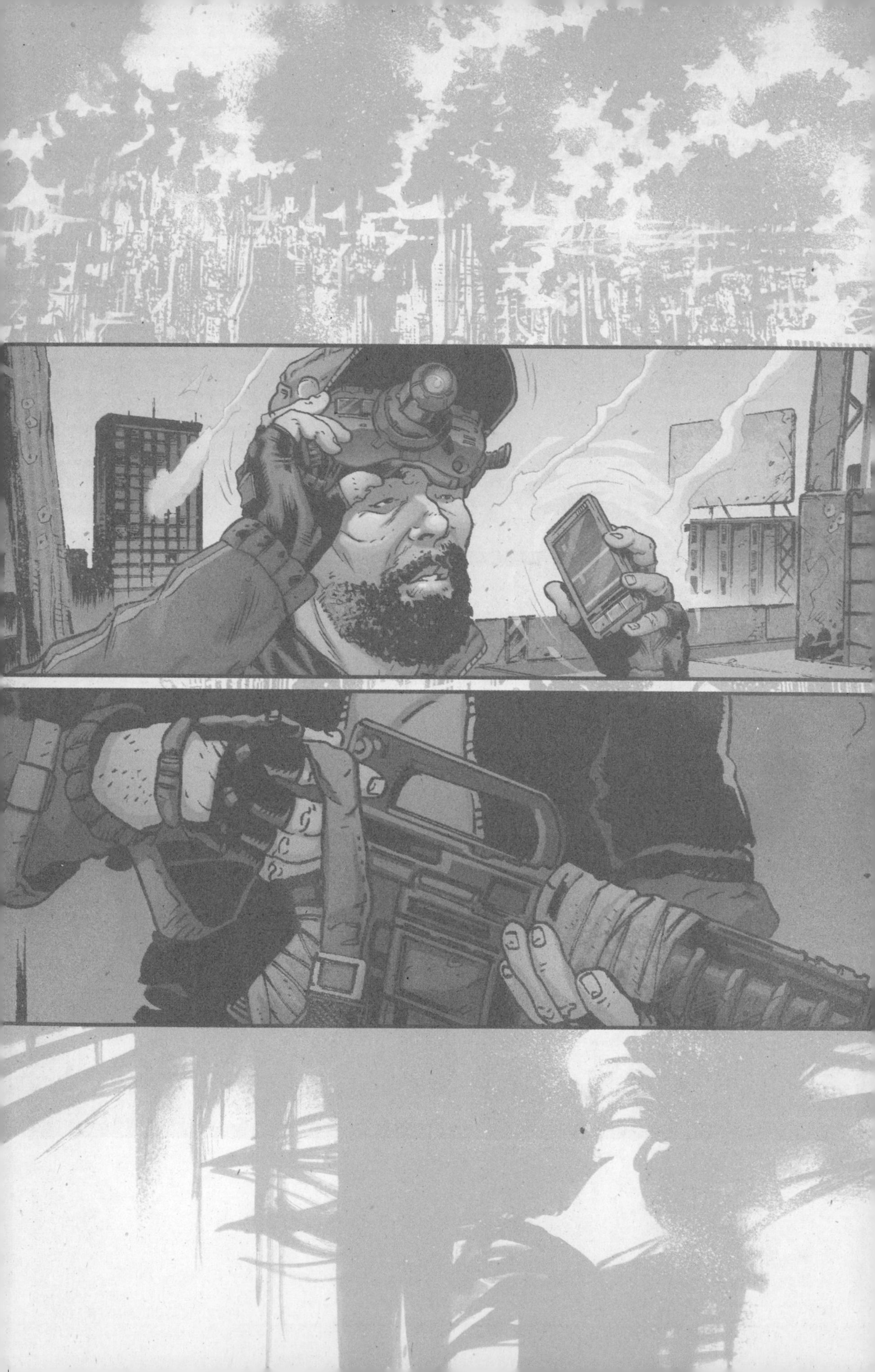

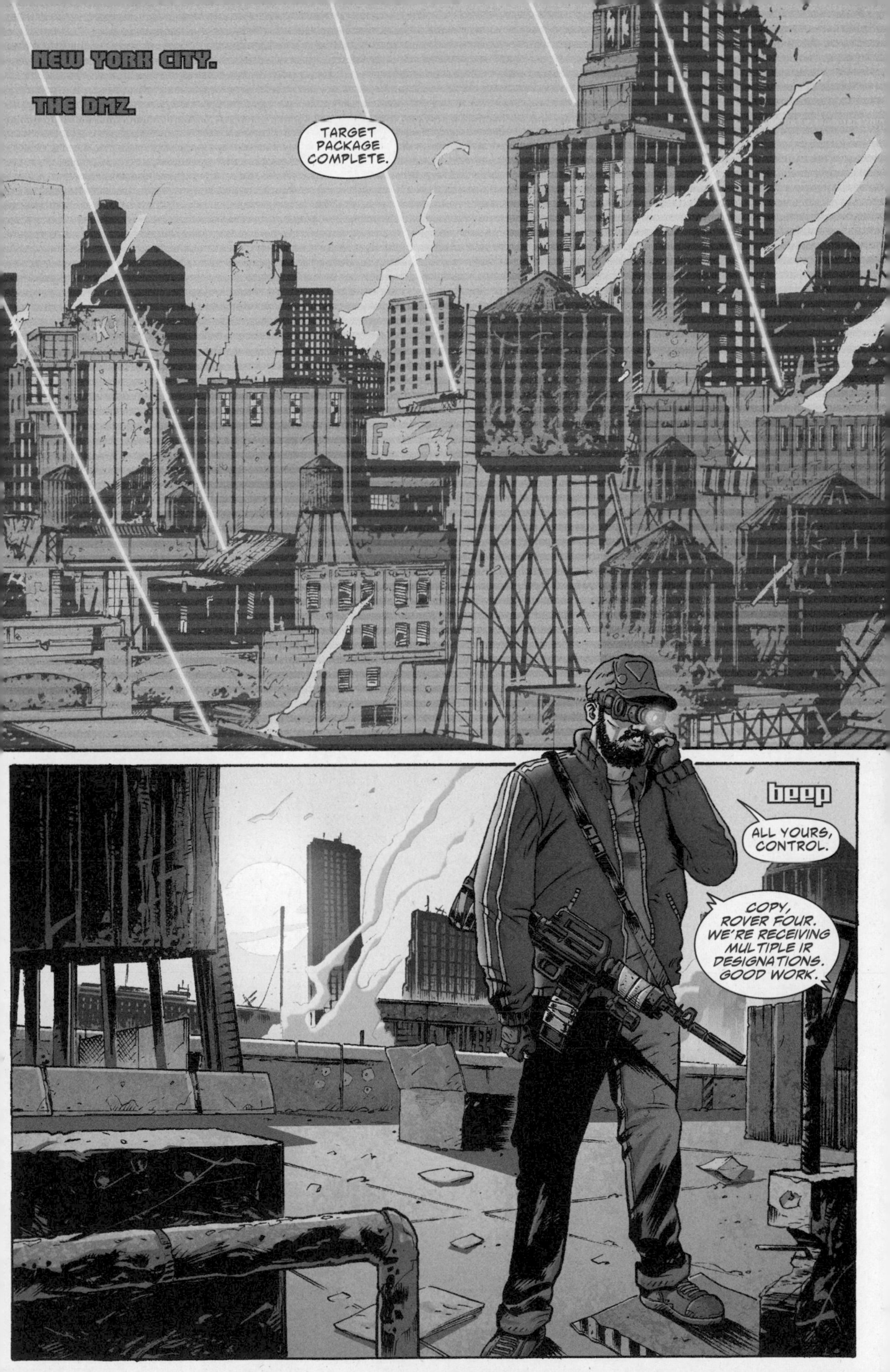
NEW YORK CITY.
THE DMZ.
TARGET PACKAGE COMPLETE.
beep
ALL YOURS, CONTROL.
COPY, ROVER FOUR. WE'RE RECEIVING MULTIPLE IR DESIGNATIONS. GOOD WORK.

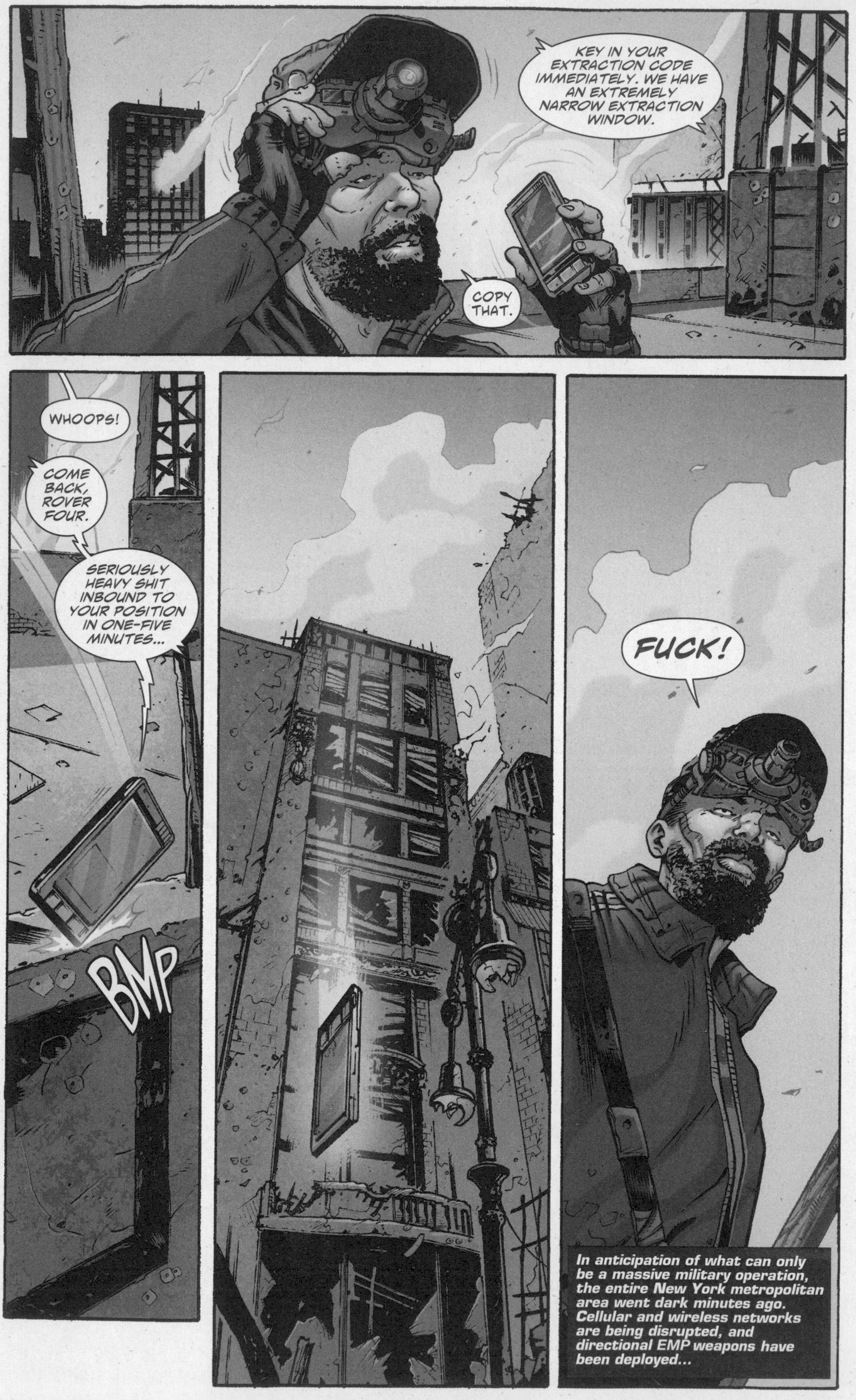
KEY IN YOUR EXTRACTION CODE IMMEDIATELY. WE HAVE AN EXTREMELY NARROW EXTRACTION WINDOW.
COPY THAT.
WHOOPS!
COME BACK, ROVER FOUR.
SERIOUSLY HEAVY SHIT INBOUND TO YOUR POSITION IN ONE-FIVE MINUTES...
BMP
FUCK!
In anticipation of what can only be a massive military operation, the entire New York metropolitan area went dark minutes ago. Cellular and wireless networks are being disrupted, and directional EMP weapons have been deployed...

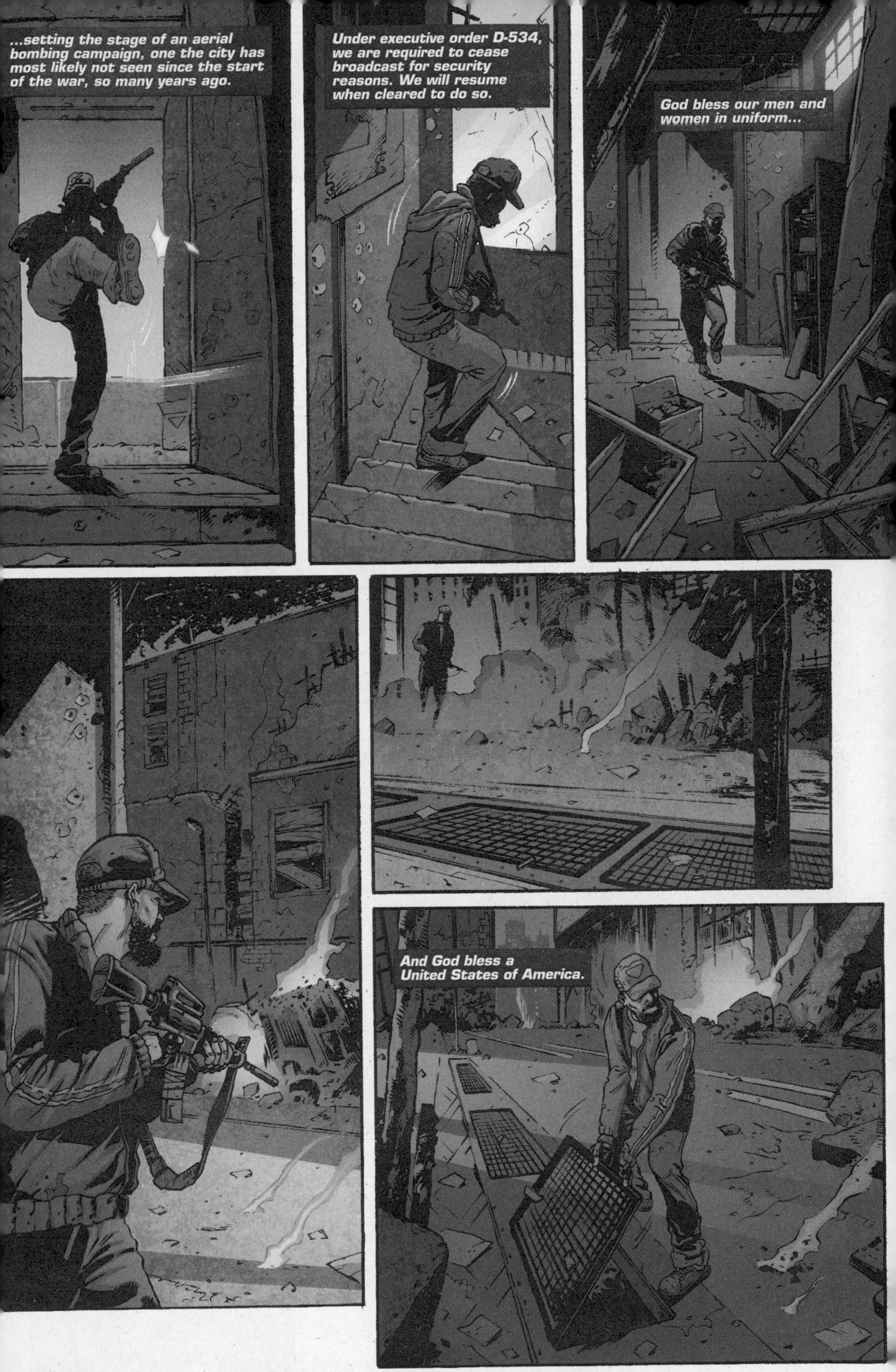

...setting the stage of an aerial bombing campaign, one the city has most likely not seen since the start of the war, so many years ago.
Under executive order D-534, we are required to cease broadcast for security reasons. We will resume when cleared to do so.
God bless our men and women in uniform...
And God bless a United States of America.

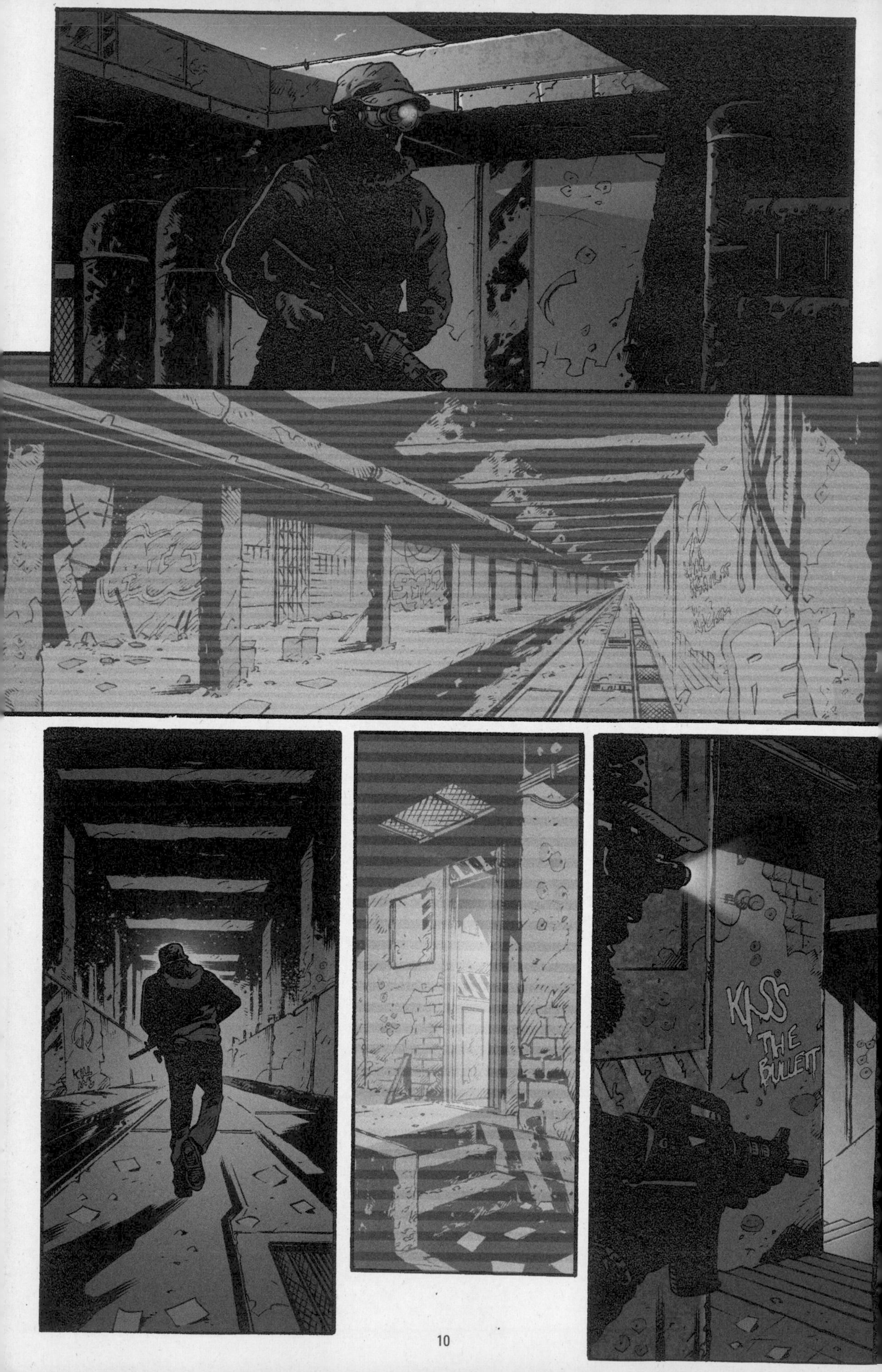
KASS
THE
BULLETT

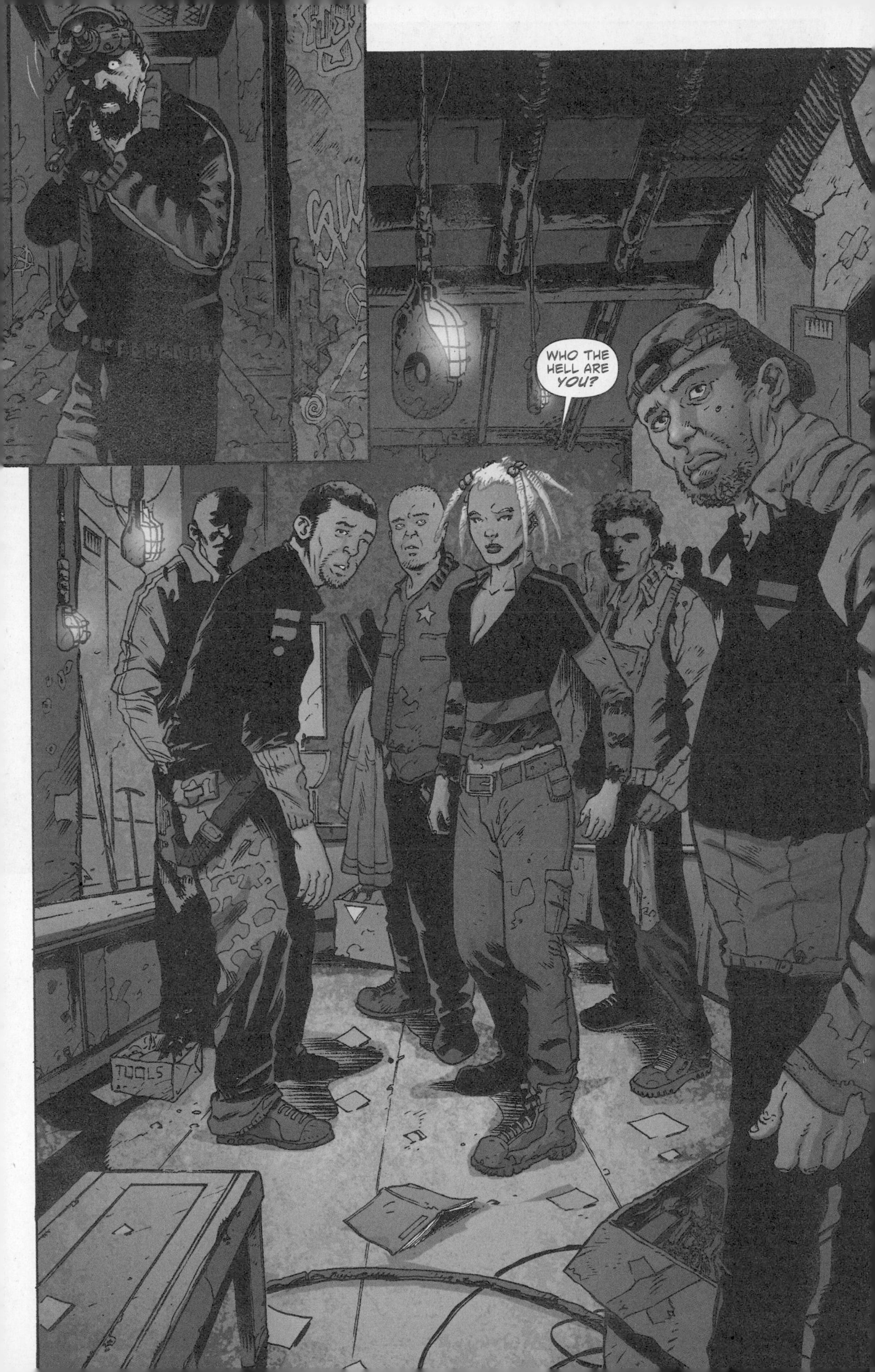
WHO THE HELL ARE YOU?
TOOLS

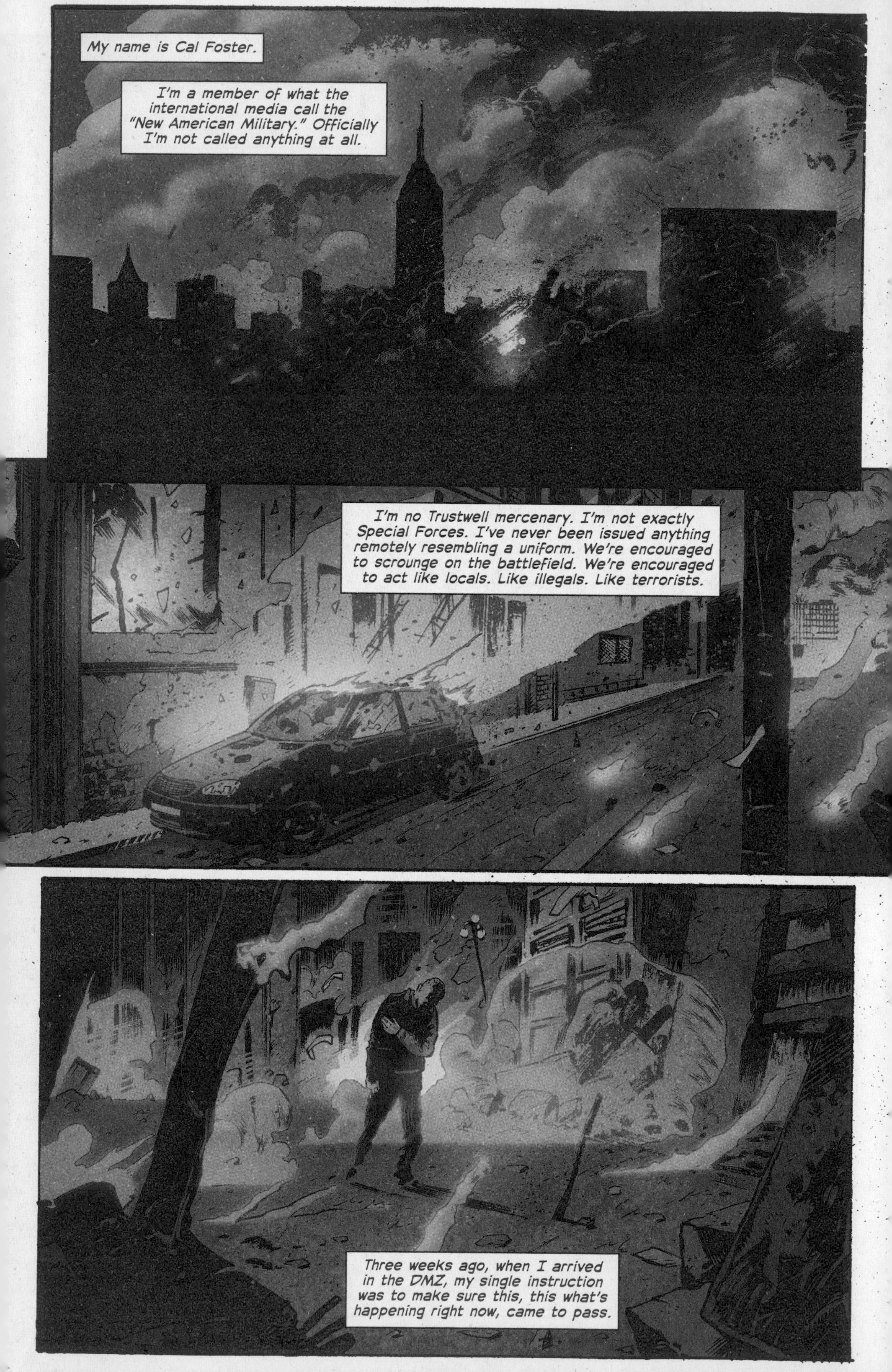
My name is Cal Foster.
I'm a member of what the international media call the "New American Military." Officially I'm not called anything at all.
I'm no Trustwell mercenary. I'm not exactly Special Forces. I've never been issued anything remotely resembling a uniform. We're encouraged to scrounge on the battlefield. We're encouraged to act like locals. Like illegals. Like terrorists.
Three weeks ago, when I arrived in the DMZ, my single instruction was to make sure this, this what's happening right now, came to pass.

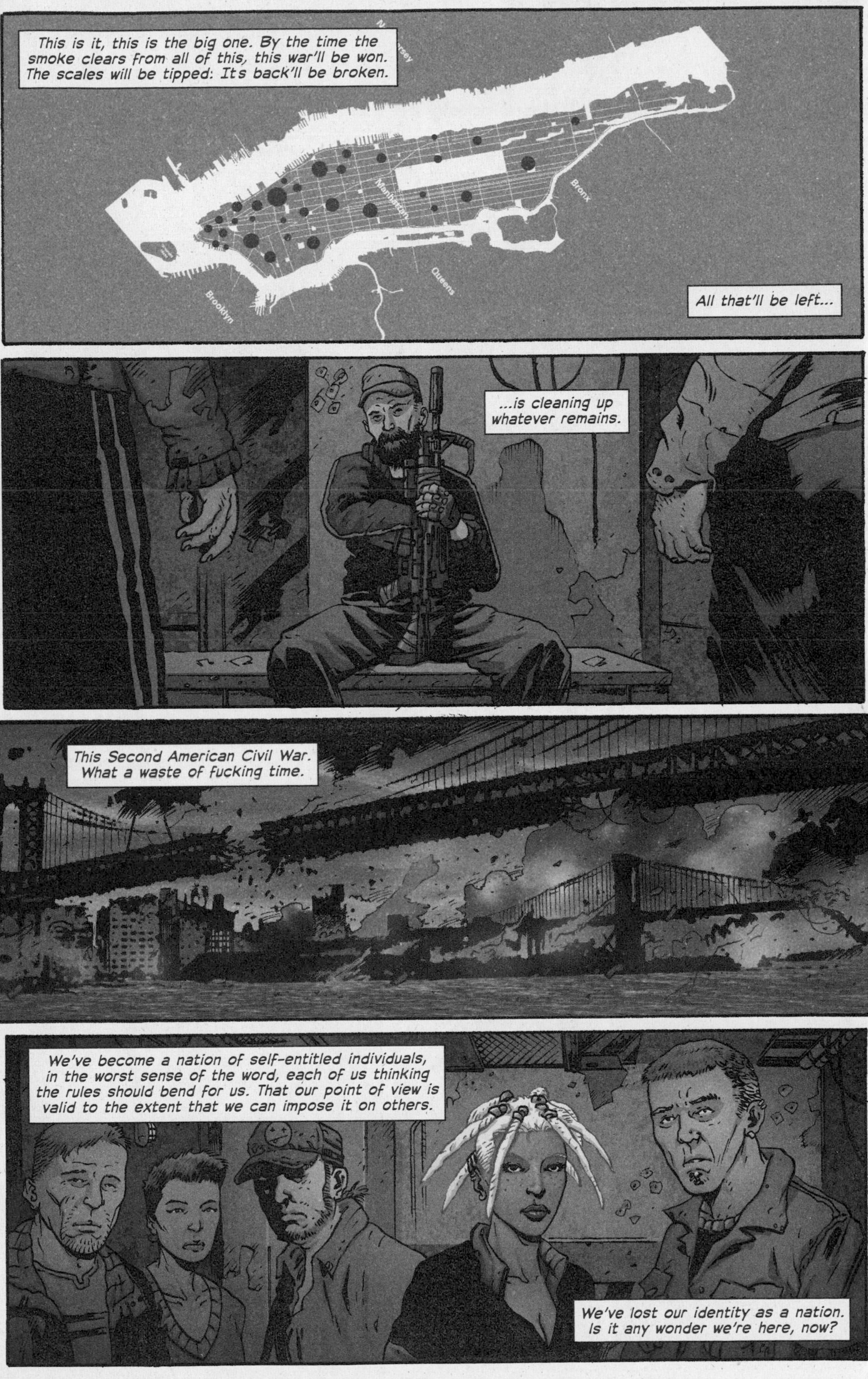
This is it, this is the big one. By the time the smoke clears from all of this, this war'll be won. The scales will be tipped: It's back'll be broken.
Manhattan
Bronx
Queens
Brooklyn
All that'll be left...
...is cleaning up whatever remains.
This Second American Civil War. What a waste of fucking time.
We've become a nation of self-entitled individuals, in the worst sense of the word, each of us thinking the rules should bend for us. That our point of view is valid to the extent that we can impose it on others.
We've lost our identity as a nation. Is it any wonder we're here, now?

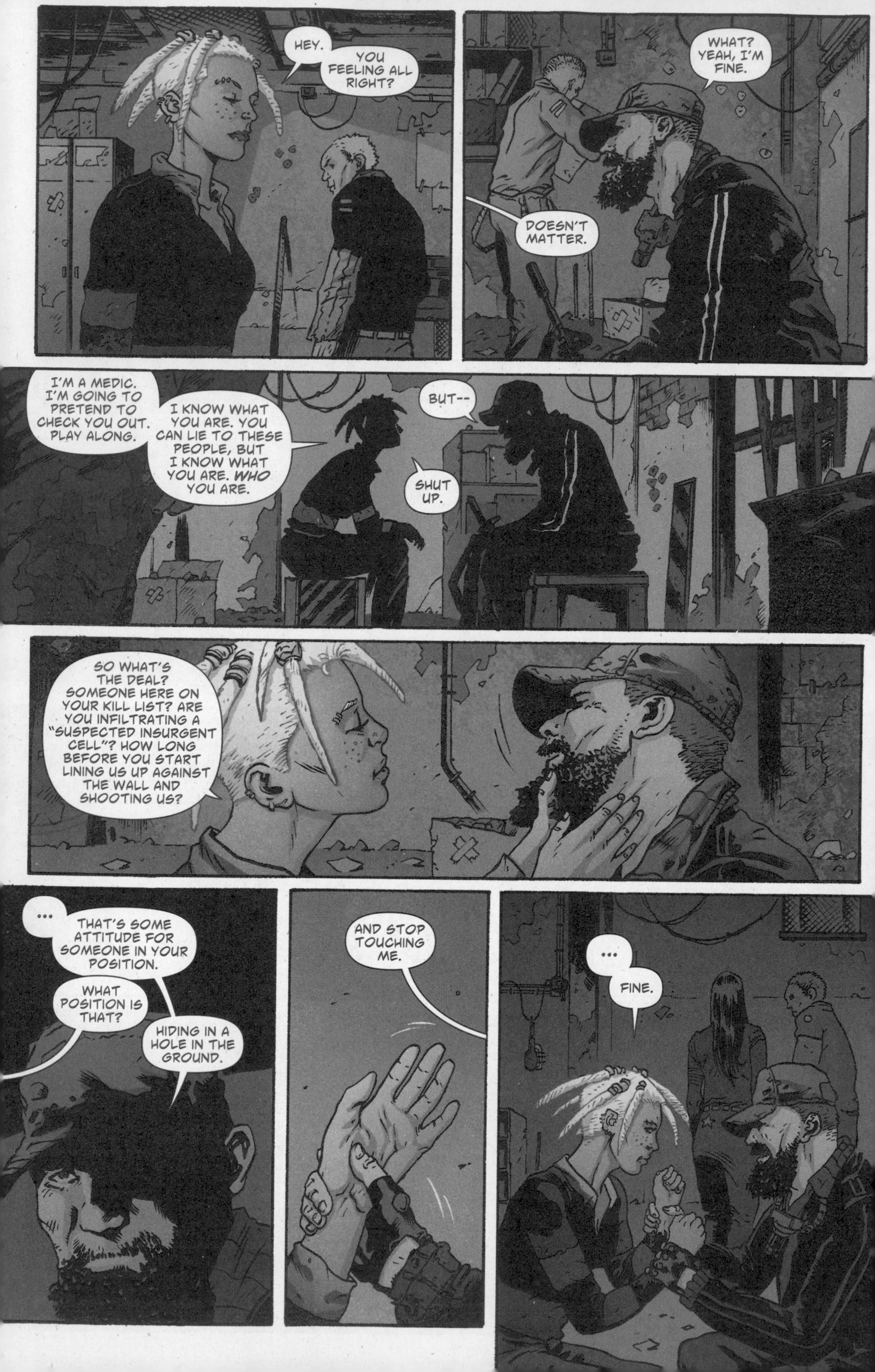
HEY.
YOU FEELING ALL RIGHT?
WHAT? YEAH, I'M FINE.
DOESN'T MATTER.
I'M A MEDIC. I'M GOING TO PRETEND TO CHECK YOU OUT. PLAY ALONG.
I KNOW WHAT YOU ARE. YOU CAN LIE TO THESE PEOPLE, BUT I KNOW WHAT YOU ARE. *WHO* YOU ARE.
BUT--
SHUT UP.
SO WHAT'S THE DEAL? SOMEONE HERE ON YOUR KILL LIST? ARE YOU INFILTRATING A "SUSPECTED INSURGENT CELL"? HOW LONG BEFORE YOU START LINING US UP AGAINST THE WALL AND SHOOTING US?
...
THAT'S SOME ATTITUDE FOR SOMEONE IN YOUR POSITION.
WHAT POSITION IS THAT?
HIDING IN A HOLE IN THE GROUND.
AND STOP TOUCHING ME.
...
FINE.

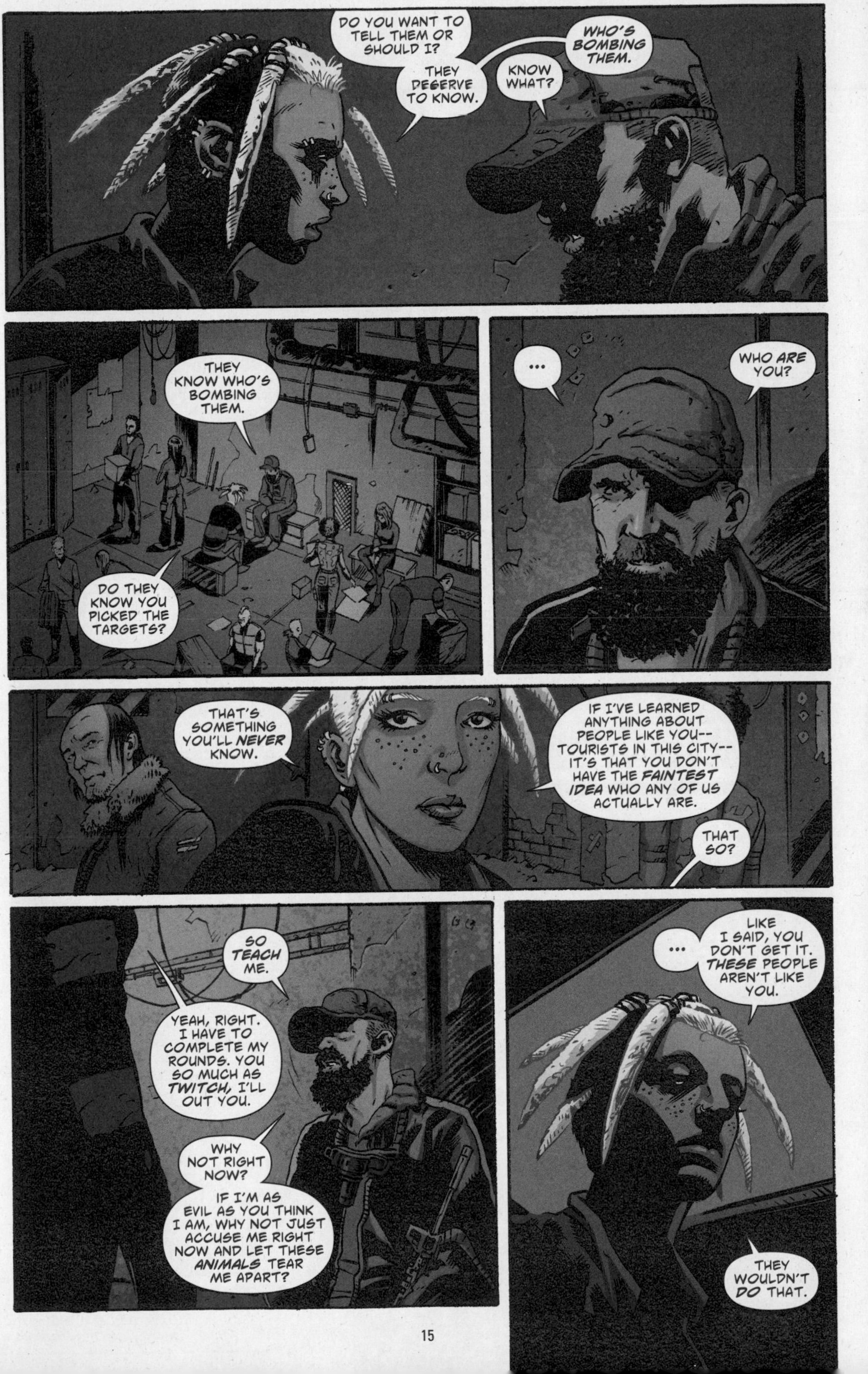
DO YOU WANT TO TELL THEM OR SHOULD I?
THEY DESERVE TO KNOW.
KNOW WHAT?
WHO'S BOMBING THEM.
THEY KNOW WHO'S BOMBING THEM.
DO THEY KNOW YOU PICKED THE TARGETS?
...
WHO ARE YOU?
THAT'S SOMETHING YOU'LL NEVER KNOW.
IF I'VE LEARNED ANYTHING ABOUT PEOPLE LIKE YOU-- TOURISTS IN THIS CITY-- IT'S THAT YOU DON'T HAVE THE FAINTEST IDEA WHO ANY OF US ACTUALLY ARE.
THAT SO?
SO TEACH ME.
YEAH, RIGHT. I HAVE TO COMPLETE MY ROUNDS. YOU SO MUCH AS TWITCH, I'LL OUT YOU.
WHY NOT RIGHT NOW?
IF I'M AS EVIL AS YOU THINK I AM, WHY NOT JUST ACCUSE ME RIGHT NOW AND LET THESE ANIMALS TEAR ME APART?
...
LIKE I SAID, YOU DON'T GET IT. THESE PEOPLE AREN'T LIKE YOU.
THEY WOULDN'T DO THAT.

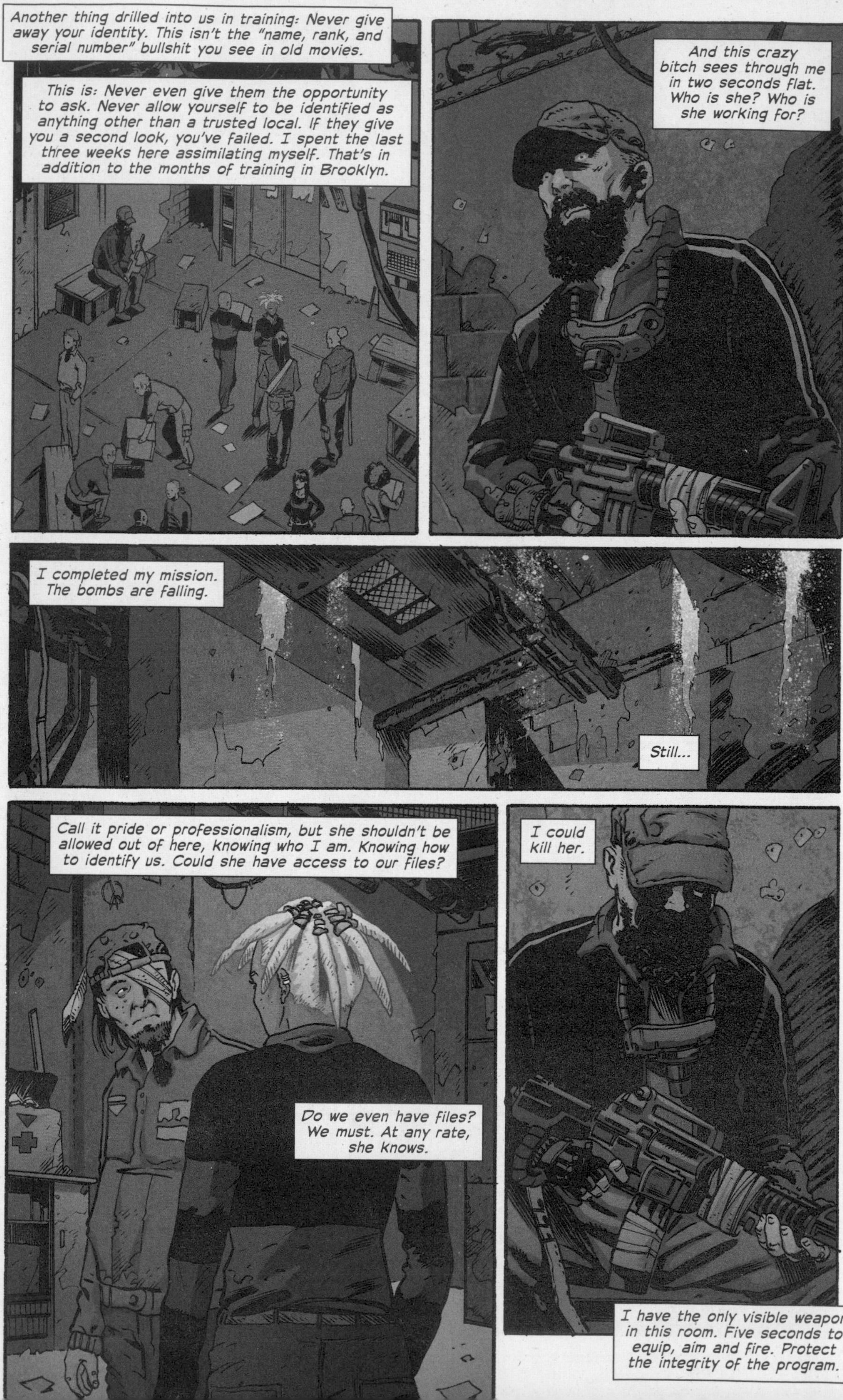
Another thing drilled into us in training: Never give away your identity. This isn't the "name, rank, and serial number" bullshit you see in old movies.
This is: Never even give them the opportunity to ask. Never allow yourself to be identified as anything other than a trusted local. If they give you a second look, you've failed. I spent the last three weeks here assimilating myself. That's in addition to the months of training in Brooklyn.
And this crazy bitch sees through me in two seconds flat. Who is she? Who is she working for?
I completed my mission. The bombs are falling.
Still...
Call it pride or professionalism, but she shouldn't be allowed out of here, knowing who I am. Knowing how to identify us. Could she have access to our files?
Do we even have files? We must. At any rate, she knows.
I could kill her.
I have the only visible weapon in this room. Five seconds to equip, aim and fire. Protect the integrity of the program.

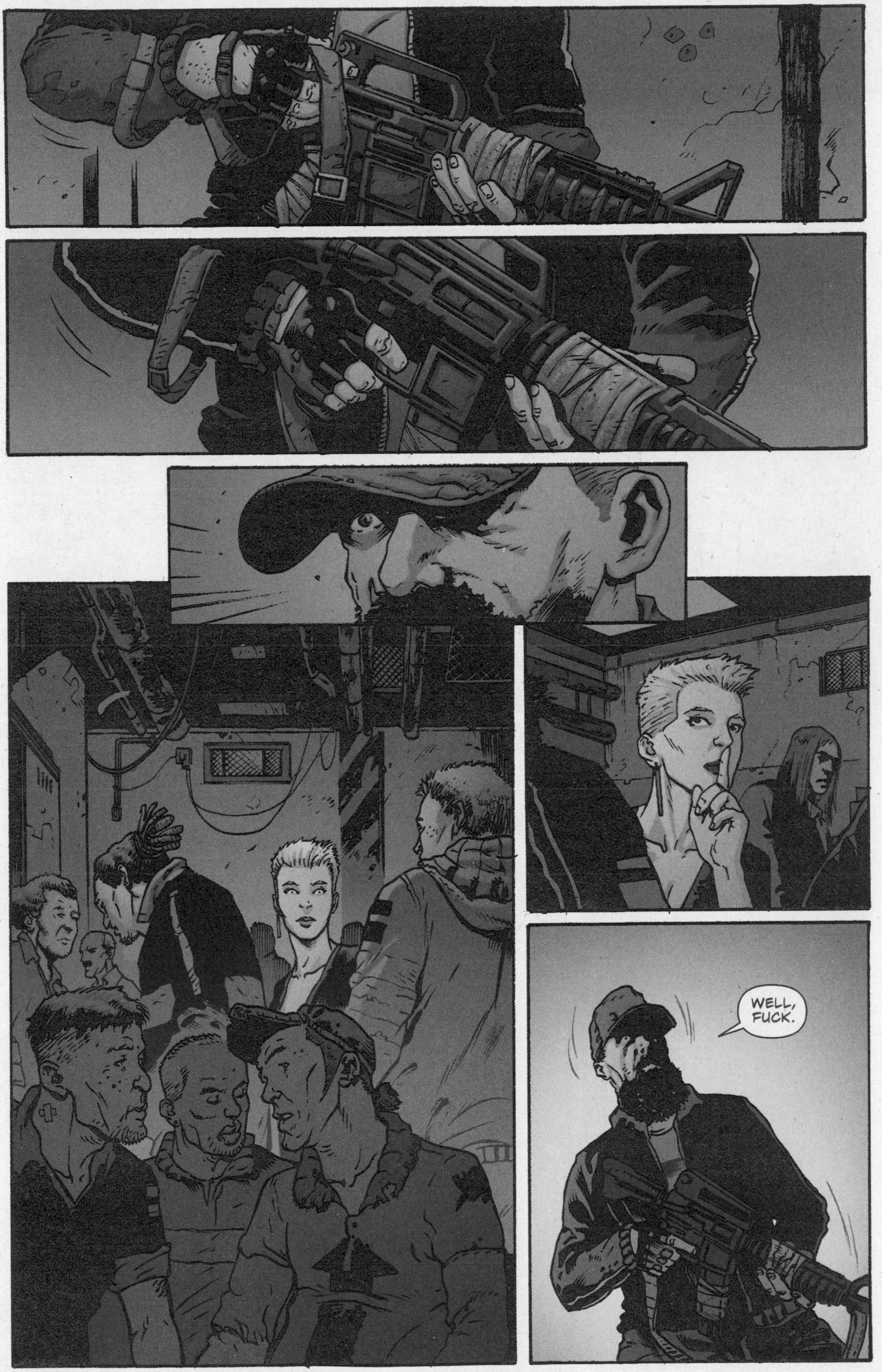
WELL, FUCK.

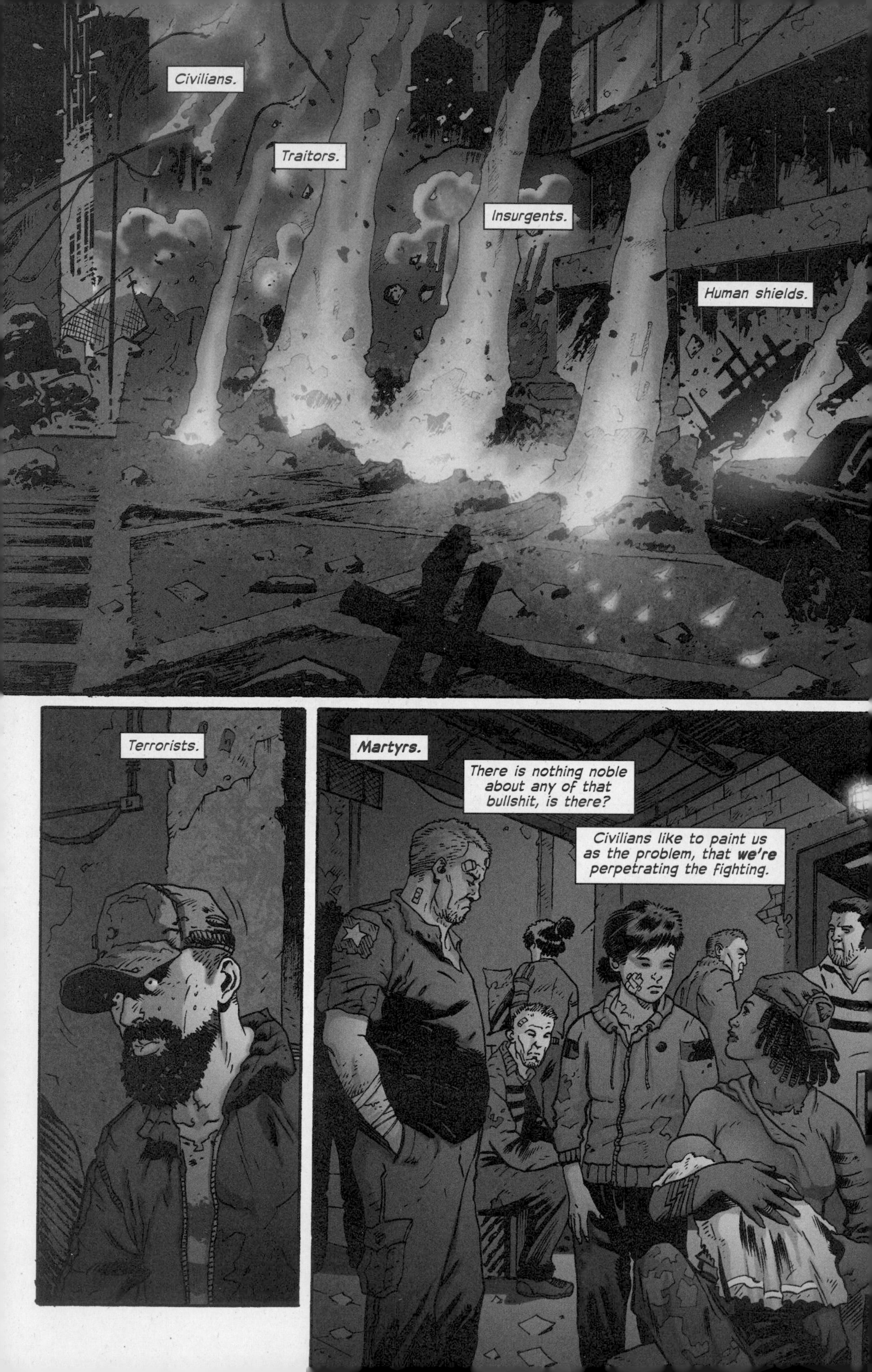
Civilians.
Traitors.
Insurgents.
Human shields.
Terrorists.
Martyrs.
There is nothing noble about any of that bullshit, is there?
Civilians like to paint us as the problem, that we're perpetrating the fighting.

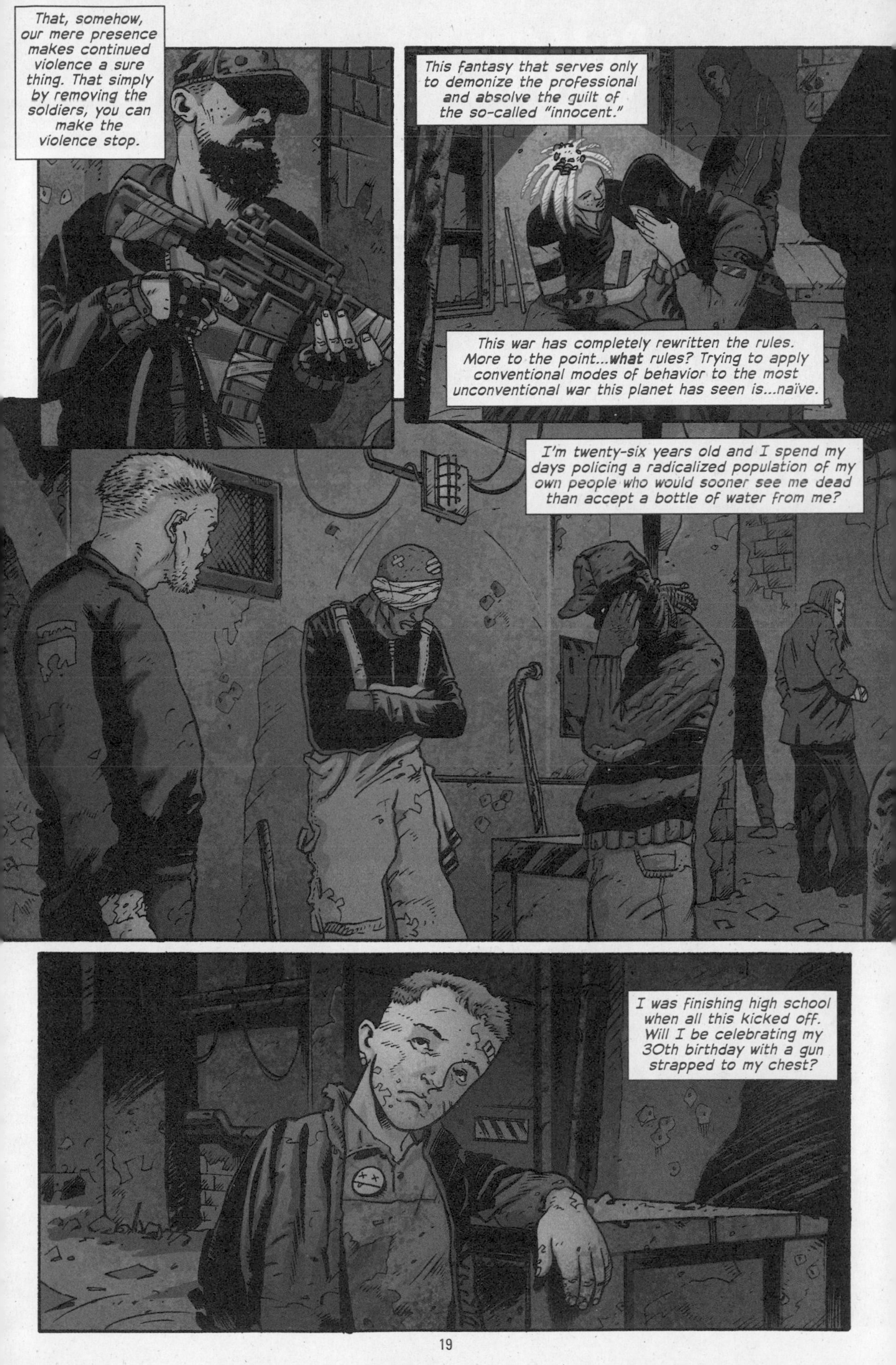
That, somehow, our mere presence makes continued violence a sure thing. That simply by removing the soldiers, you can make the violence stop.
This fantasy that serves only to demonize the professional and absolve the guilt of the so-called "innocent."
This war has completely rewritten the rules. More to the point...**what** rules? Trying to apply conventional modes of behavior to the most unconventional war this planet has seen is...naïve.
I'm twenty-six years old and I spend my days policing a radicalized population of my own people who would sooner see me dead than accept a bottle of water from me?
I was finishing high school when all this kicked off. Will I be celebrating my 30th birthday with a gun strapped to my chest?

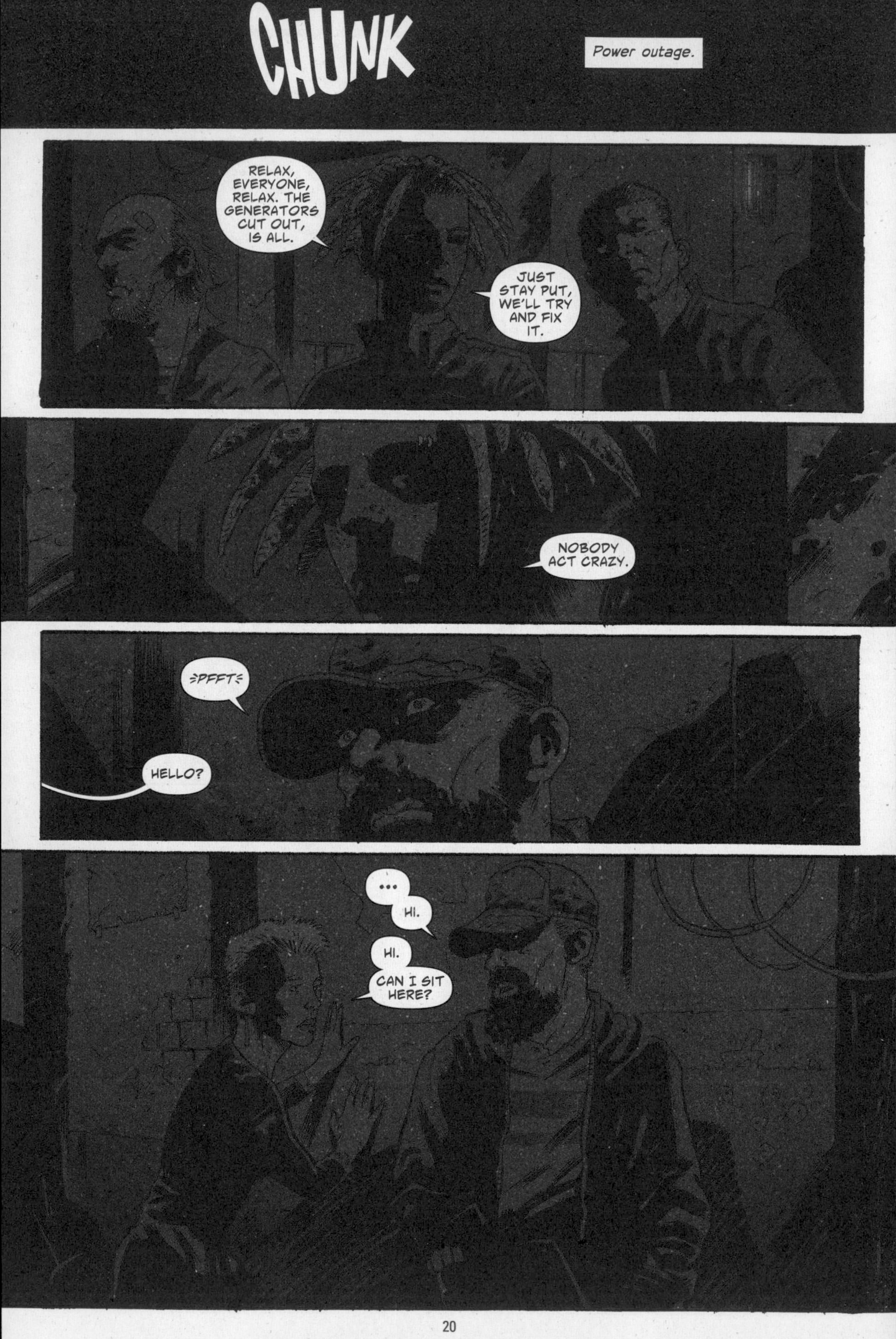
CHUNK
Power outage.
RELAX, EVERYONE, RELAX. THE GENERATORS CUT OUT, IS ALL.
JUST STAY PUT, WE'LL TRY AND FIX IT.
NOBODY ACT CRAZY.
=PFFT=
HELLO?
...
HI.
HI.
CAN I SIT HERE?

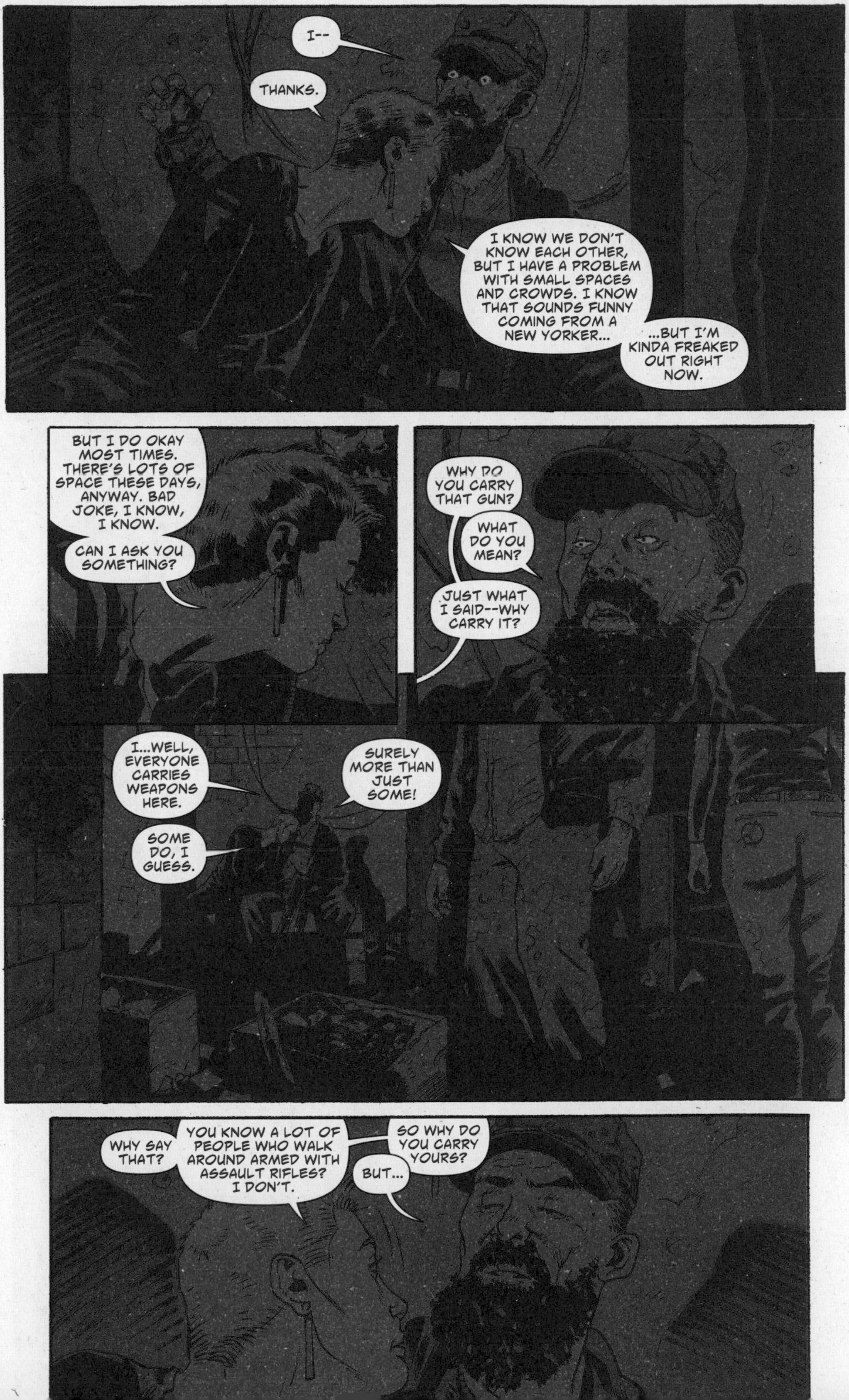
I--
THANKS.
I KNOW WE DON'T KNOW EACH OTHER, BUT I HAVE A PROBLEM WITH SMALL SPACES AND CROWDS. I KNOW THAT SOUNDS FUNNY COMING FROM A NEW YORKER...
...BUT I'M KINDA FREAKED OUT RIGHT NOW.
BUT I DO OKAY MOST TIMES. THERE'S LOTS OF SPACE THESE DAYS, ANYWAY. BAD JOKE, I KNOW, I KNOW.
CAN I ASK YOU SOMETHING?
WHY DO YOU CARRY THAT GUN?
WHAT DO YOU MEAN?
JUST WHAT I SAID--WHY CARRY IT?
I...WELL, EVERYONE CARRIES WEAPONS HERE.
SURELY MORE THAN JUST SOME!
SOME DO, I GUESS.
WHY SAY THAT?
YOU KNOW A LOT OF PEOPLE WHO WALK AROUND ARMED WITH ASSAULT RIFLES? I DON'T.
BUT...
SO WHY DO YOU CARRY YOURS?

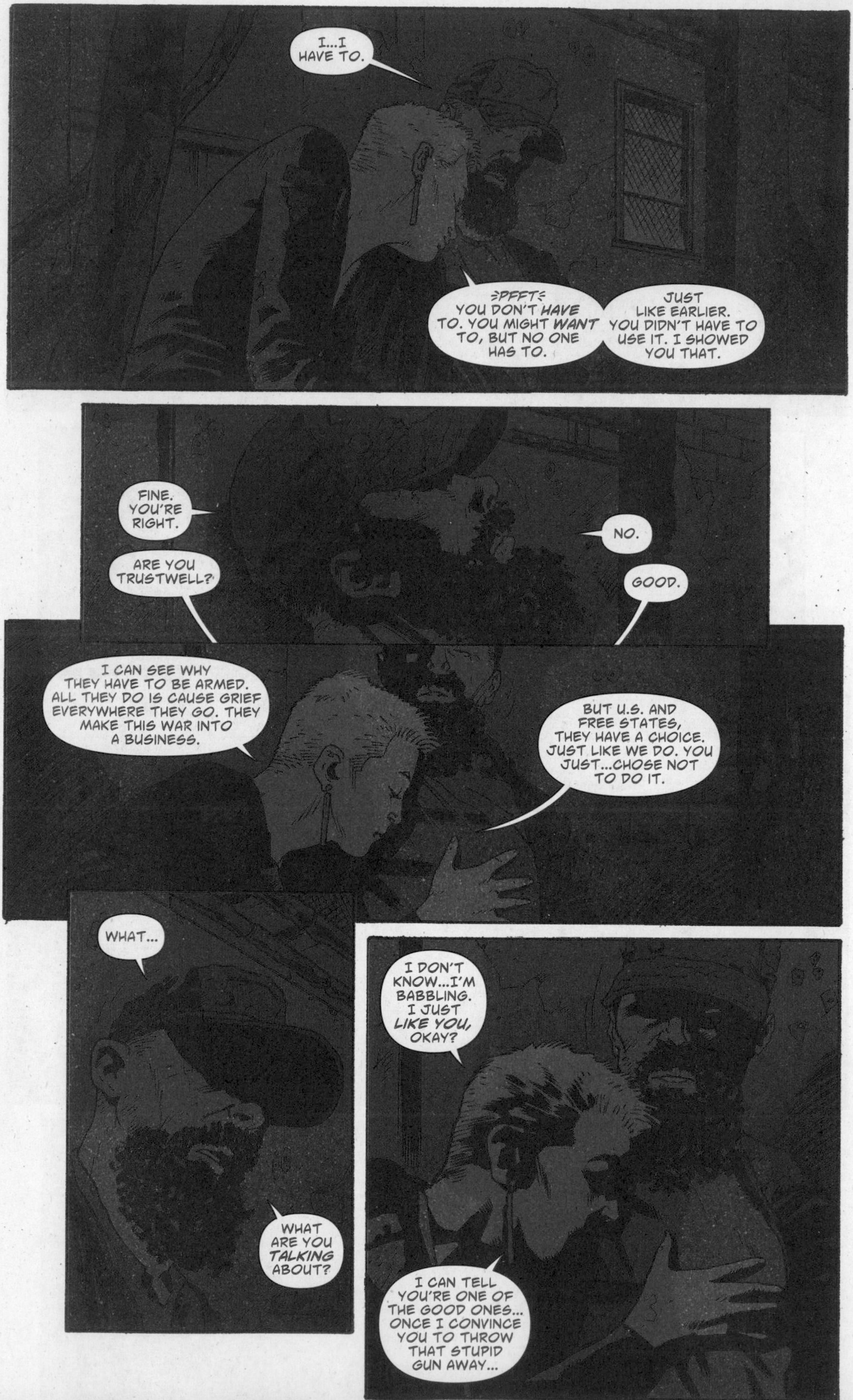
I...I HAVE TO.
=PFFT= YOU DON'T HAVE TO. YOU MIGHT WANT TO, BUT NO ONE HAS TO.
JUST LIKE EARLIER. YOU DIDN'T HAVE TO USE IT. I SHOWED YOU THAT.
FINE. YOU'RE RIGHT.
NO.
ARE YOU TRUSTWELL?
GOOD.
I CAN SEE WHY THEY HAVE TO BE ARMED. ALL THEY DO IS CAUSE GRIEF EVERYWHERE THEY GO. THEY MAKE THIS WAR INTO A BUSINESS.
BUT U.S. AND FREE STATES, THEY HAVE A CHOICE. JUST LIKE WE DO. YOU JUST...CHOSE NOT TO DO IT.
WHAT...
WHAT ARE YOU TALKING ABOUT?
I DON'T KNOW...I'M BABBLING. I JUST LIKE YOU, OKAY?
I CAN TELL YOU'RE ONE OF THE GOOD ONES... ONCE I CONVINCE YOU TO THROW THAT STUPID GUN AWAY...

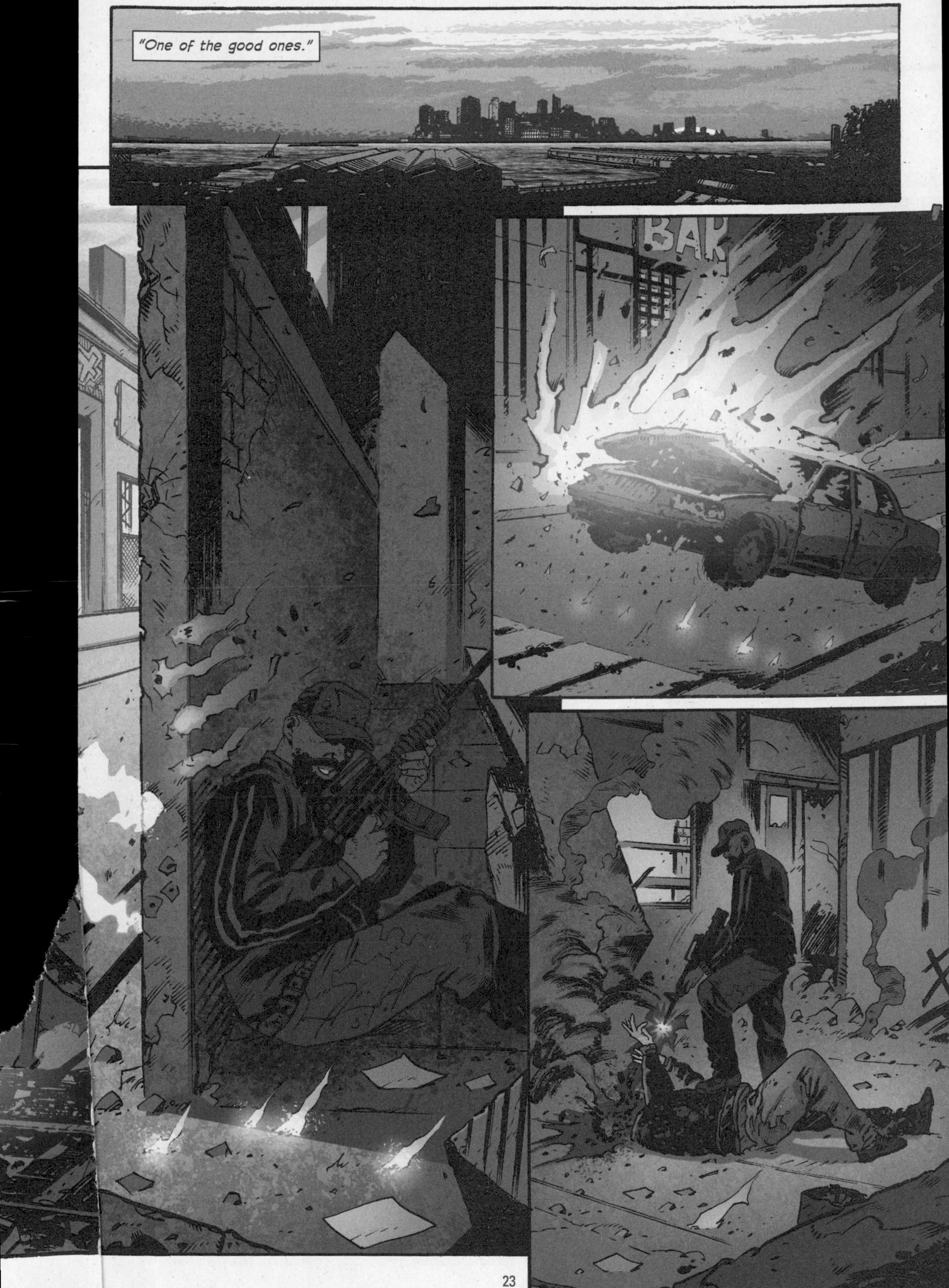
"One of the good ones."
BAR

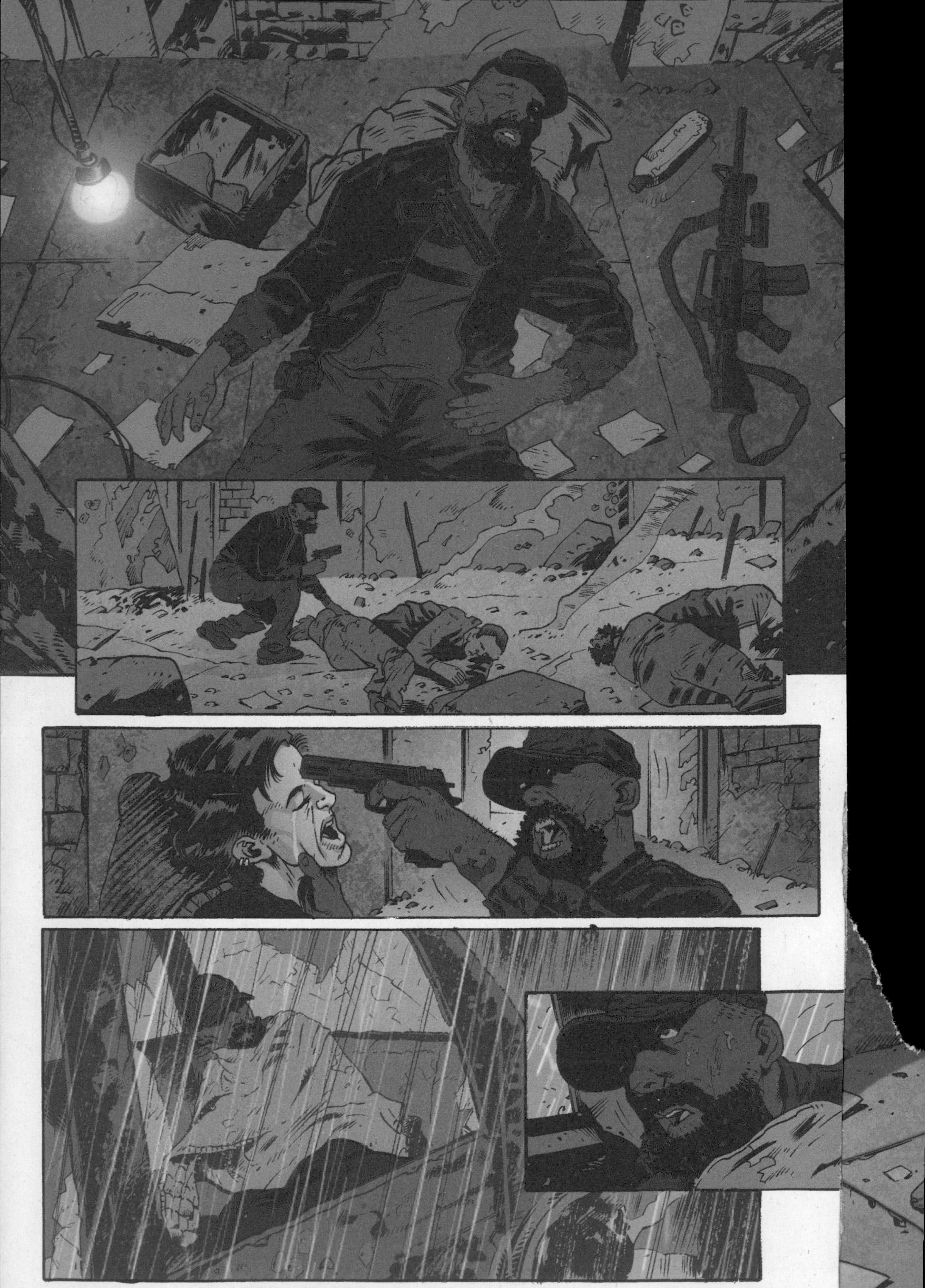

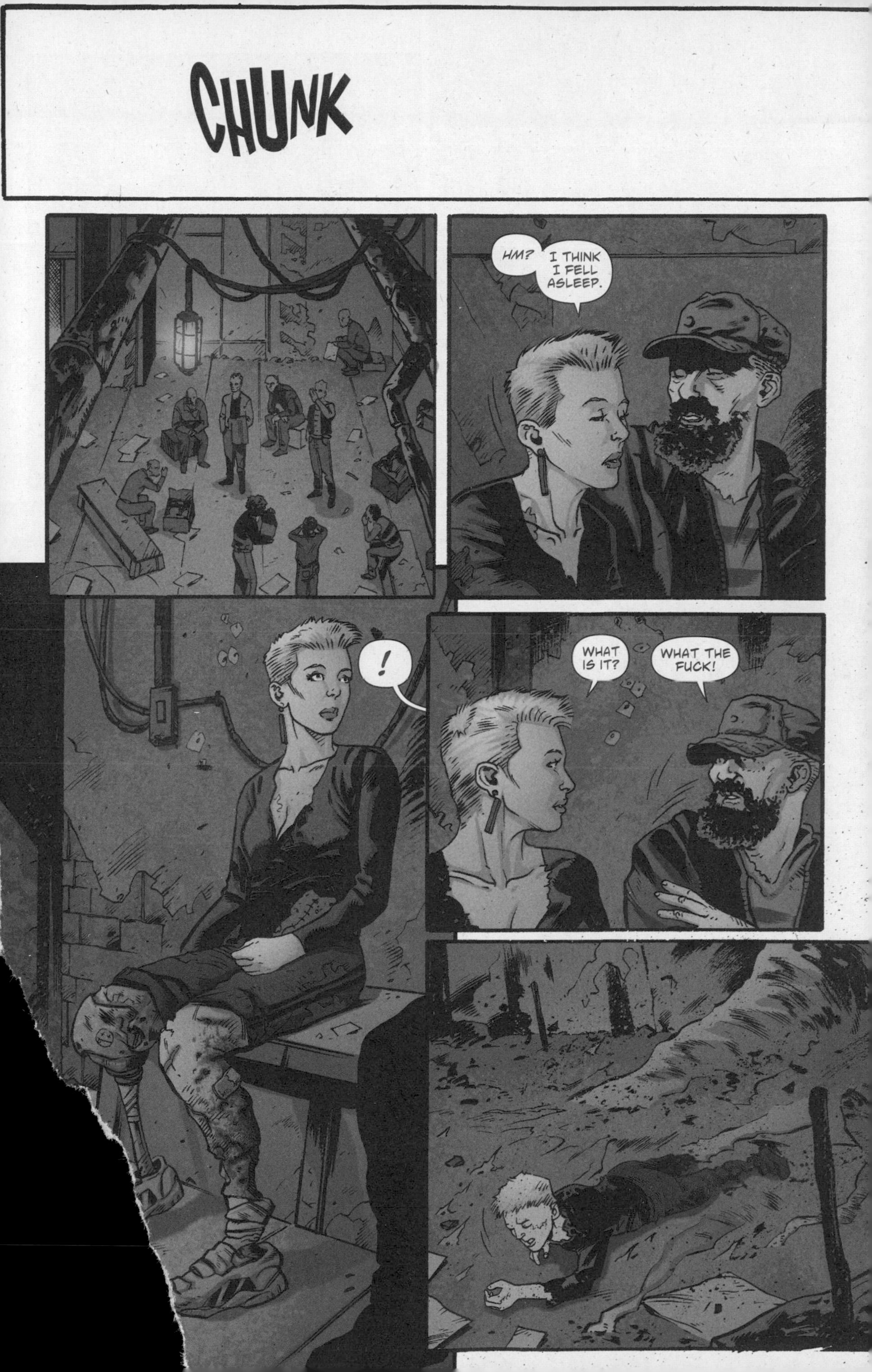
CHUNK
HM?
I THINK I FELL ASLEEP.
!
WHAT IS IT?
WHAT THE FUCK!

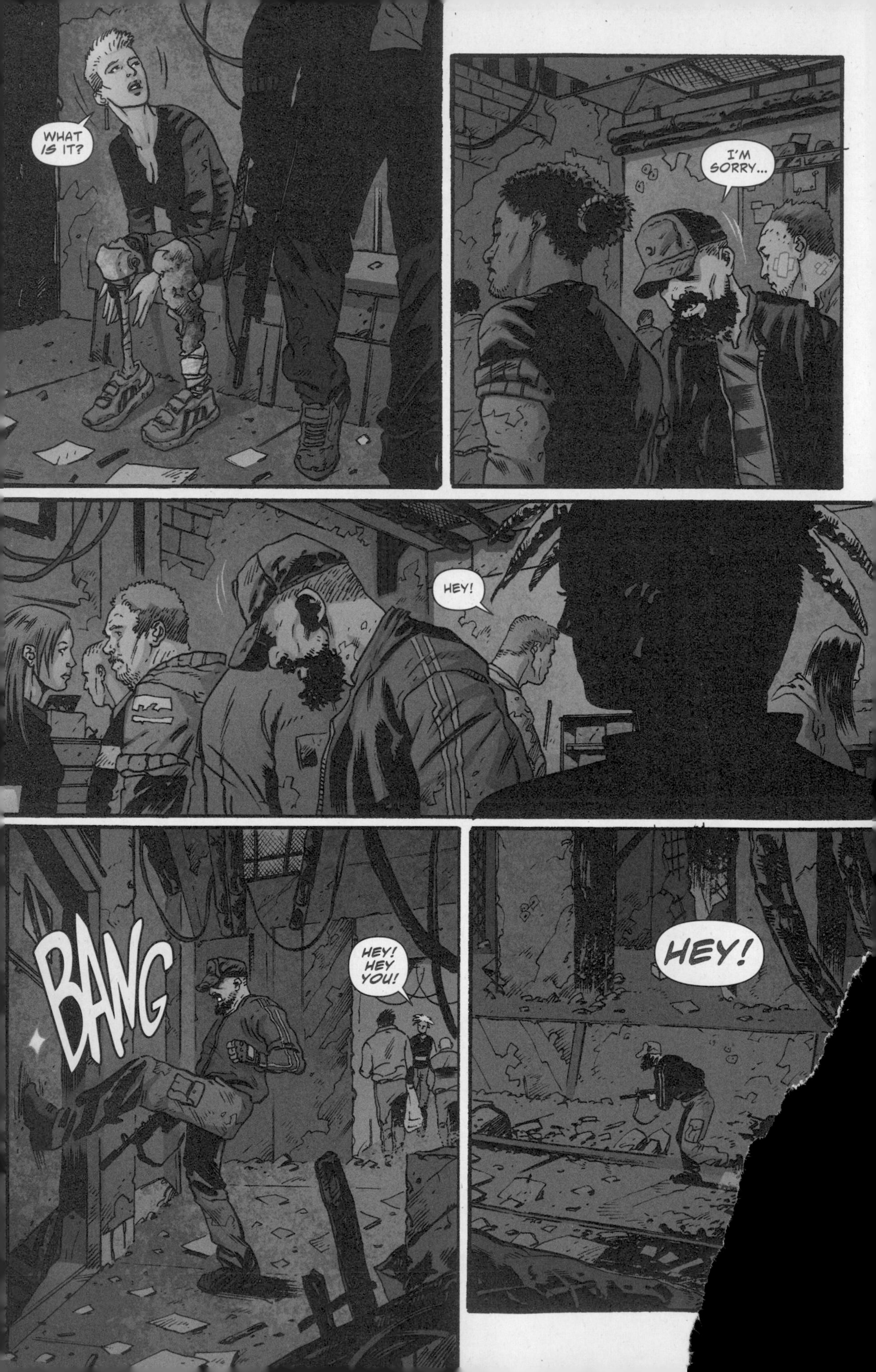
WHAT IS IT?
I'M SORRY...
HEY!
BANG
HEY! HEY YOU!
HEY!

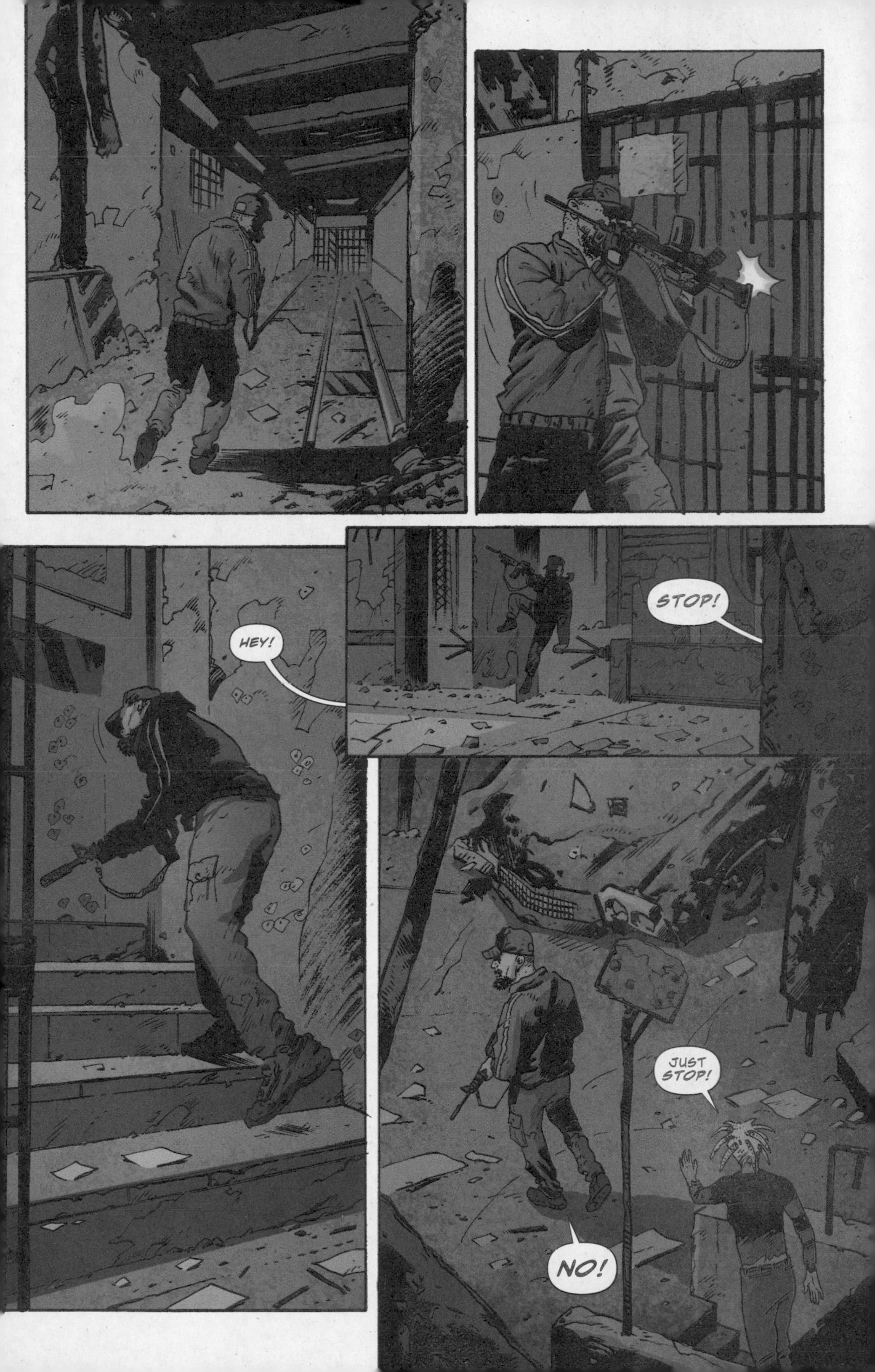
STOP!
HEY!
JUST STOP!
NO!

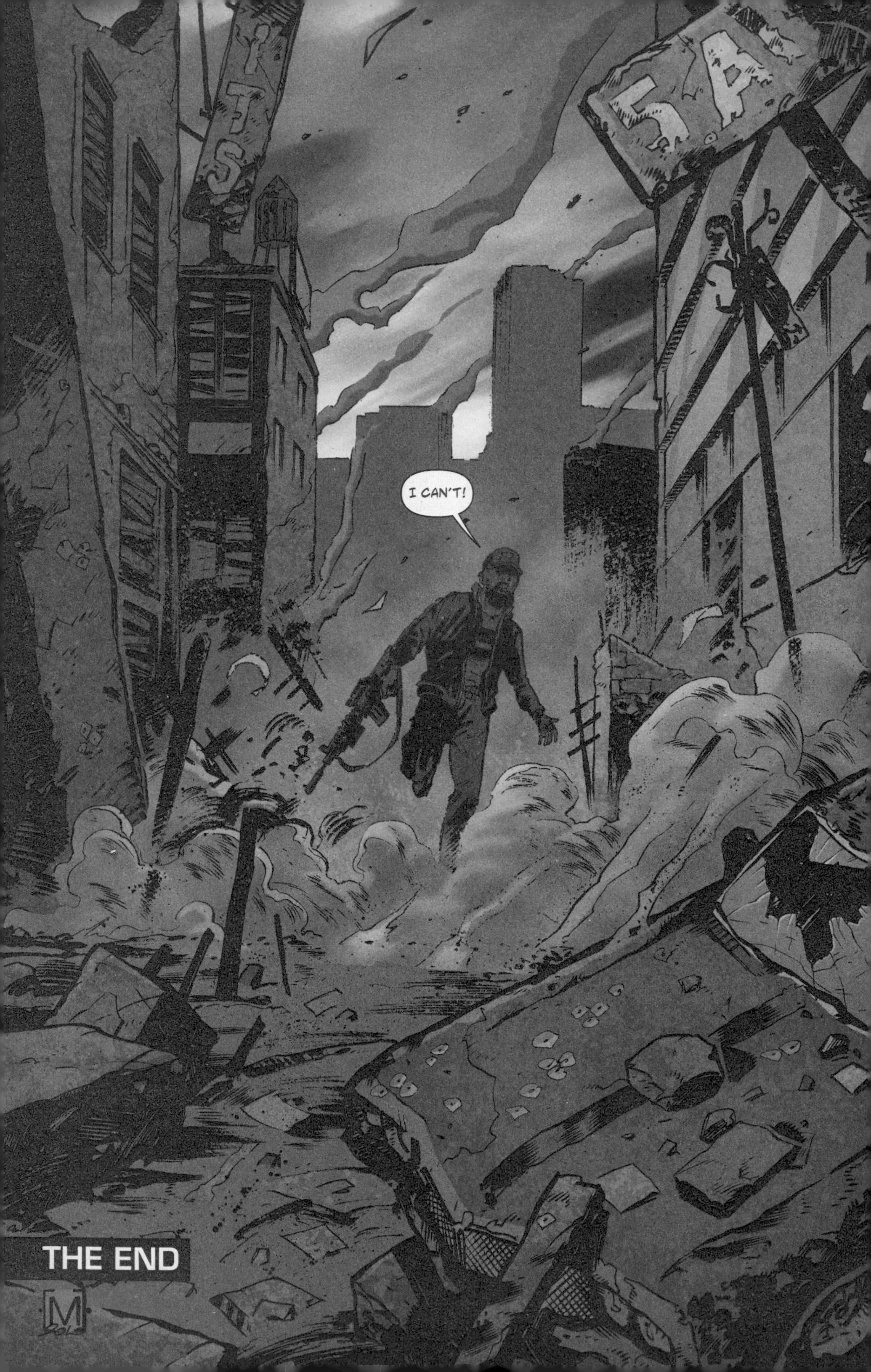
I CAN'T!
THE END

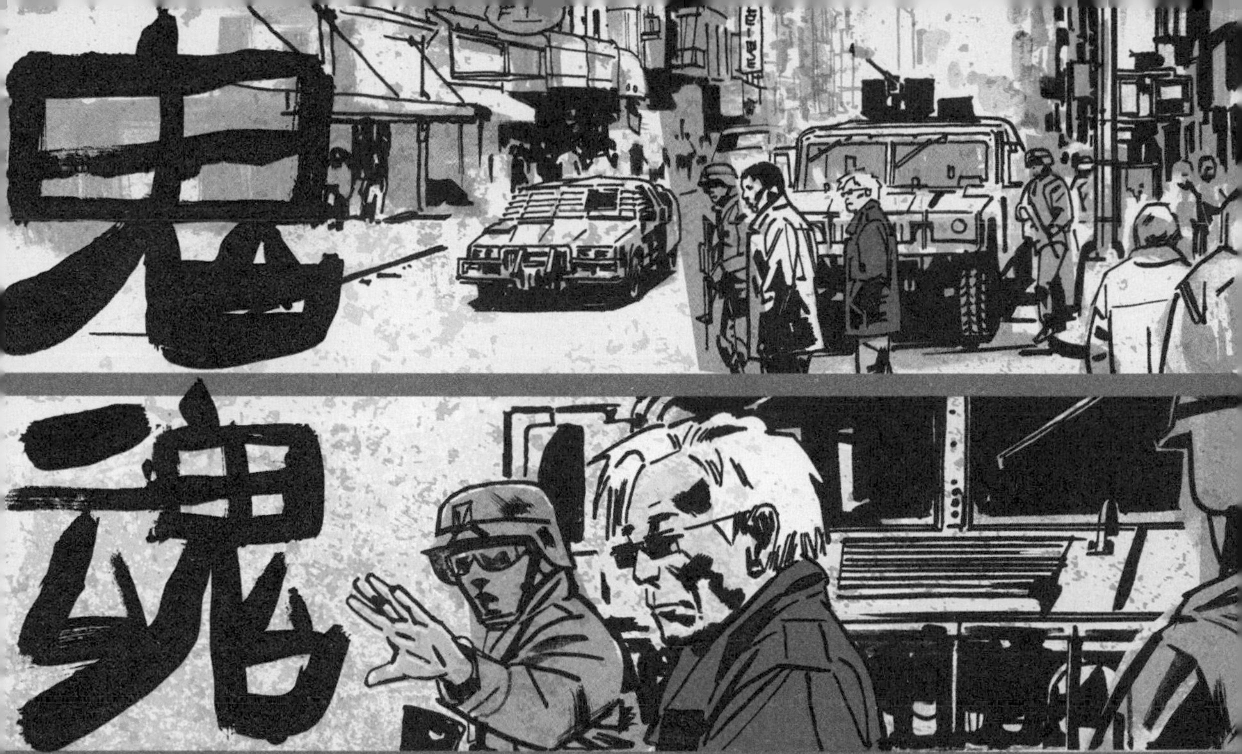
鬼
魂

GHOST PROTECTOR

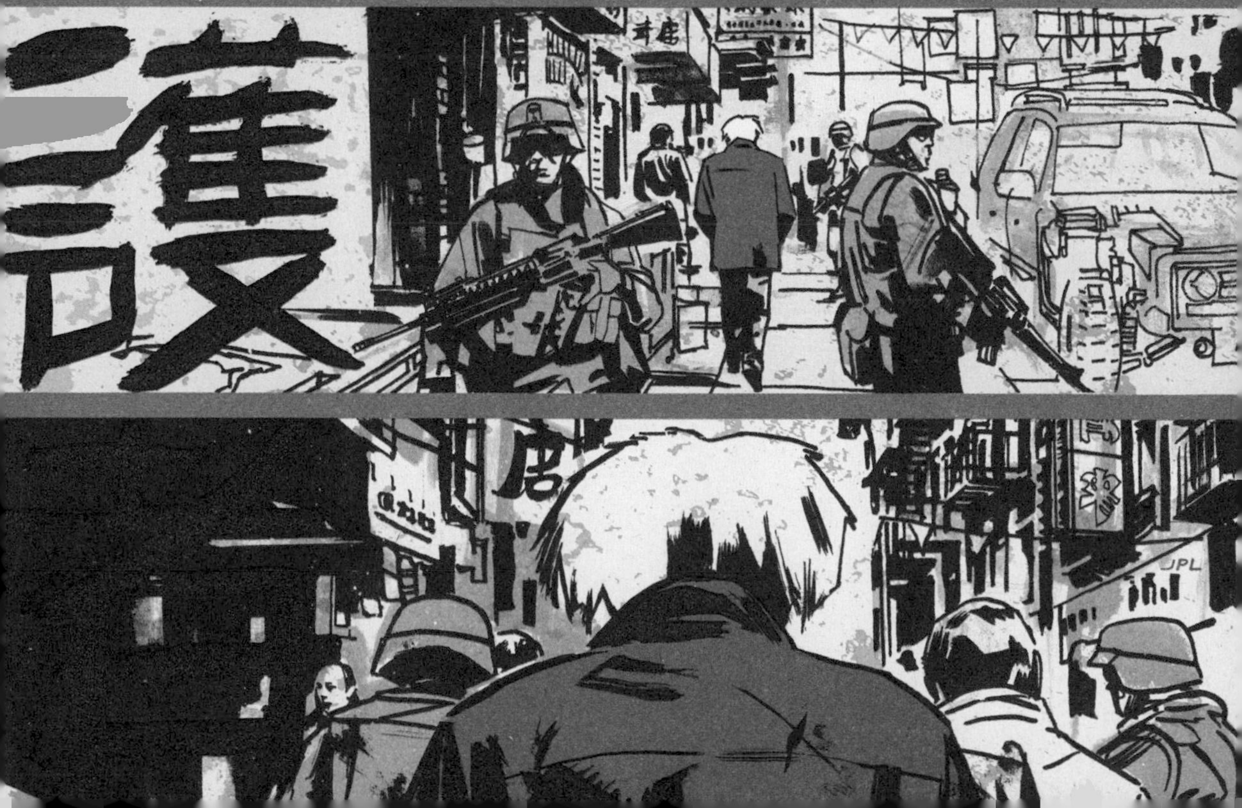
護
店

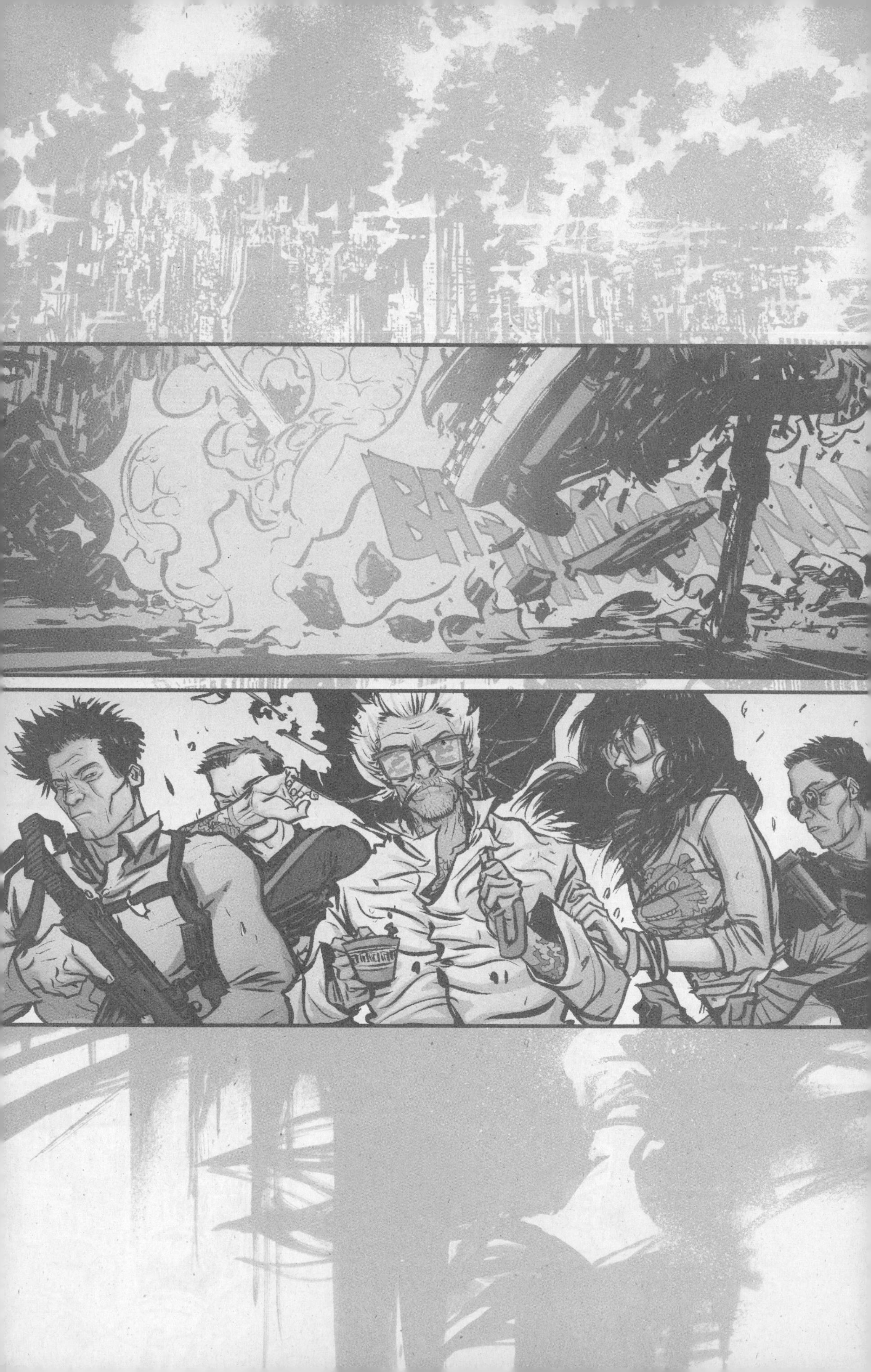
BA

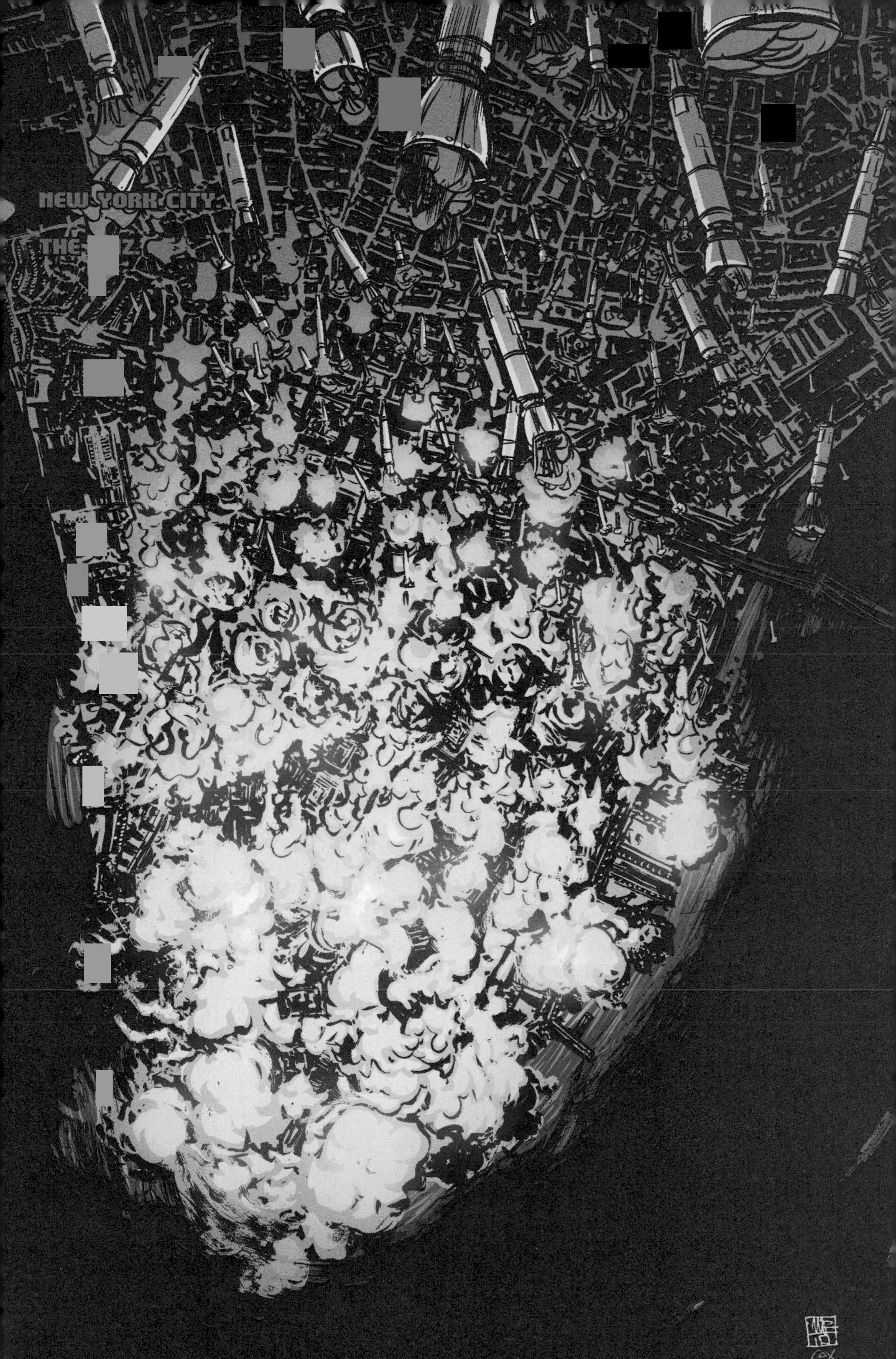
NEW YORK CITY.
THE

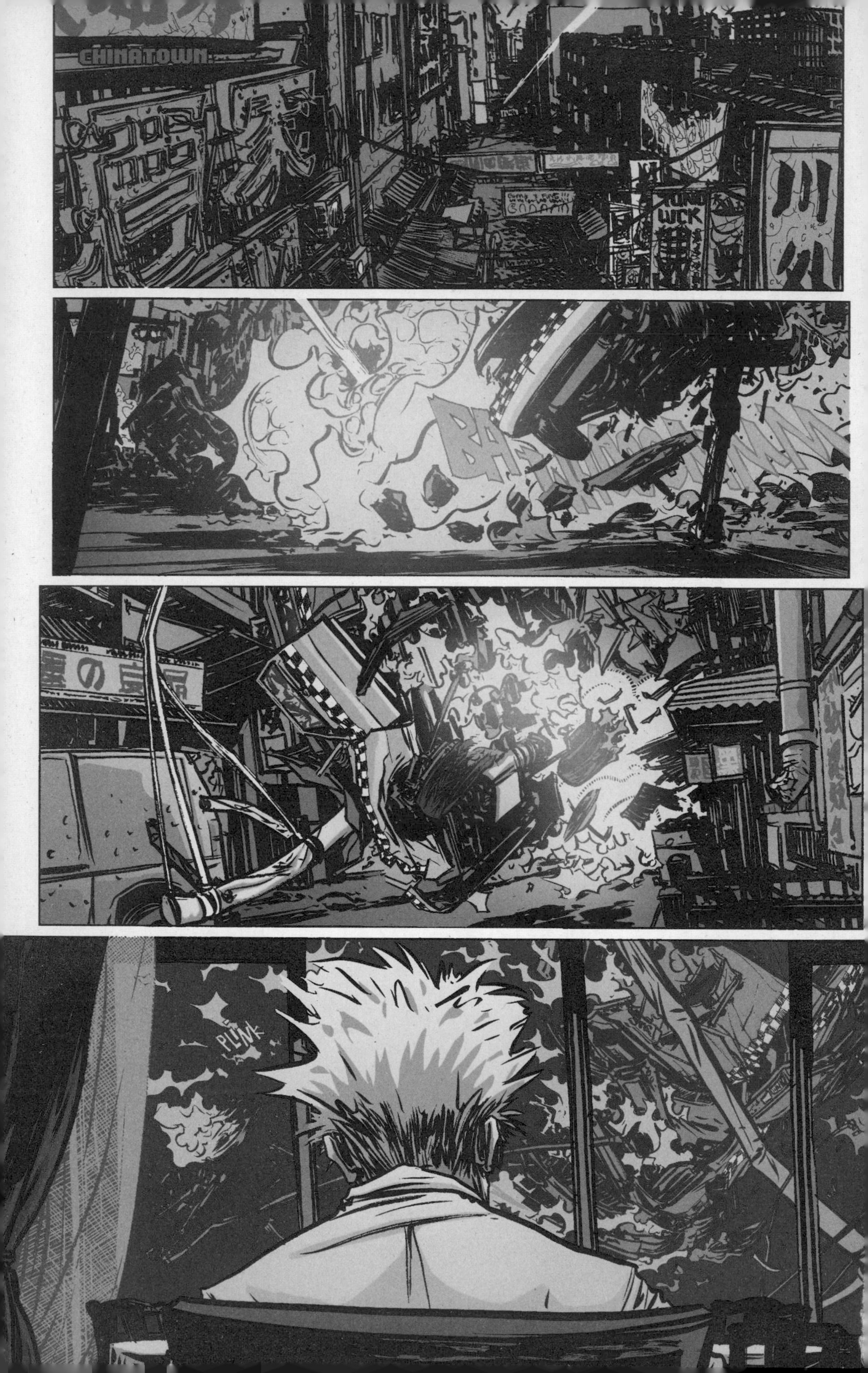
CHINATOWN
PLINK

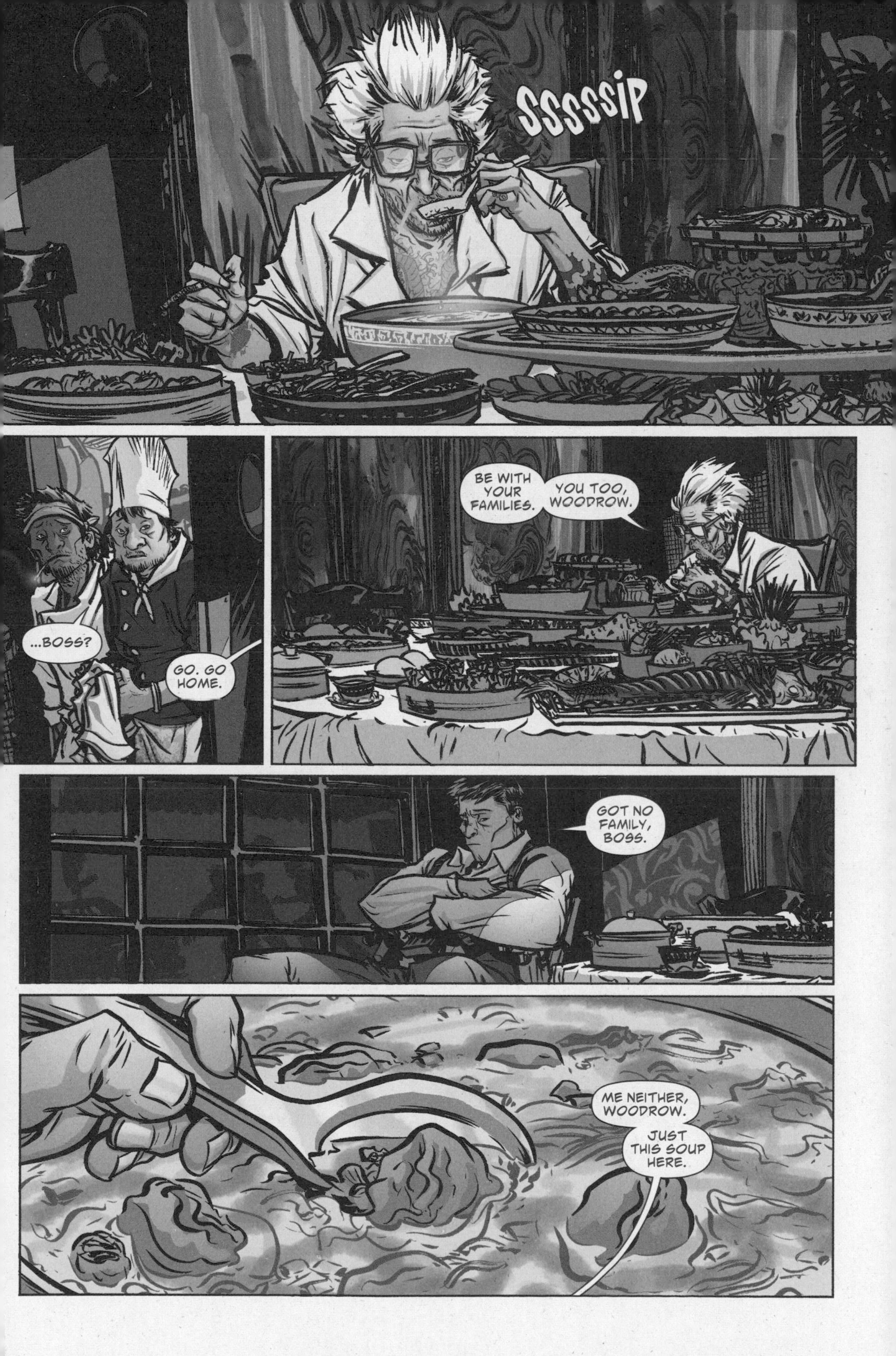
SSSSSIP
...BOSS?
GO. GO HOME.
BE WITH YOUR FAMILIES.
YOU TOO, WOODROW.
GOT NO FAMILY, BOSS.
ME NEITHER, WOODROW.
JUST THIS SOUP HERE.

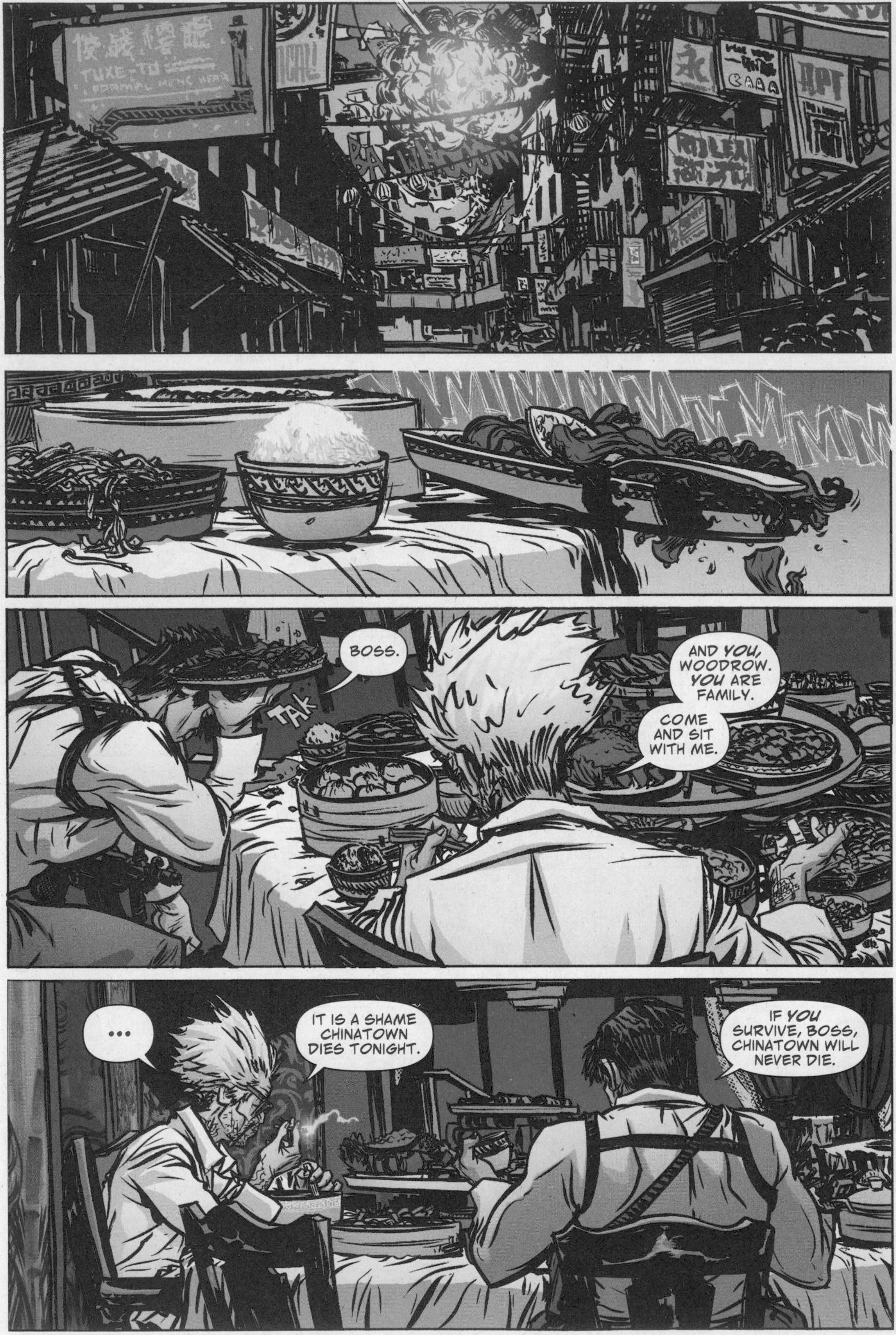
BOSS.
TAK
AND YOU, WOODROW. YOU ARE FAMILY.
COME AND SIT WITH ME.
...
IT IS A SHAME CHINATOWN DIES TONIGHT.
IF YOU SURVIVE, BOSS, CHINATOWN WILL NEVER DIE.

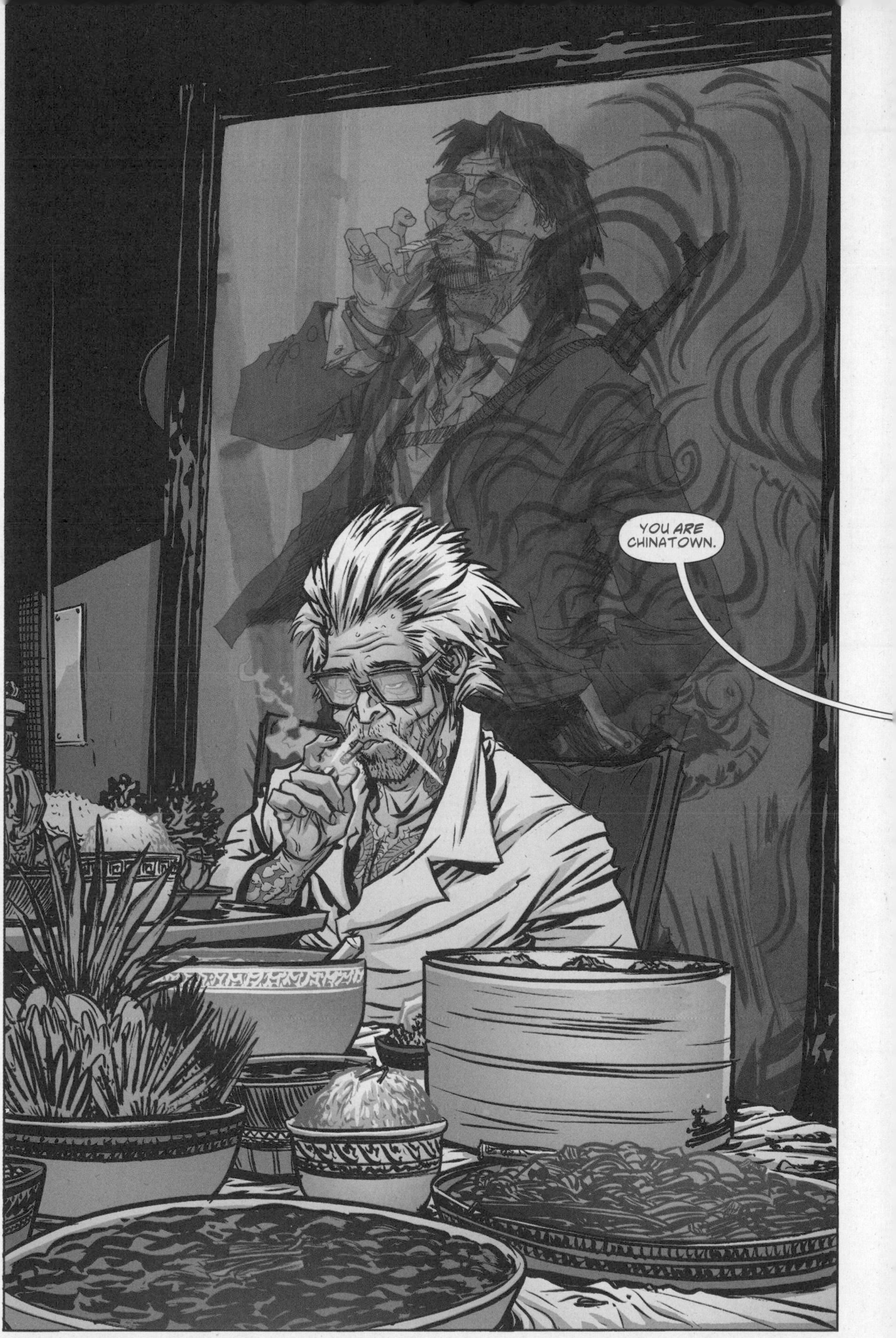
YOU ARE CHINATOWN.

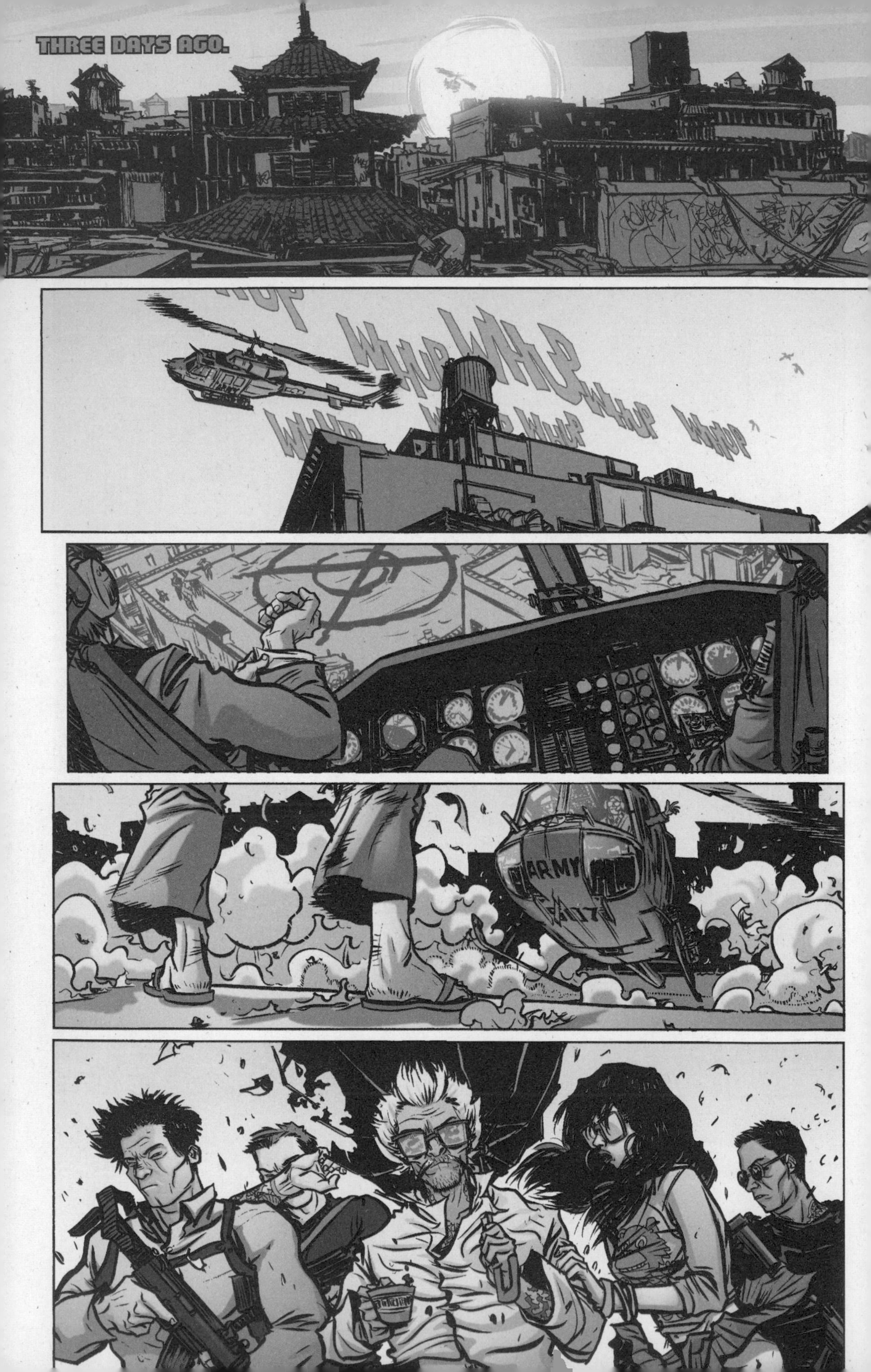
THREE DAYS AGO.
ARMY

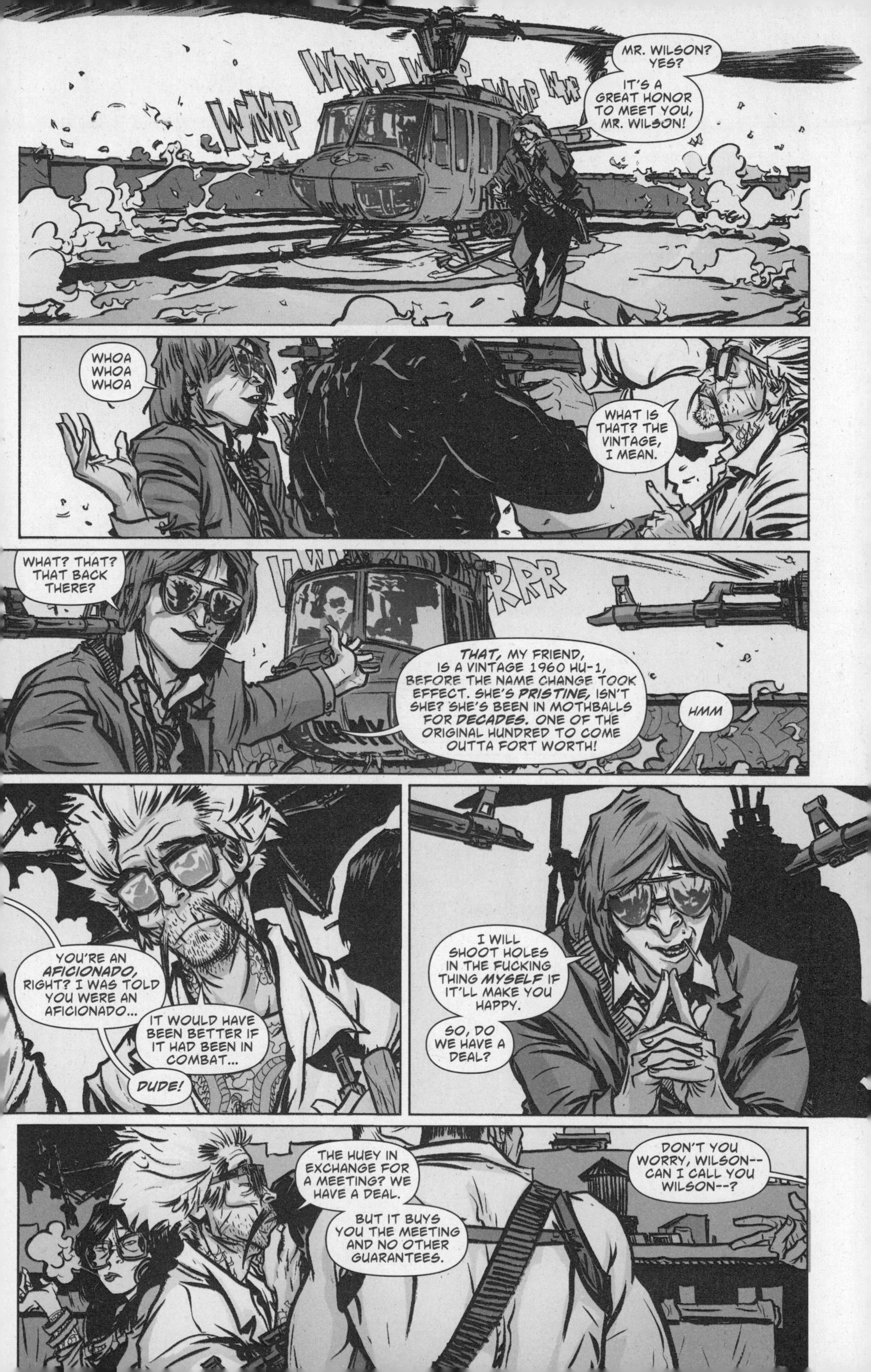
WMP
WMP WMP WMP WMP
MR. WILSON? YES?
IT'S A GREAT HONOR TO MEET YOU, MR. WILSON!
WHOA WHOA WHOA
WHAT IS THAT? THE VINTAGE, I MEAN.
WHAT? THAT? THAT BACK THERE?
RRR
THAT, MY FRIEND, IS A VINTAGE 1960 HU-1, BEFORE THE NAME CHANGE TOOK EFFECT. SHE'S PRISTINE, ISN'T SHE? SHE'S BEEN IN MOTHBALLS FOR DECADES. ONE OF THE ORIGINAL HUNDRED TO COME OUTTA FORT WORTH!
HMM
YOU'RE AN AFICIONADO, RIGHT? I WAS TOLD YOU WERE AN AFICIONADO...
IT WOULD HAVE BEEN BETTER IF IT HAD BEEN IN COMBAT...
DUDE!
I WILL SHOOT HOLES IN THE FUCKING THING MYSELF IF IT'LL MAKE YOU HAPPY.
SO, DO WE HAVE A DEAL?
THE HUEY IN EXCHANGE FOR A MEETING? WE HAVE A DEAL.
BUT IT BUYS YOU THE MEETING AND NO OTHER GUARANTEES.
DON'T YOU WORRY, WILSON-- CAN I CALL YOU WILSON--?

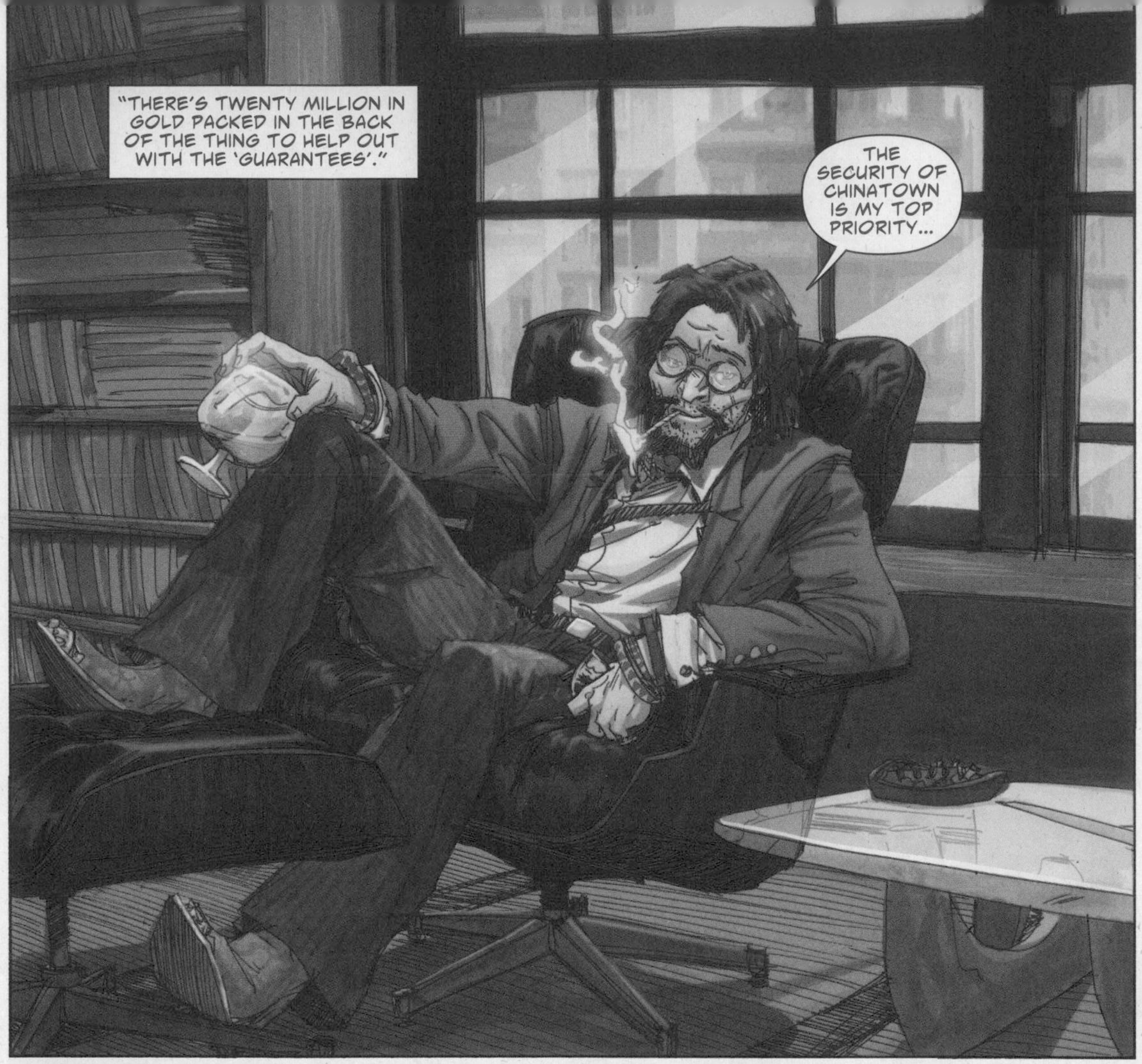
"THERE'S TWENTY MILLION IN GOLD PACKED IN THE BACK OF THE THING TO HELP OUT WITH THE 'GUARANTEES'."
THE SECURITY OF CHINATOWN IS MY TOP PRIORITY...

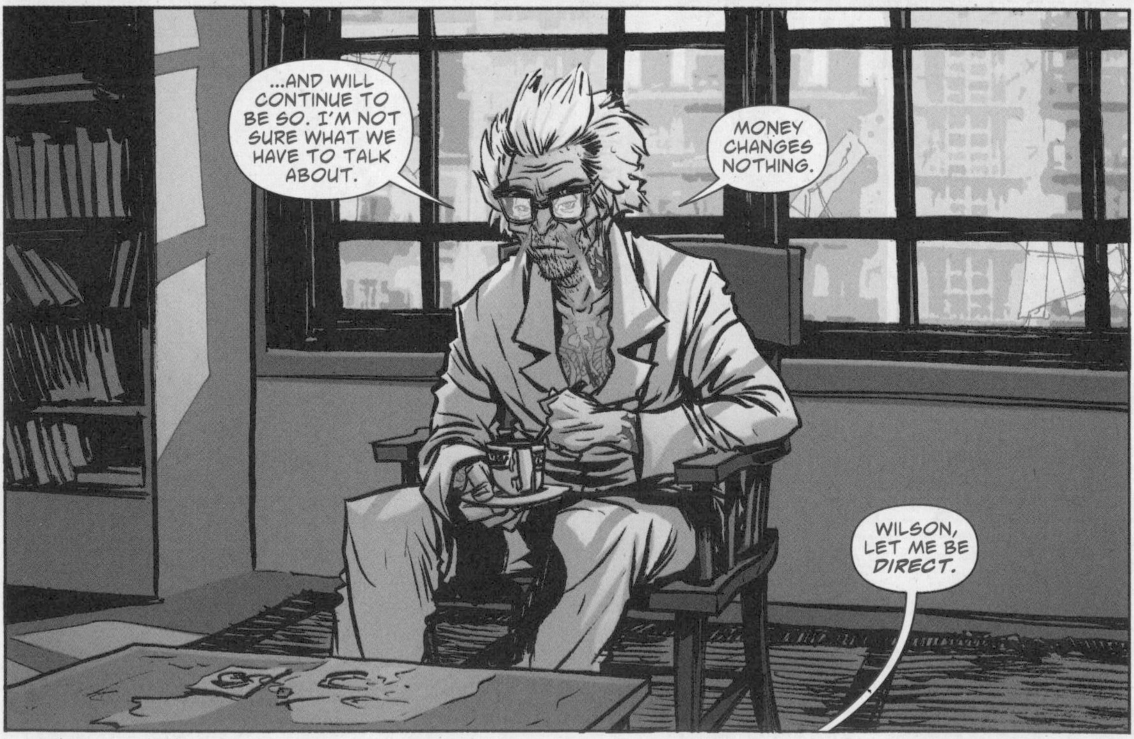
...AND WILL CONTINUE TO BE SO. I'M NOT SURE WHAT WE HAVE TO TALK ABOUT.
MONEY CHANGES NOTHING.
WILSON, LET ME BE *DIRECT*.

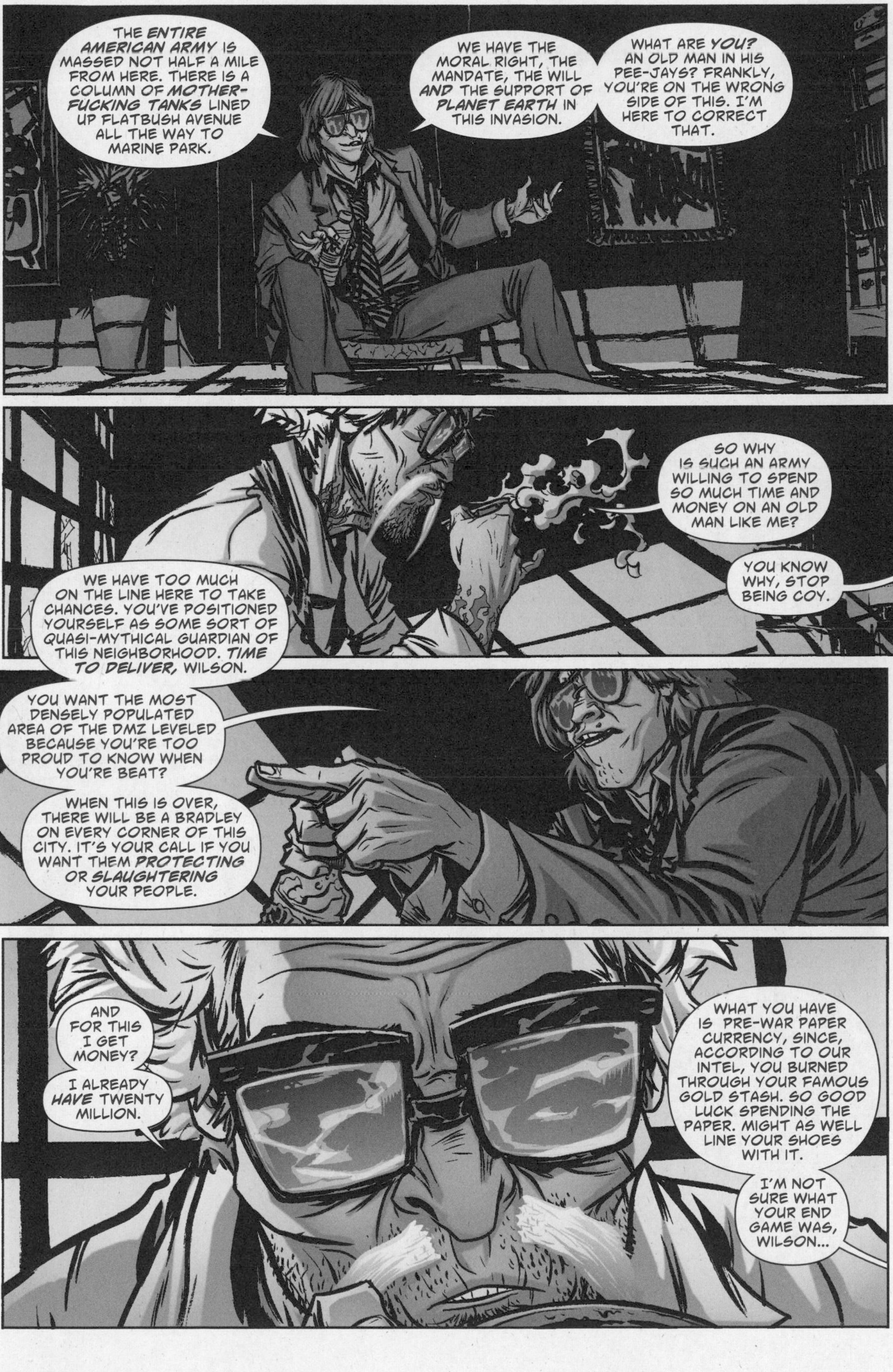
THE ENTIRE AMERICAN ARMY IS MASSED NOT HALF A MILE FROM HERE. THERE IS A COLUMN OF MOTHER-FUCKING TANKS LINED UP FLATBUSH AVENUE ALL THE WAY TO MARINE PARK.
WE HAVE THE MORAL RIGHT, THE MANDATE, THE WILL AND THE SUPPORT OF PLANET EARTH IN THIS INVASION.
WHAT ARE YOU? AN OLD MAN IN HIS PEE-JAYS? FRANKLY, YOU'RE ON THE WRONG SIDE OF THIS. I'M HERE TO CORRECT THAT.
SO WHY IS SUCH AN ARMY WILLING TO SPEND SO MUCH TIME AND MONEY ON AN OLD MAN LIKE ME?
YOU KNOW WHY, STOP BEING COY.
WE HAVE TOO MUCH ON THE LINE HERE TO TAKE CHANCES. YOU'VE POSITIONED YOURSELF AS SOME SORT OF QUASI-MYTHICAL GUARDIAN OF THIS NEIGHBORHOOD. TIME TO DELIVER, WILSON.
YOU WANT THE MOST DENSELY POPULATED AREA OF THE DMZ LEVELED BECAUSE YOU'RE TOO PROUD TO KNOW WHEN YOU'RE BEAT?
WHEN THIS IS OVER, THERE WILL BE A BRADLEY ON EVERY CORNER OF THIS CITY. IT'S YOUR CALL IF YOU WANT THEM PROTECTING OR SLAUGHTERING YOUR PEOPLE.
AND FOR THIS I GET MONEY?
I ALREADY HAVE TWENTY MILLION.
WHAT YOU HAVE IS PRE-WAR PAPER CURRENCY, SINCE, ACCORDING TO OUR INTEL, YOU BURNED THROUGH YOUR FAMOUS GOLD STASH. SO GOOD LUCK SPENDING THE PAPER. MIGHT AS WELL LINE YOUR SHOES WITH IT.
I'M NOT SURE WHAT YOUR END GAME WAS, WILSON...

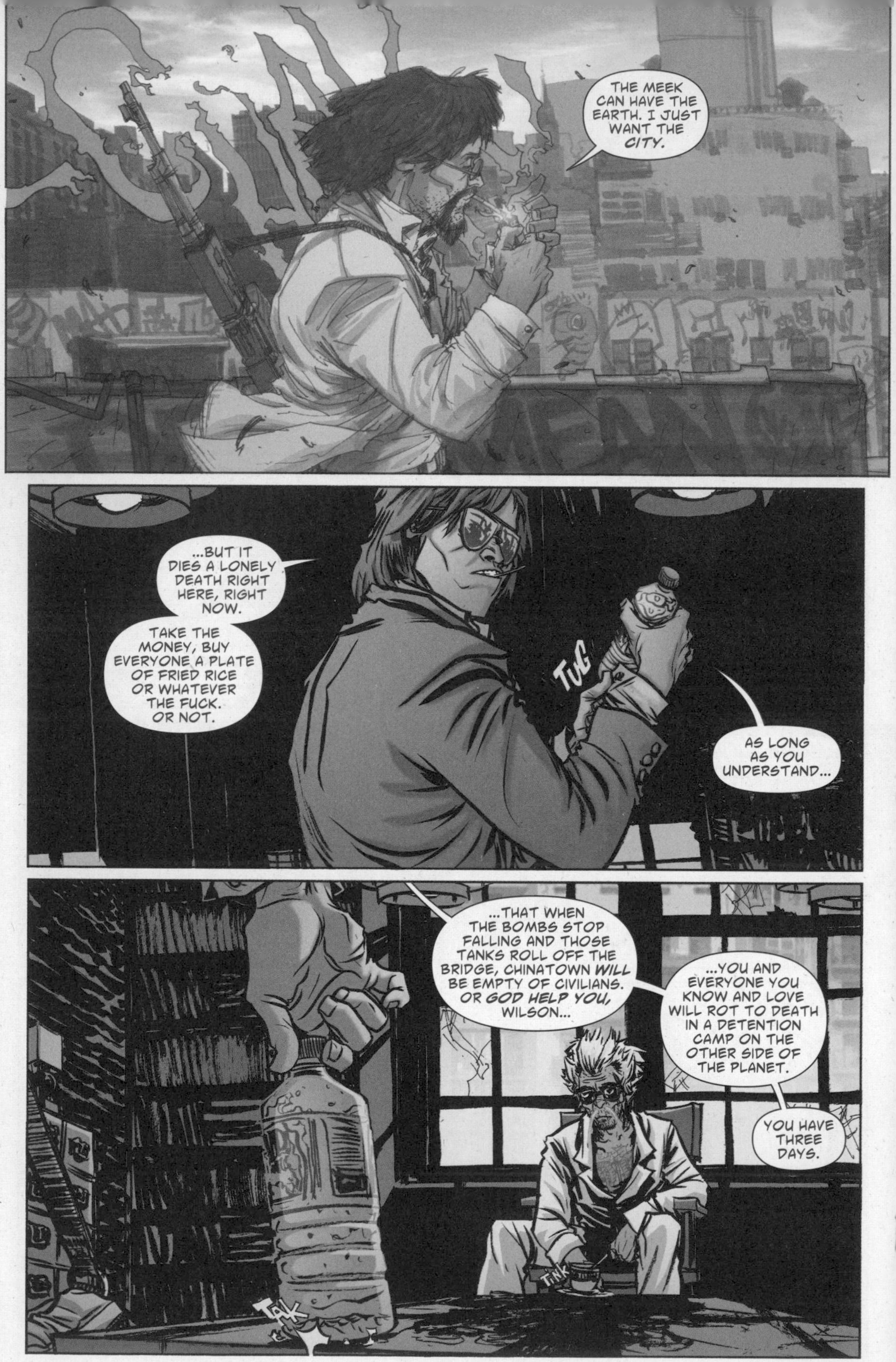
THE MEEK CAN HAVE THE EARTH. I JUST WANT THE CITY.
...BUT IT DIES A LONELY DEATH RIGHT HERE, RIGHT NOW.
TAKE THE MONEY, BUY EVERYONE A PLATE OF FRIED RICE OR WHATEVER THE FUCK. OR NOT.
TUG
AS LONG AS YOU UNDERSTAND...
...THAT WHEN THE BOMBS STOP FALLING AND THOSE TANKS ROLL OFF THE BRIDGE, CHINATOWN WILL BE EMPTY OF CIVILIANS. OR GOD HELP YOU, WILSON...
...YOU AND EVERYONE YOU KNOW AND LOVE WILL ROT TO DEATH IN A DETENTION CAMP ON THE OTHER SIDE OF THE PLANET.
YOU HAVE THREE DAYS.
TINK
TAK

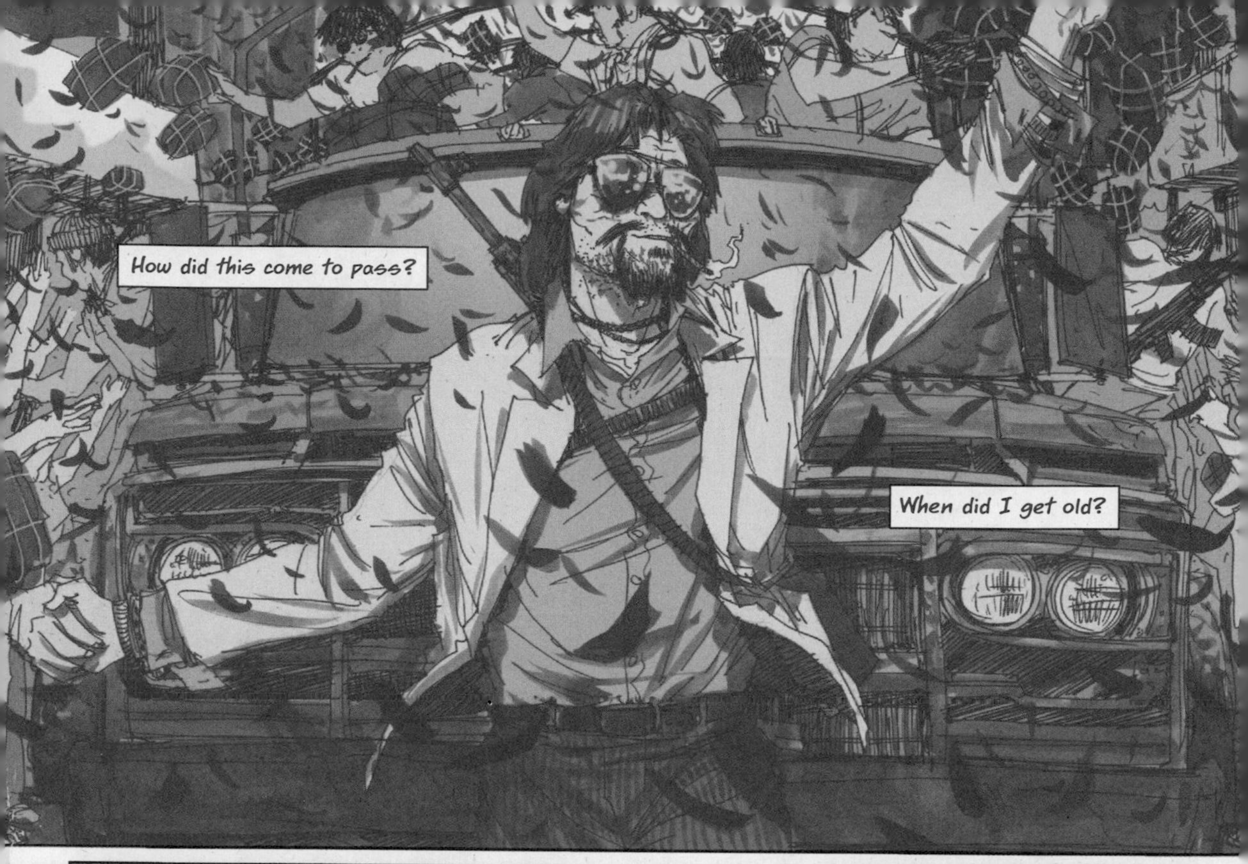
How did this come to pass?
When did I get old?

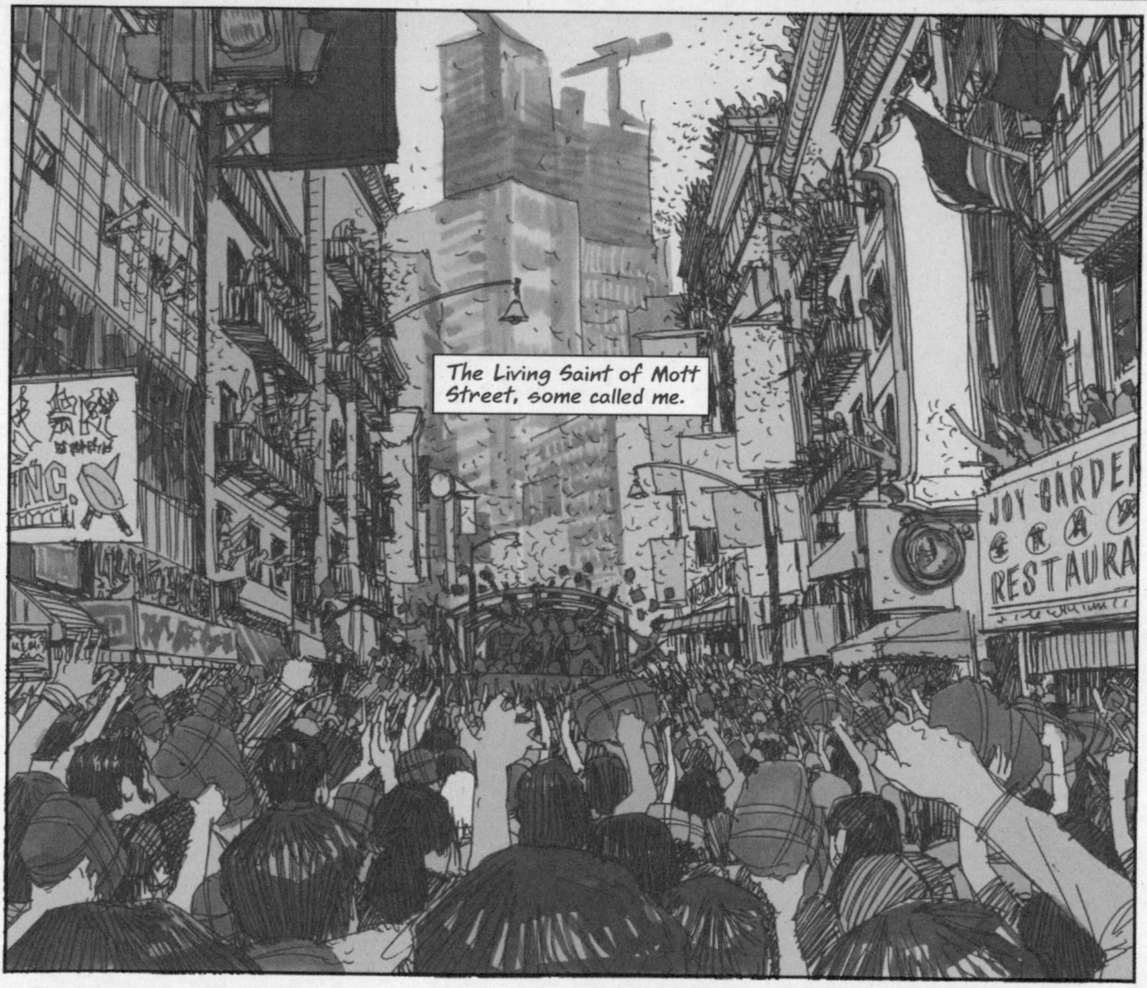
The Living Saint of Mott Street, some called me.
JOY GARDEN
RESTAURA

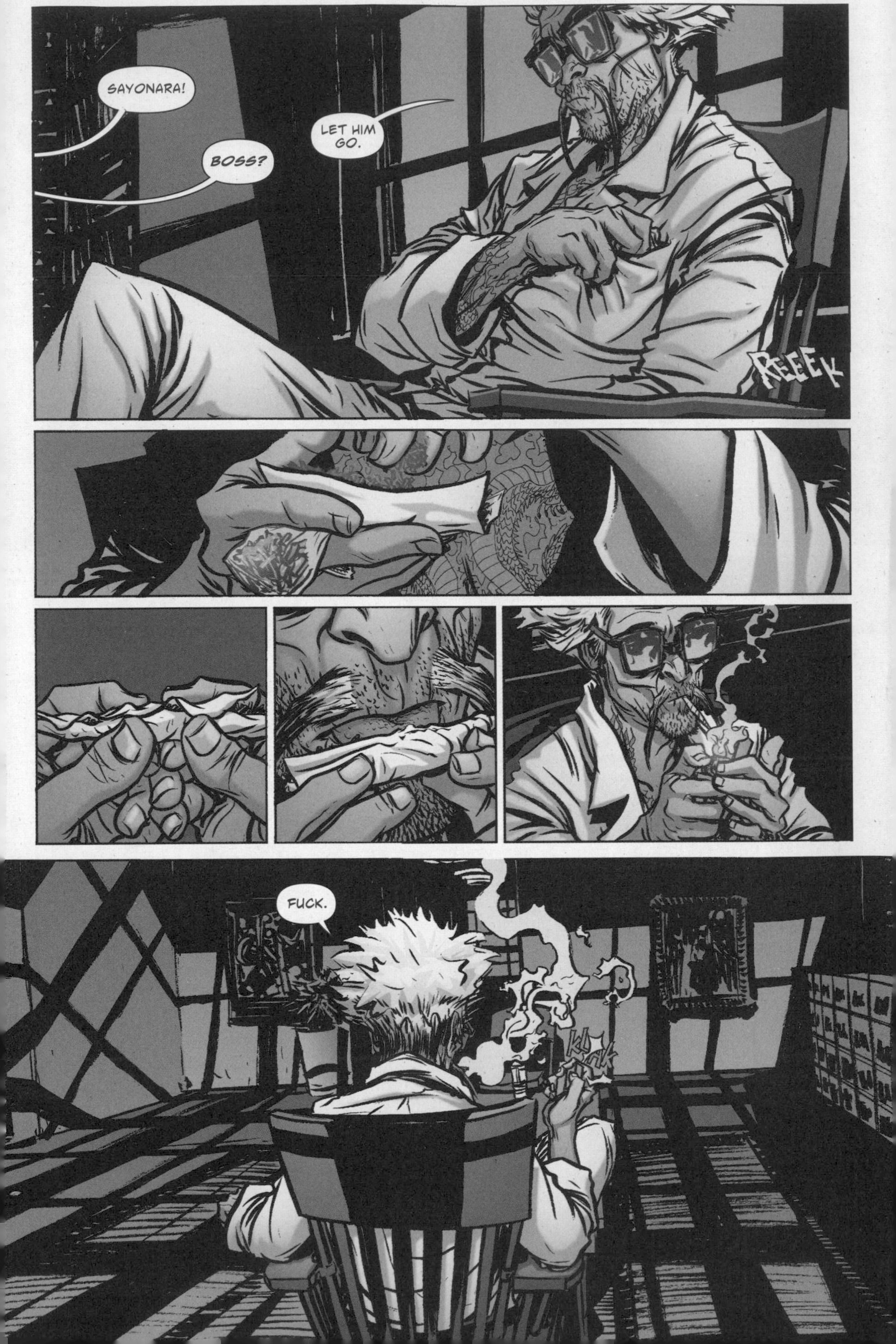
SAYONARA!
BOSS?
LET HIM GO.
REEEK
FUCK.
KLAK

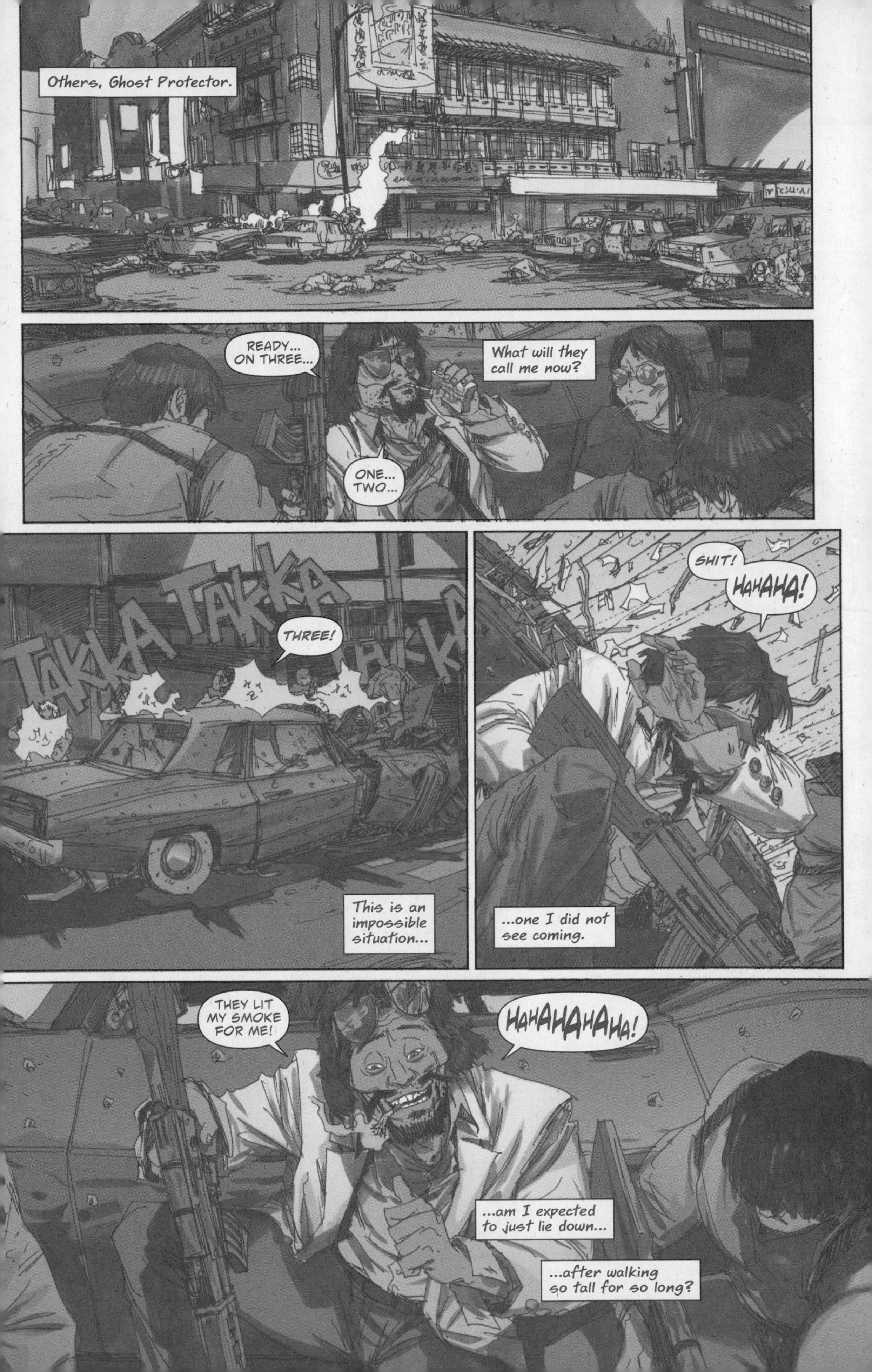
Others, Ghost Protector.
READY... ON THREE...
What will they call me now?
ONE... TWO...
TAKKA TAKKA TAKKA
THREE!
This is an impossible situation...
SHIT!
HAHAHA!
...one I did not see coming.
THEY LIT MY SMOKE FOR ME!
HAHAHAHAHAHA!
...am I expected to just lie down...
...after walking so tall for so long?

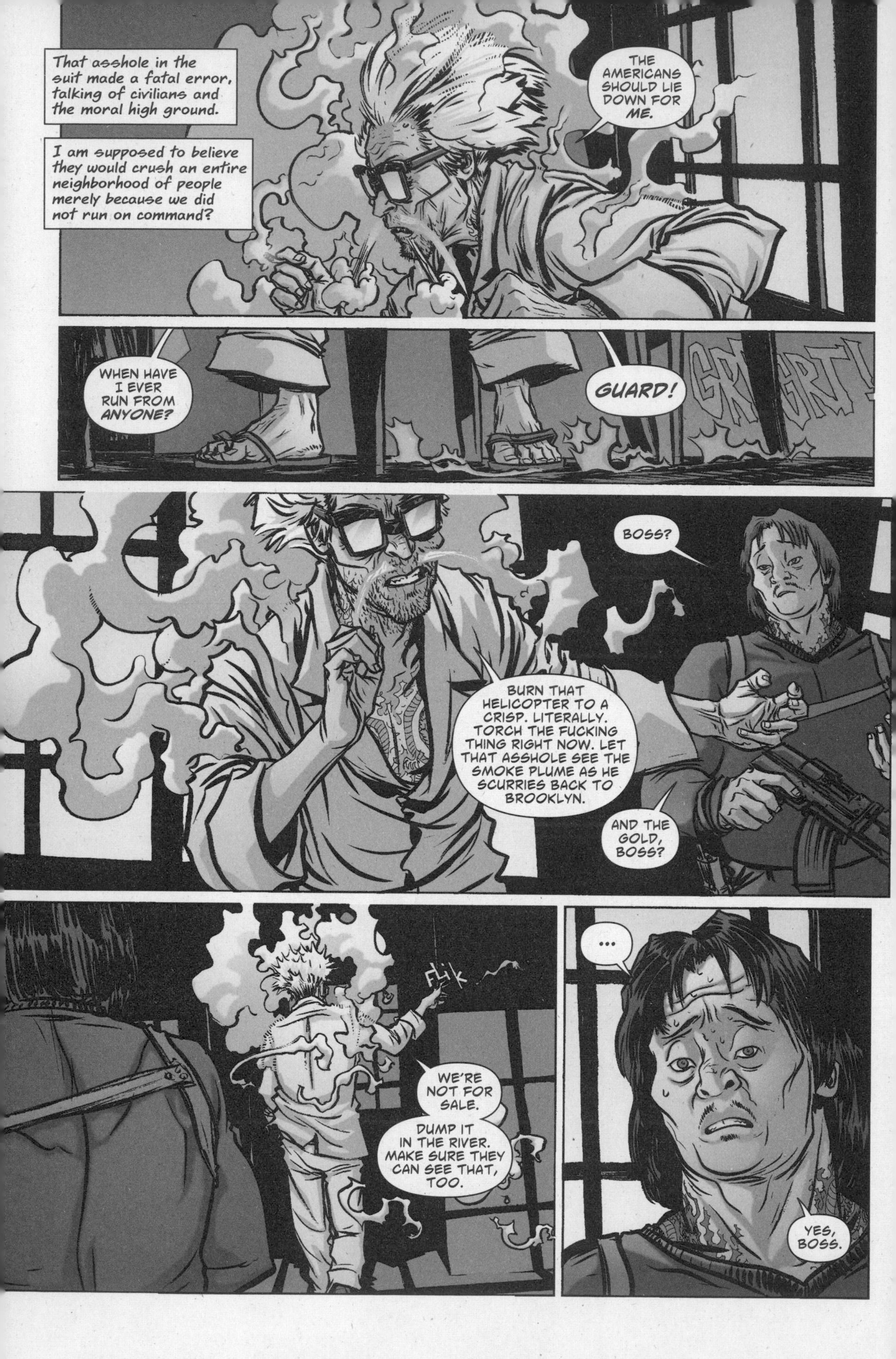
That asshole in the suit made a fatal error, talking of civilians and the moral high ground.
I am supposed to believe they would crush an entire neighborhood of people merely because we did not run on command?
THE AMERICANS SHOULD LIE DOWN FOR ME.
WHEN HAVE I EVER RUN FROM ANYONE?
GUARD!
BOSS?
BURN THAT HELICOPTER TO A CRISP. LITERALLY. TORCH THE FUCKING THING RIGHT NOW. LET THAT ASSHOLE SEE THE SMOKE PLUME AS HE SCURRIES BACK TO BROOKLYN.
AND THE GOLD, BOSS?
FLIK
WE'RE NOT FOR SALE.
DUMP IT IN THE RIVER. MAKE SURE THEY CAN SEE THAT, TOO.
...
YES, BOSS.

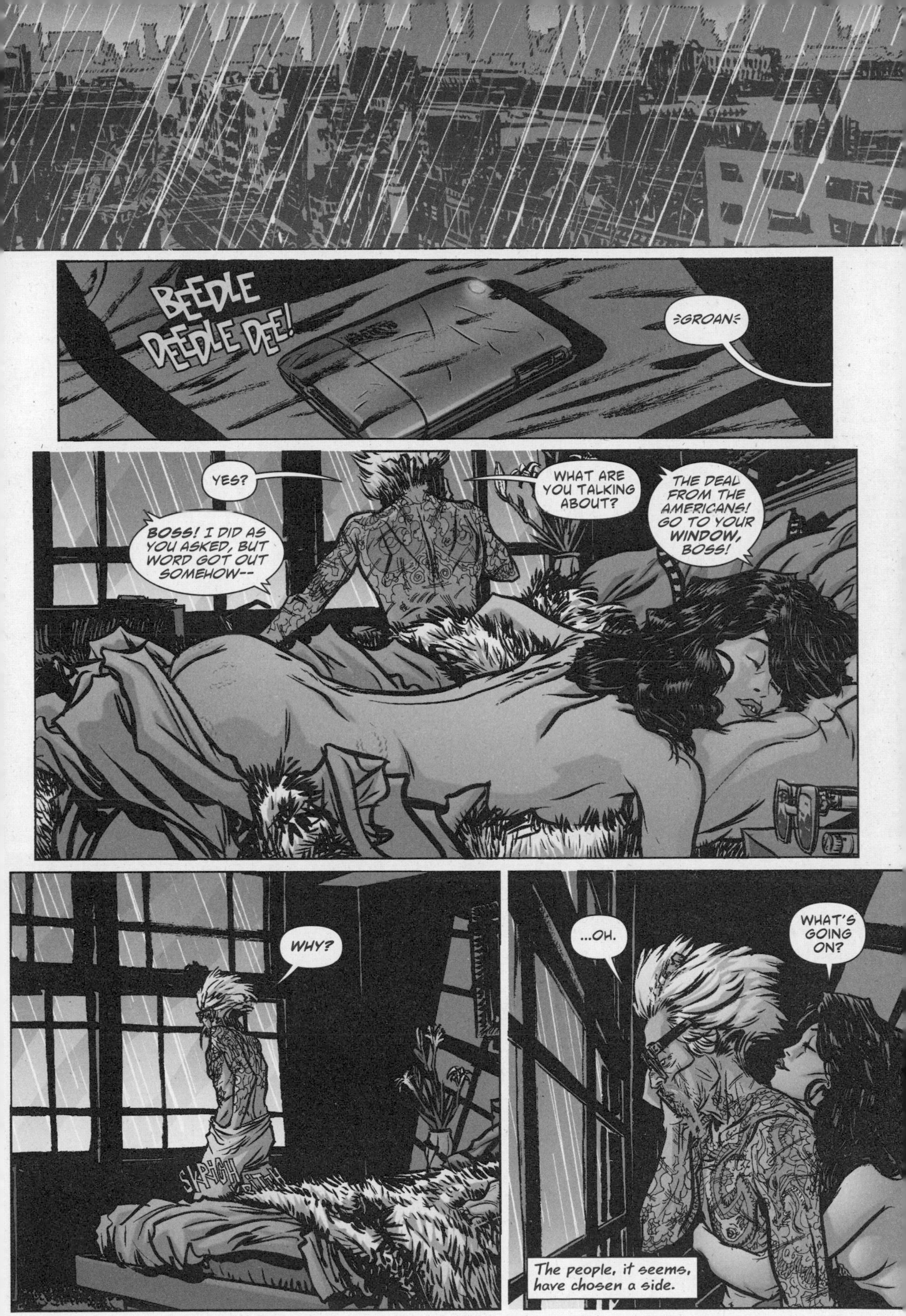
BEEDLE DEEDLE DEE!
GROAN
YES?
BOSS! I DID AS YOU ASKED, BUT WORD GOT OUT SOMEHOW--
WHAT ARE YOU TALKING ABOUT?
THE DEAL FROM THE AMERICANS! GO TO YOUR WINDOW, BOSS!
WHY?
...OH.
WHAT'S GOING ON?
The people, it seems, have chosen a side.

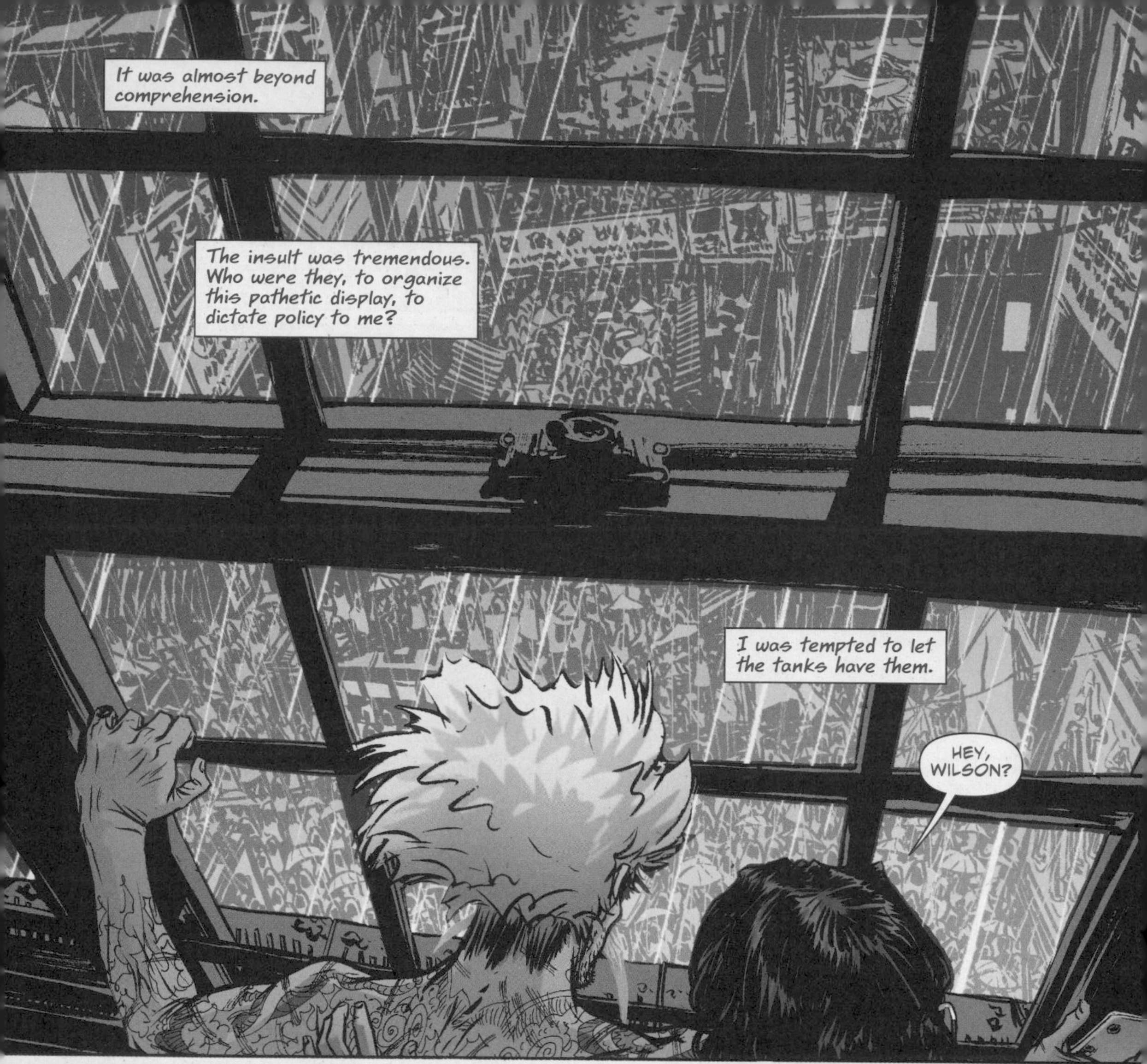
It was almost beyond comprehension.
The insult was tremendous. Who were they, to organize this pathetic display, to dictate policy to me?
I was tempted to let the tanks have them.
HEY, WILSON?

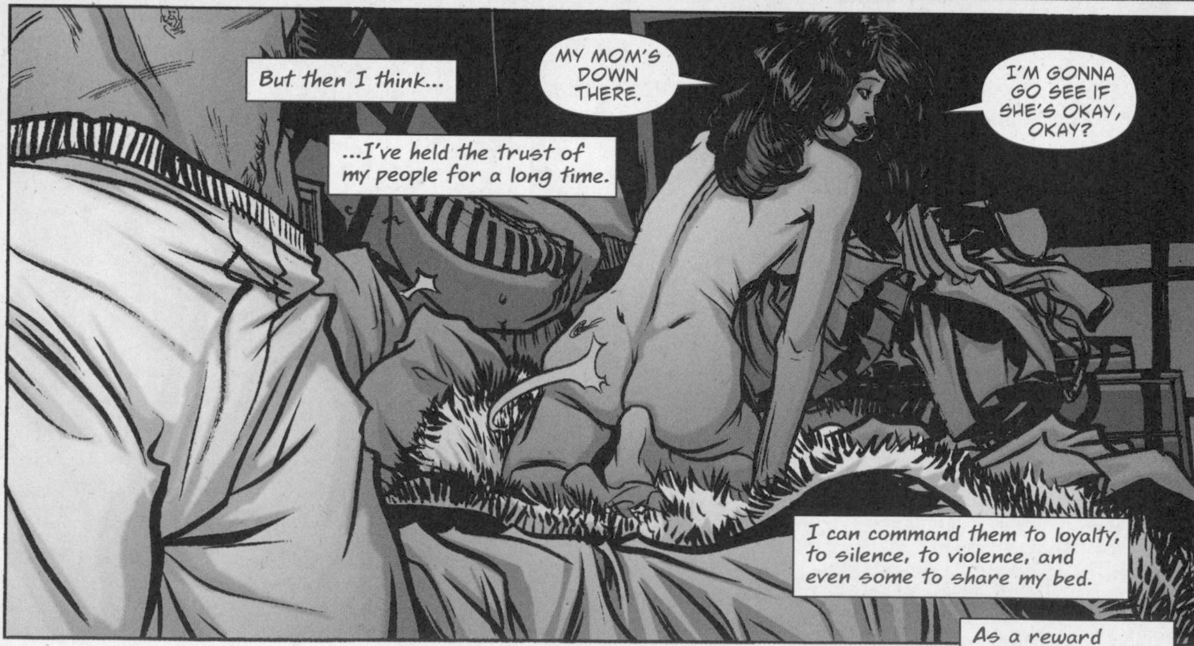
But then I think...
MY MOM'S DOWN THERE.
I'M GONNA GO SEE IF SHE'S OKAY, OKAY?
...I've held the trust of my people for a long time.
I can command them to loyalty, to silence, to violence, and even some to share my bed.
As a reward I should do what...

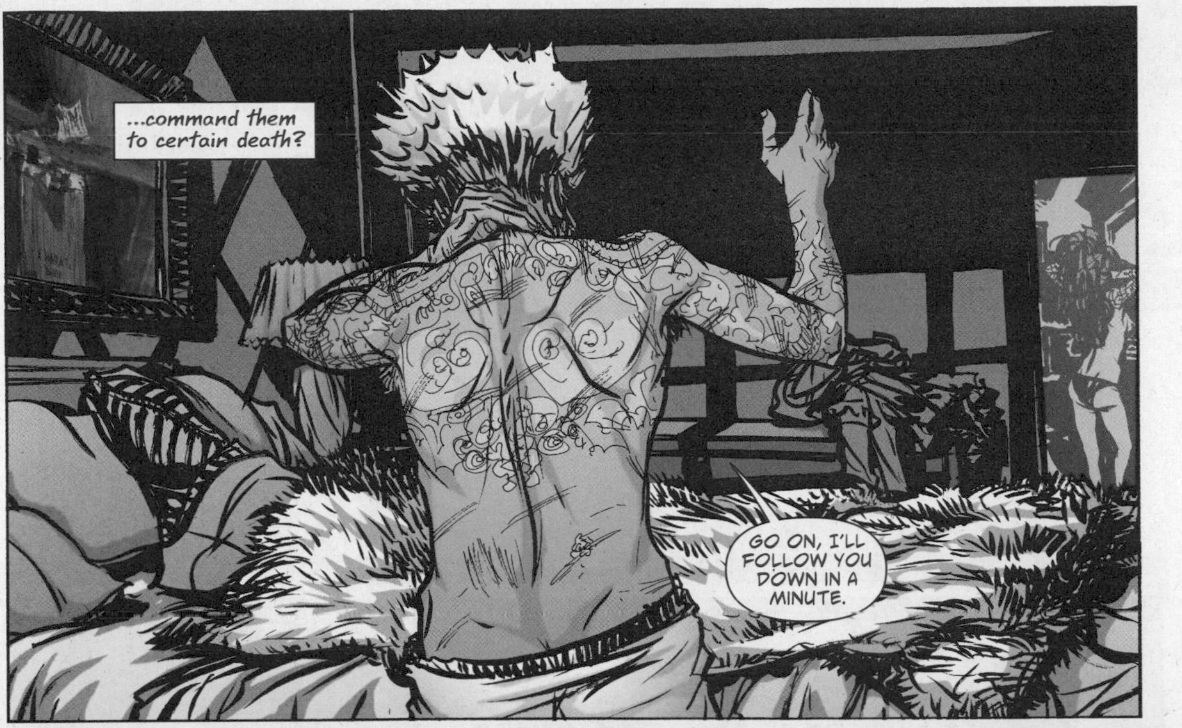
...command them to certain death?
GO ON, I'LL FOLLOW YOU DOWN IN A MINUTE.

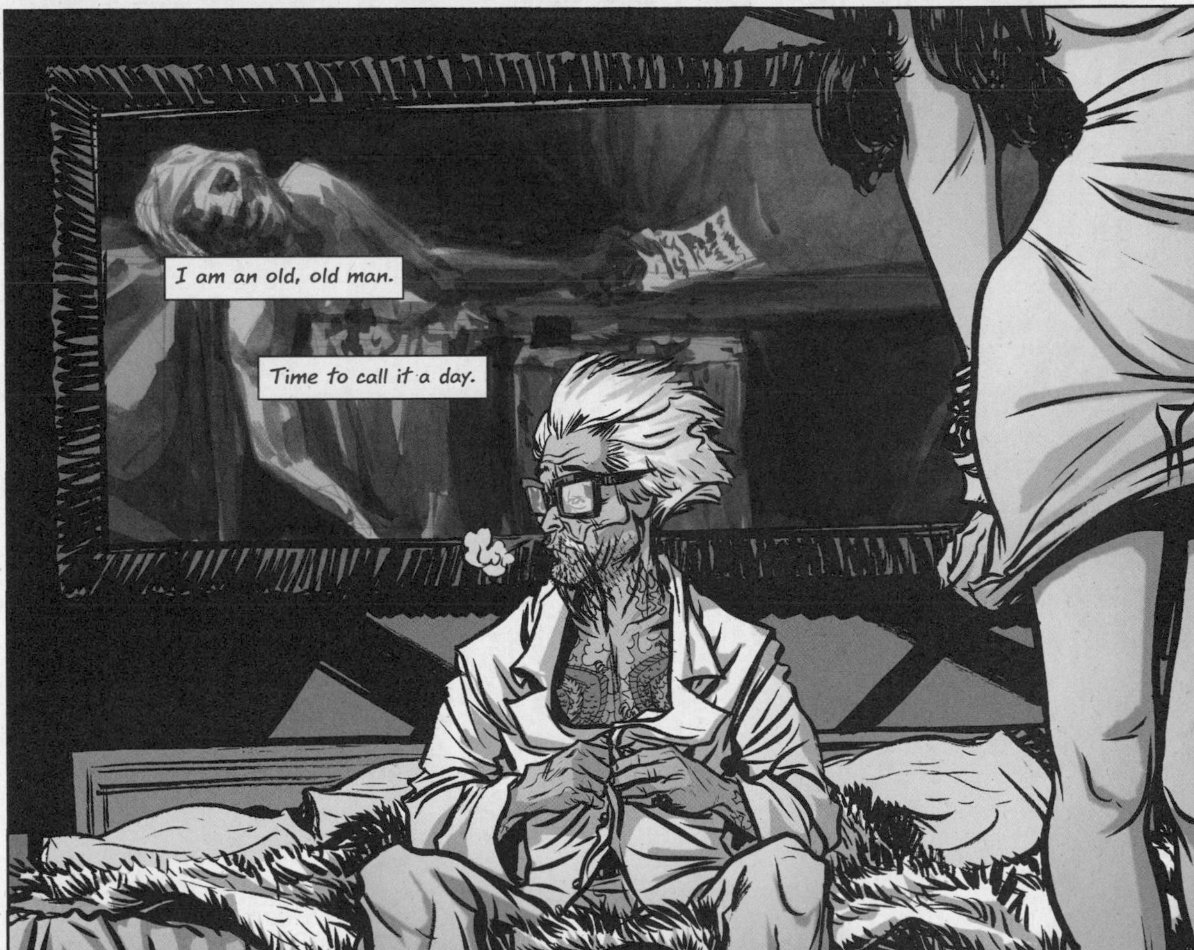
I am an old, old man.
Time to call it a day.

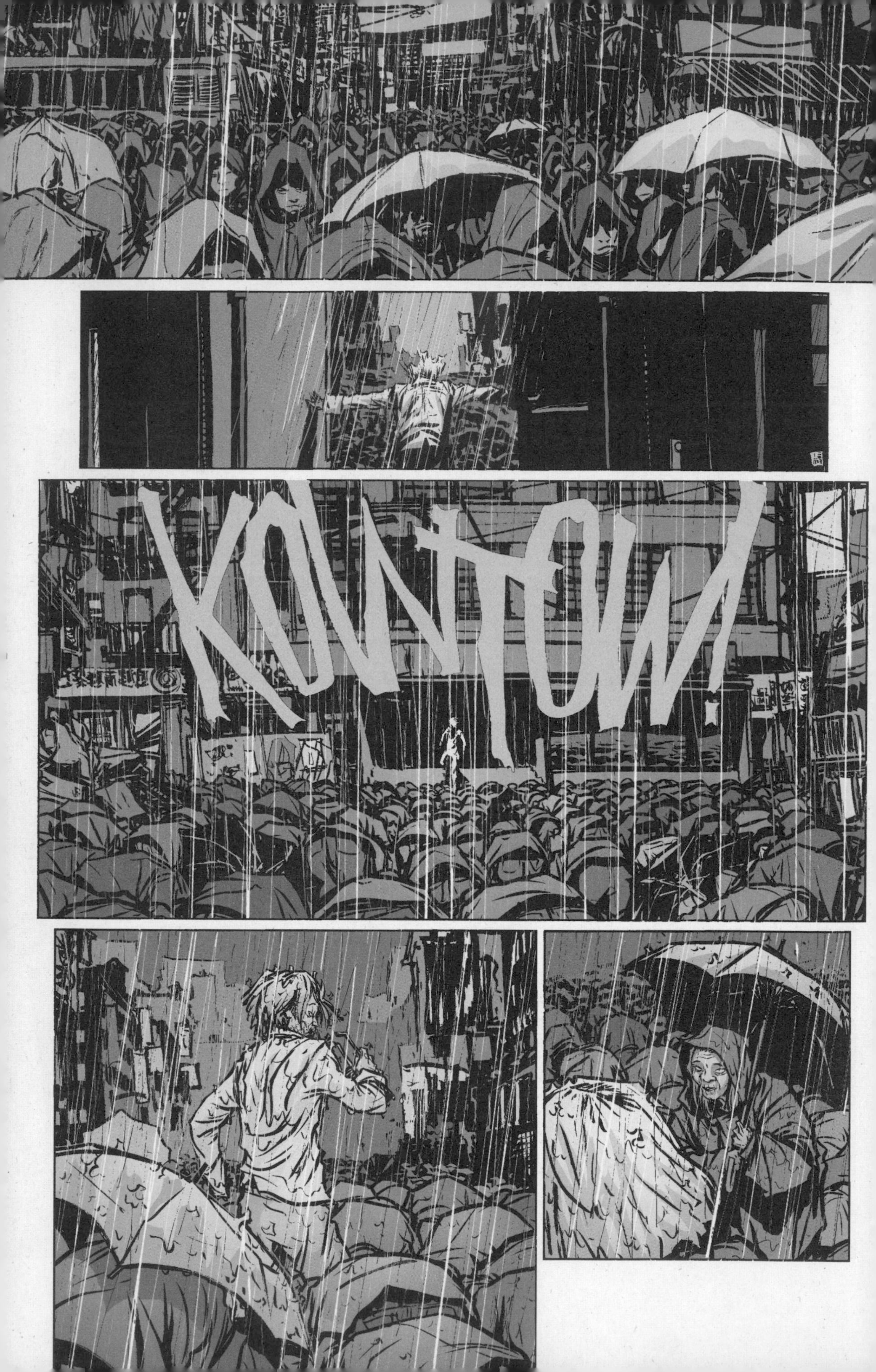
KOWTOW!

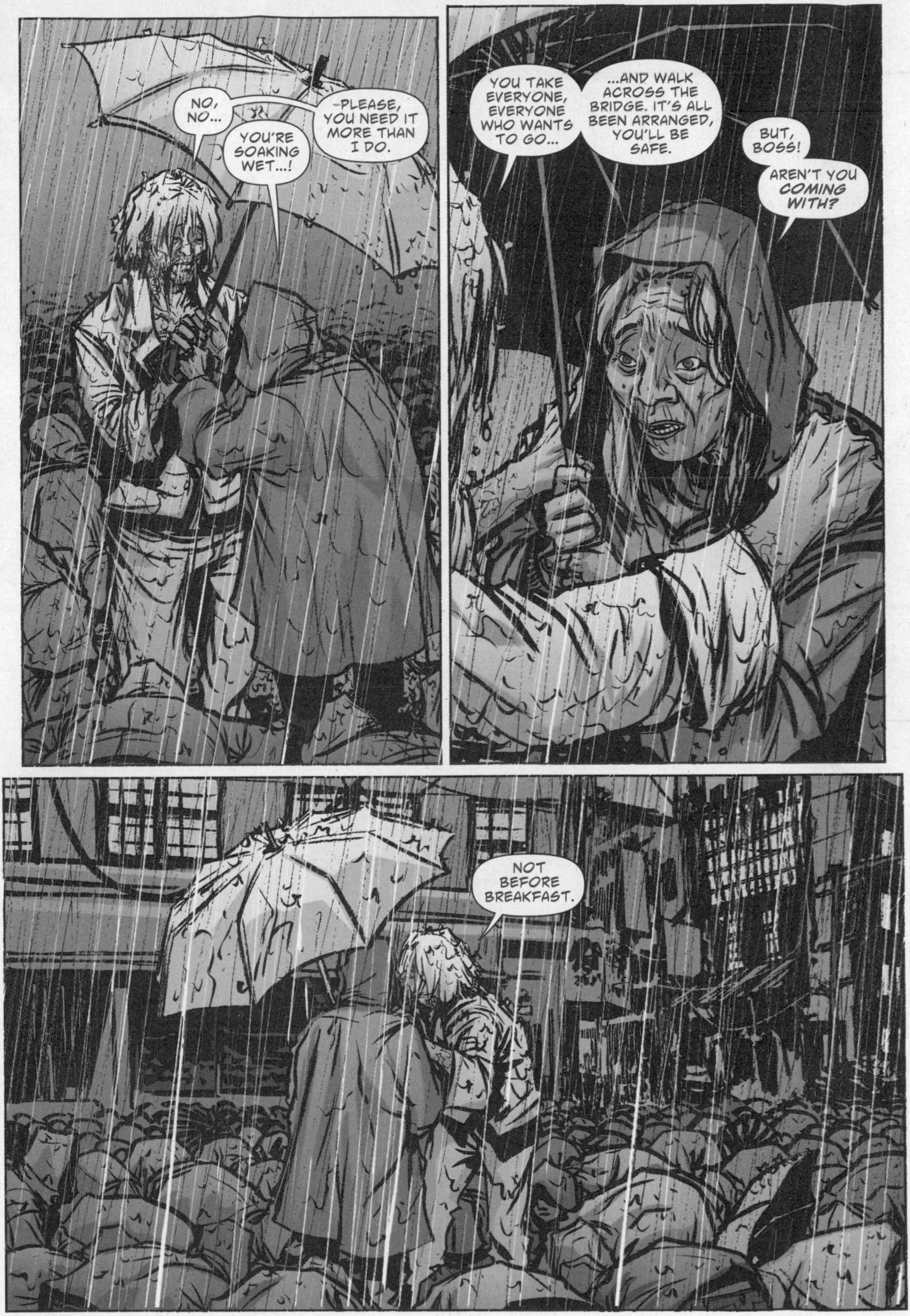
NO, NO...
YOU'RE SOAKING WET...!
-PLEASE, YOU NEED IT MORE THAN I DO.
YOU TAKE EVERYONE, EVERYONE WHO WANTS TO GO...
...AND WALK ACROSS THE BRIDGE. IT'S ALL BEEN ARRANGED, YOU'LL BE SAFE.
BUT, BOSS!
AREN'T YOU COMING WITH?
NOT BEFORE BREAKFAST.

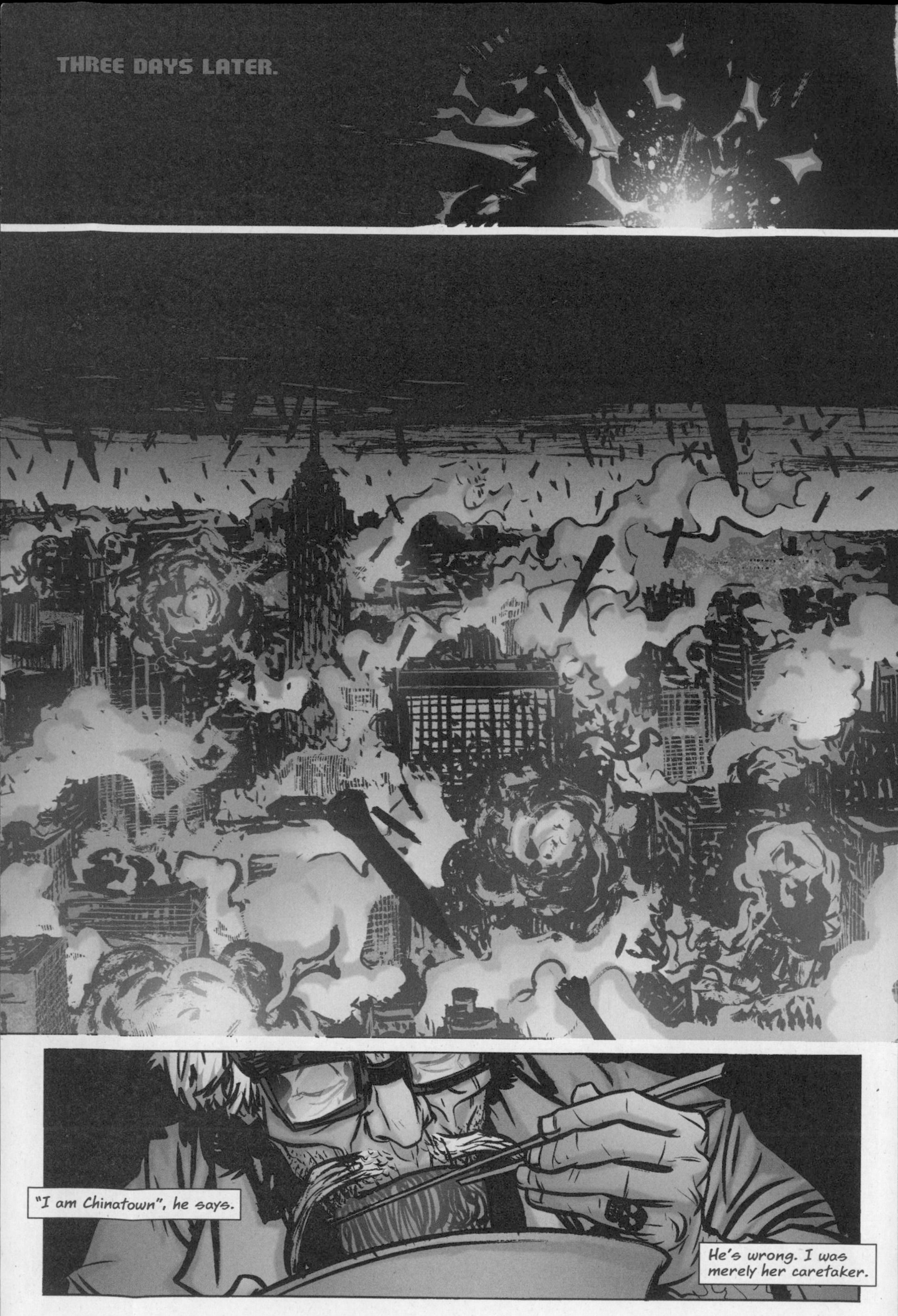
THREE DAYS LATER.
"I am Chinatown", he says.
He's wrong. I was merely her caretaker.

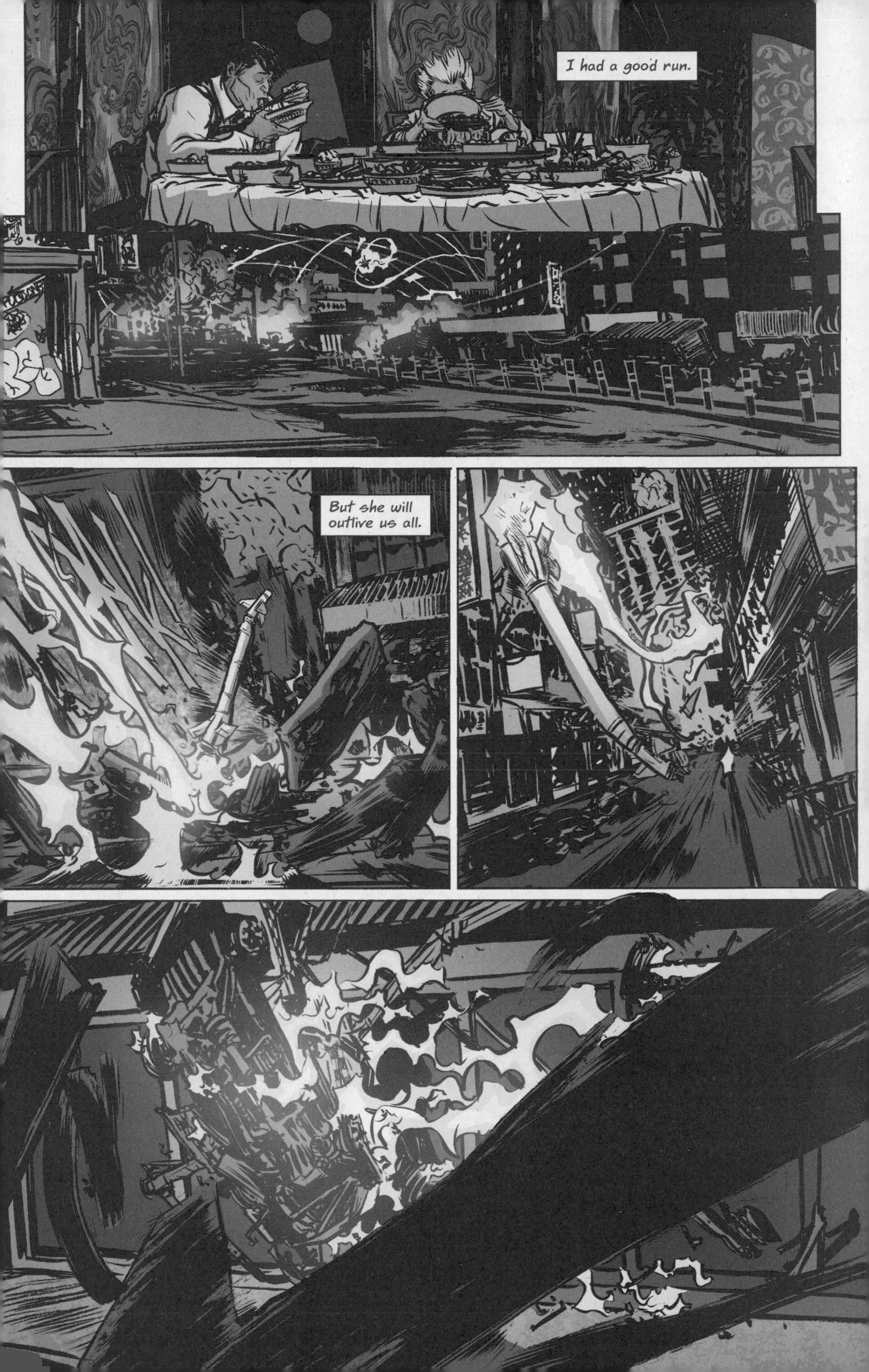
I had a good run.
But she will outlive us all.

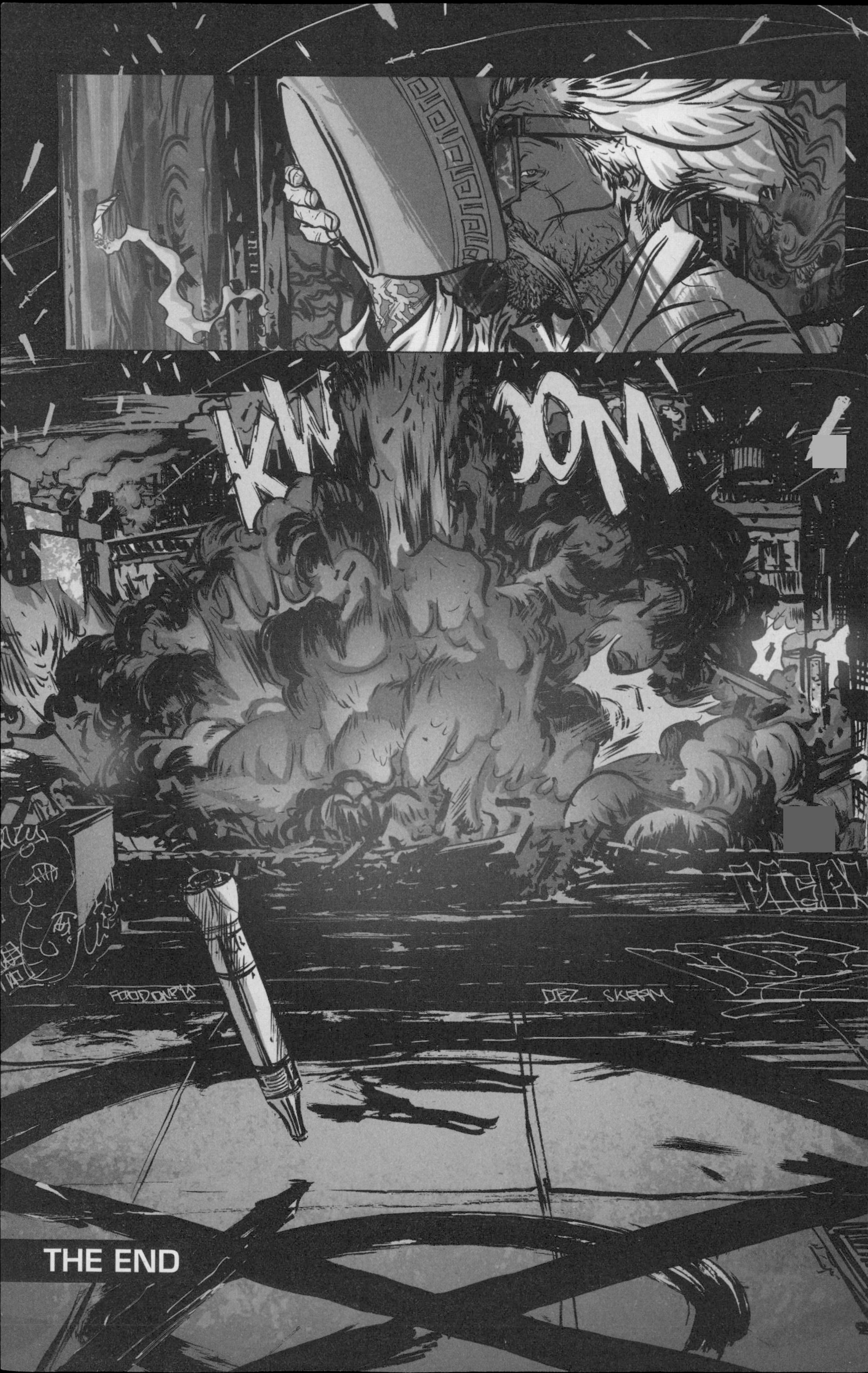
THE END

AMINA, MOTHER OF ONE

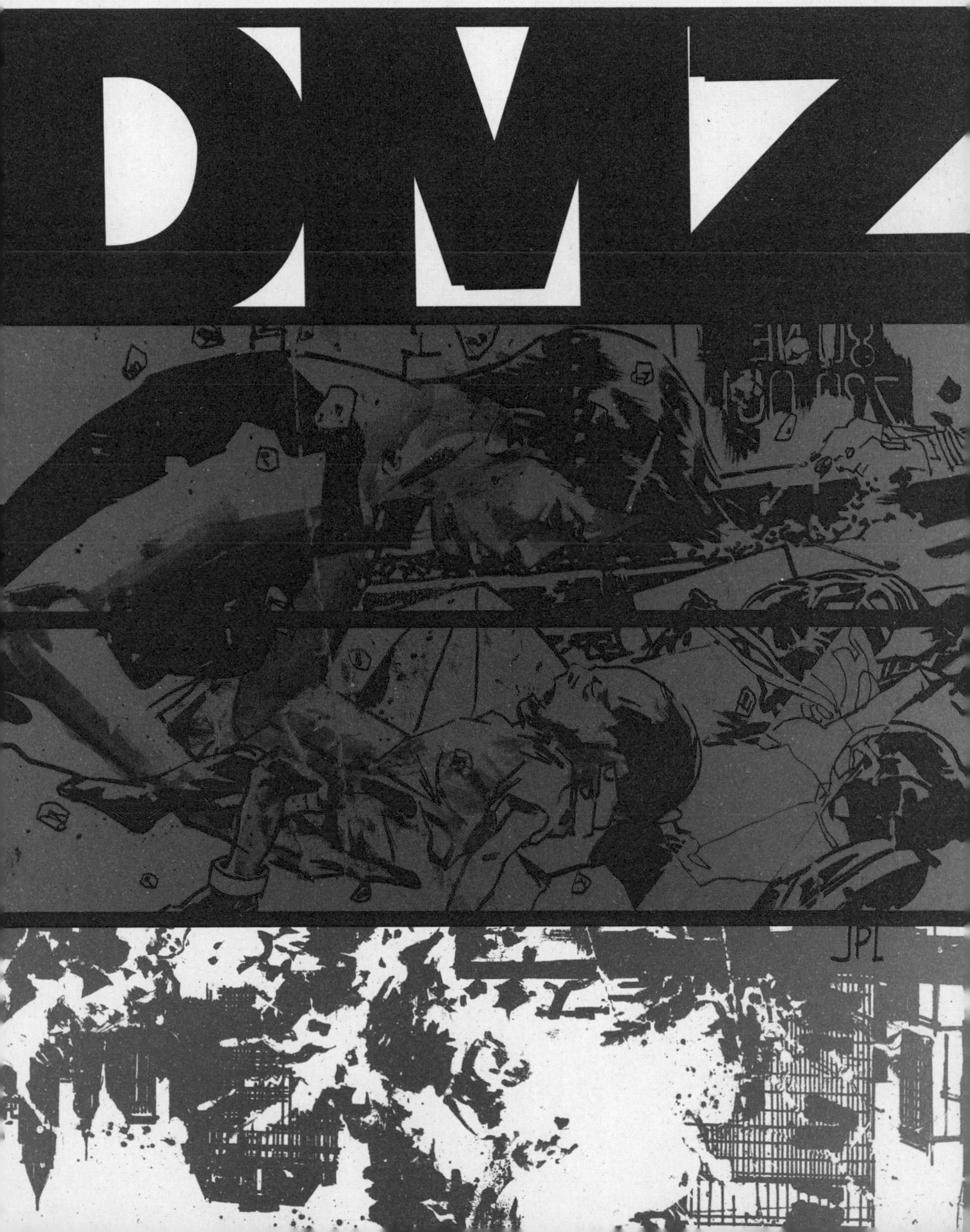
DMZ

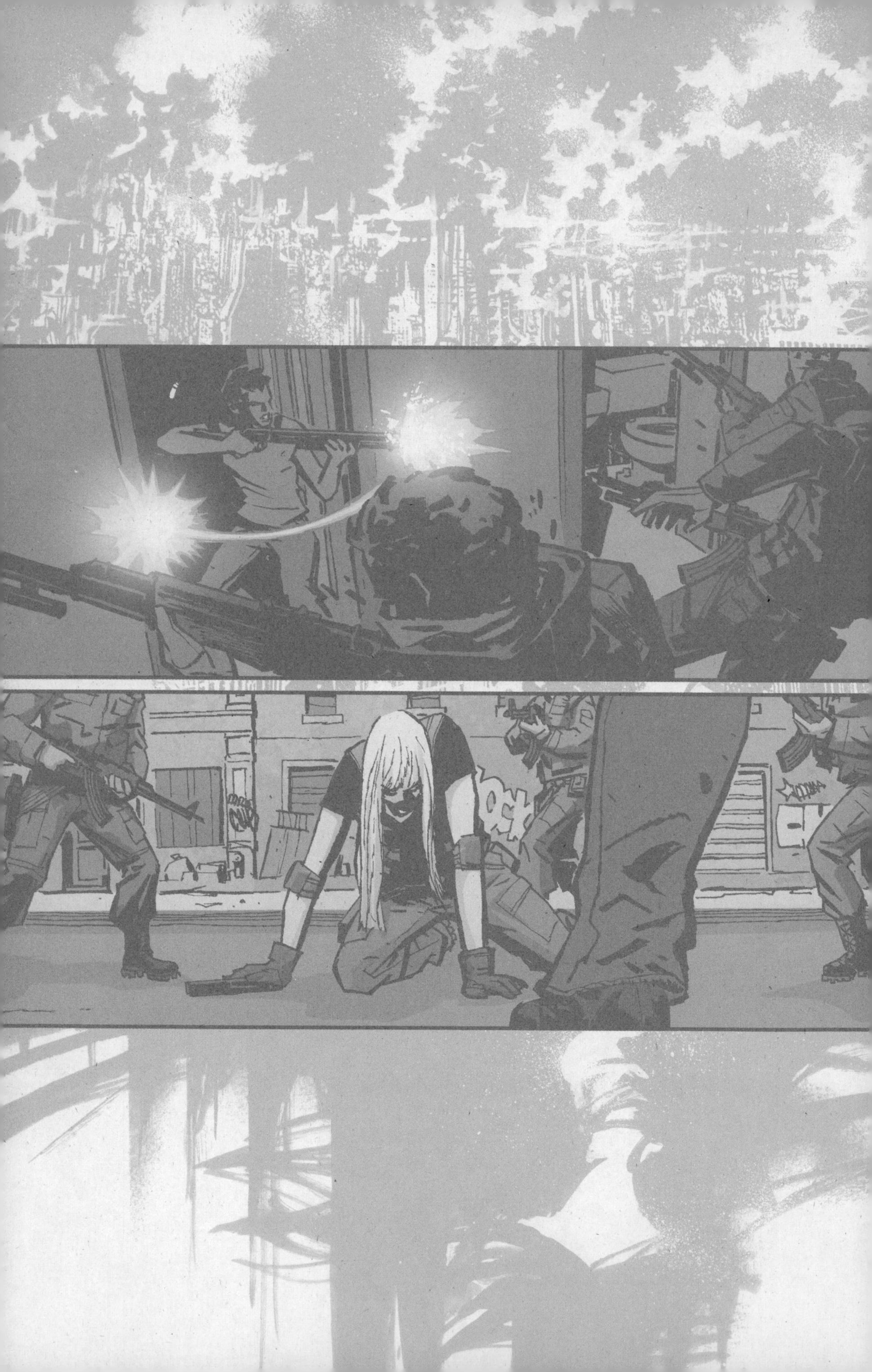

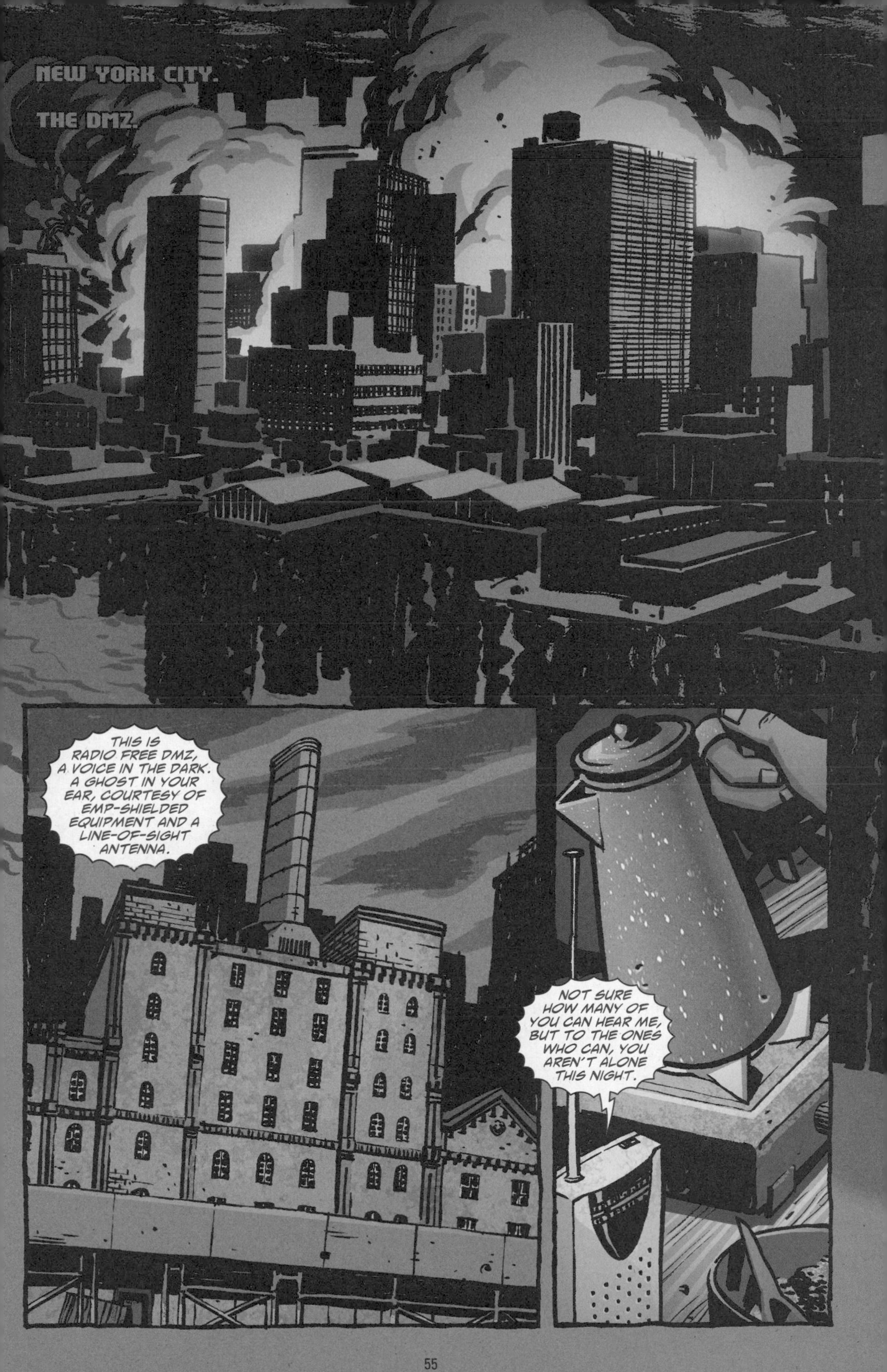
NEW YORK CITY.
THE DMZ.
THIS IS RADIO FREE DMZ, A VOICE IN THE DARK. A GHOST IN YOUR EAR, COURTESY OF EMP-SHIELDED EQUIPMENT AND A LINE-OF-SIGHT ANTENNA.
NOT SURE HOW MANY OF YOU CAN HEAR ME, BUT TO THE ONES WHO CAN, YOU AREN'T ALONE THIS NIGHT.

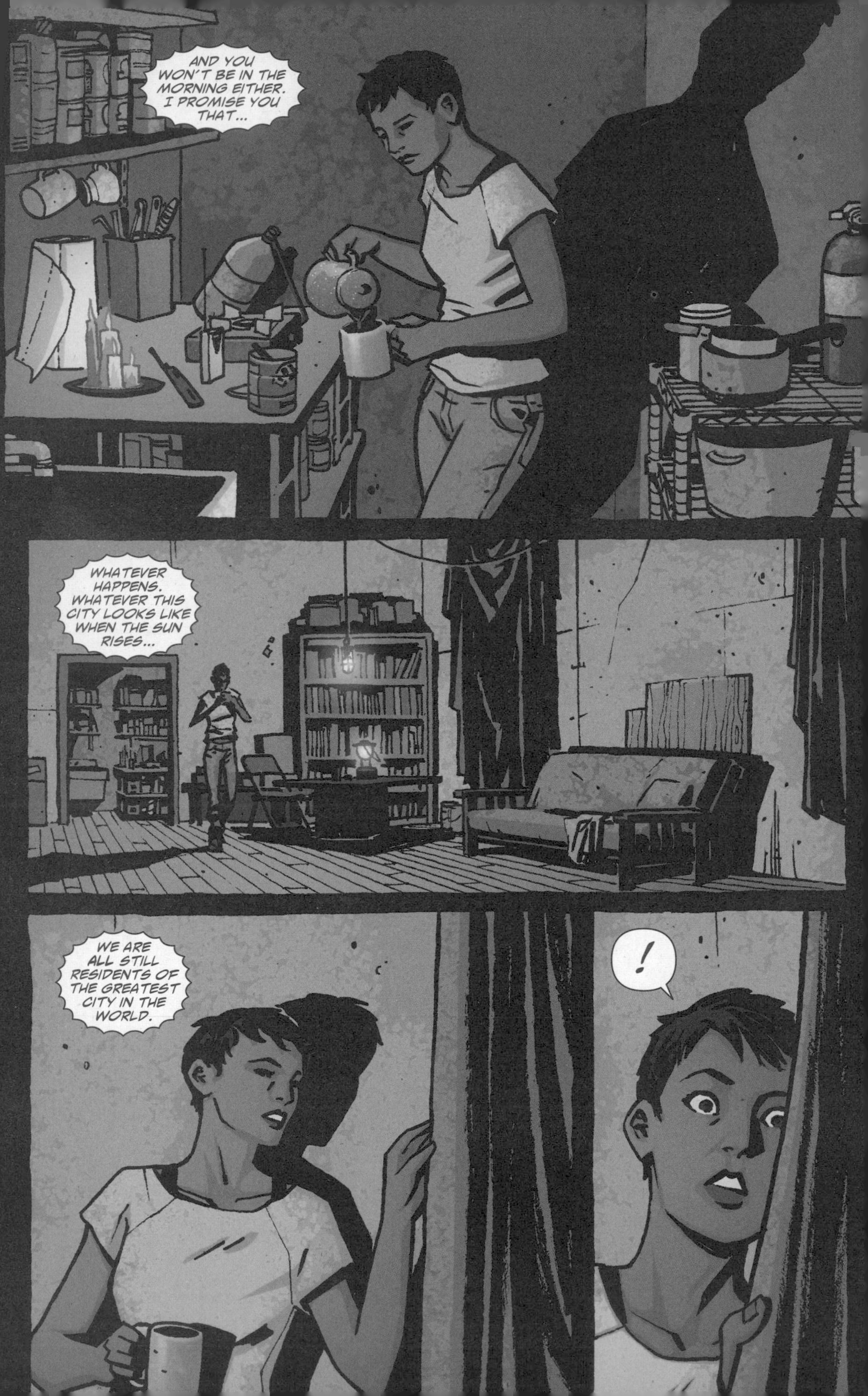
AND YOU WON'T BE IN THE MORNING EITHER. I PROMISE YOU THAT...
WHATEVER HAPPENS. WHATEVER THIS CITY LOOKS LIKE WHEN THE SUN RISES...
WE ARE ALL STILL RESIDENTS OF THE GREATEST CITY IN THE WORLD.
!

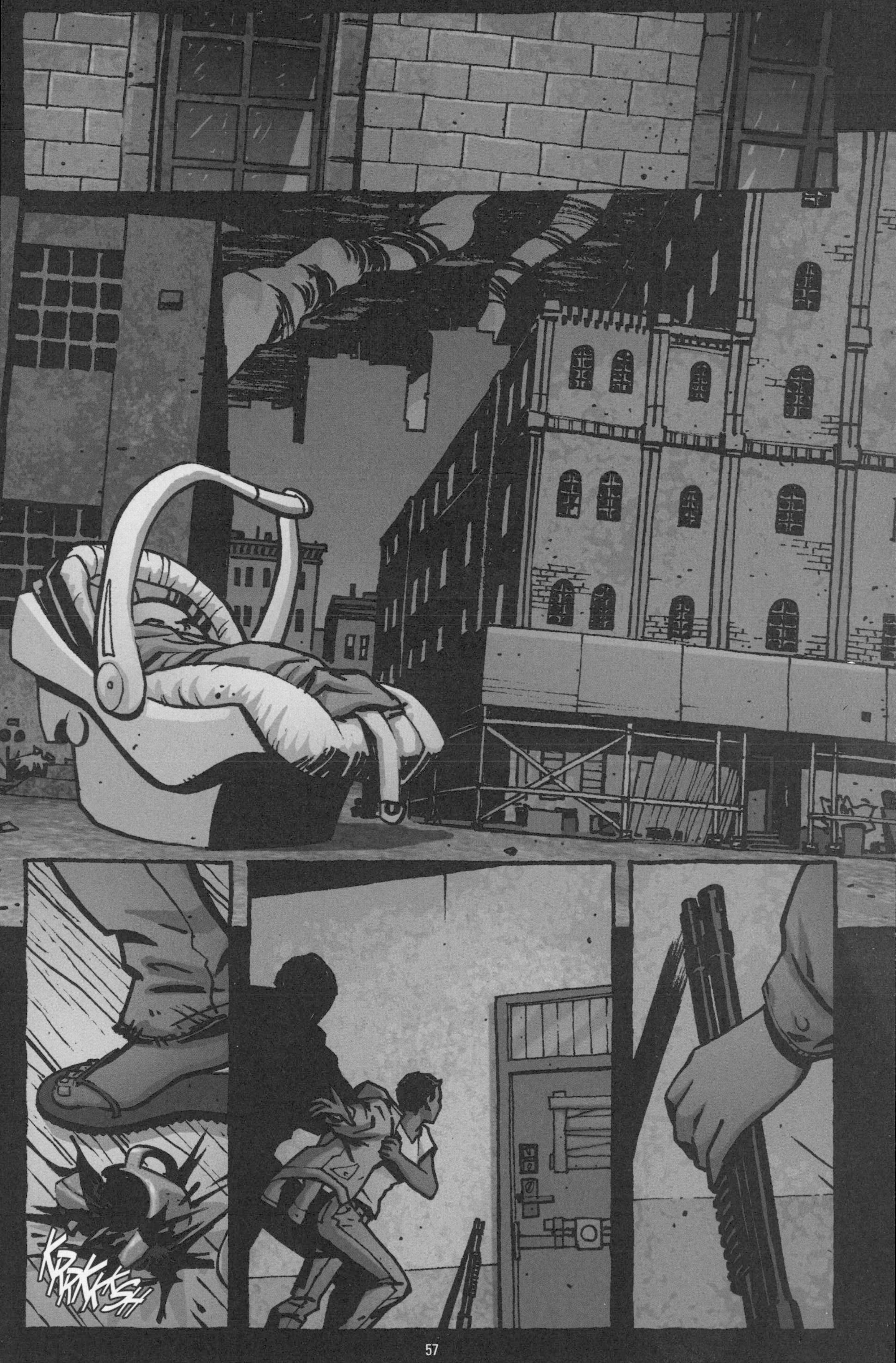
KRRKKKSH

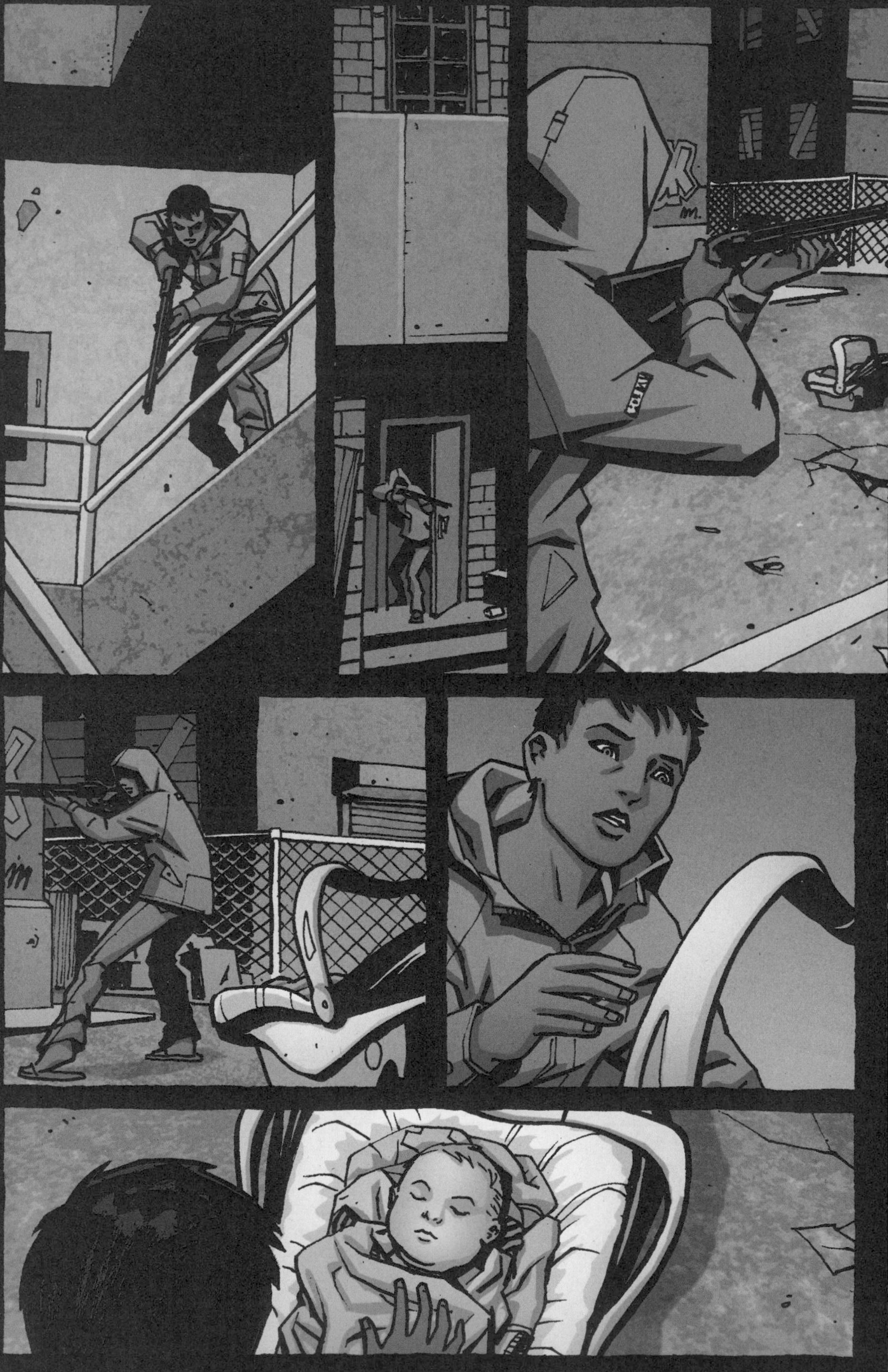

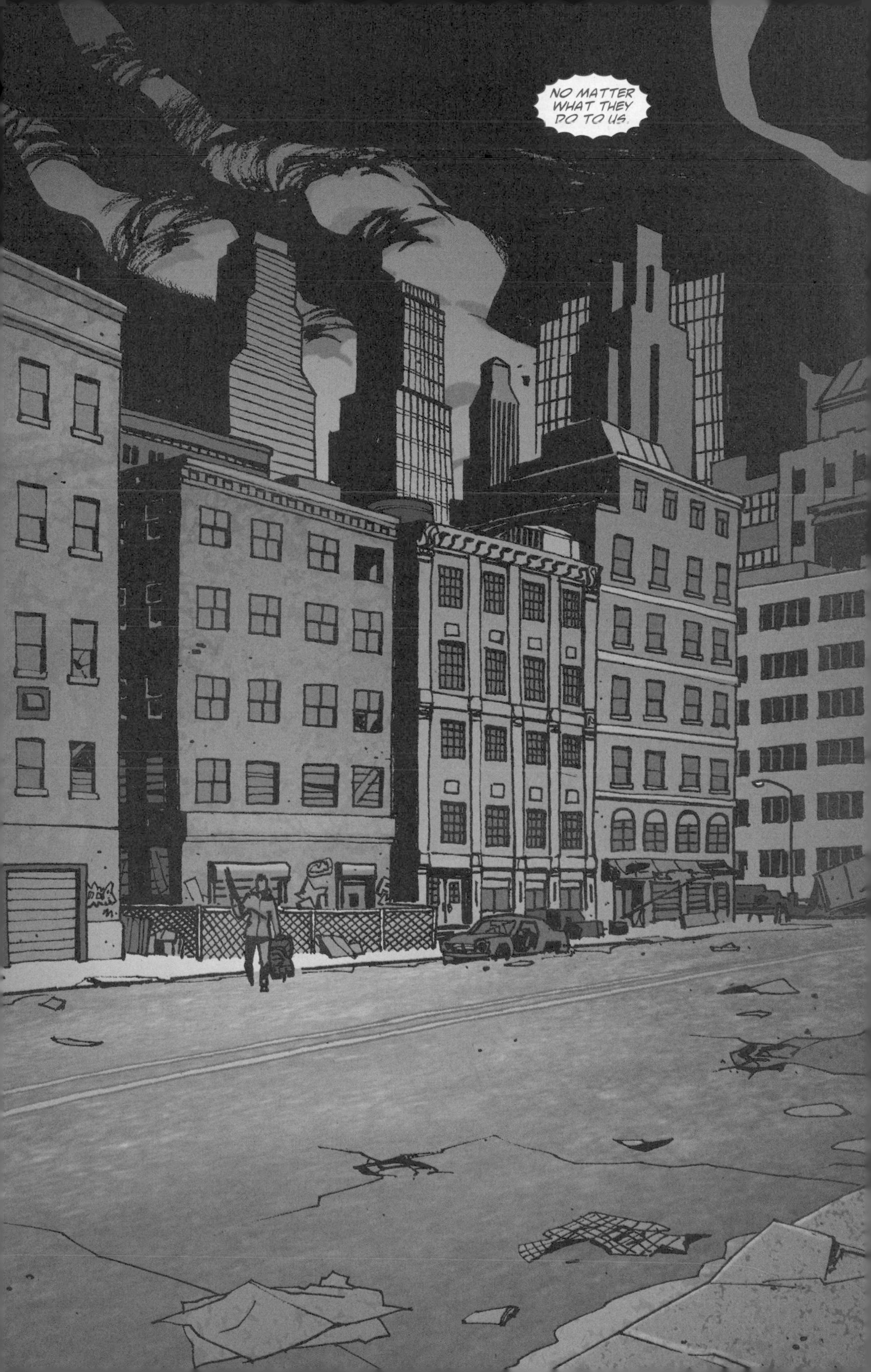
NO MATTER WHAT THEY DO TO US.

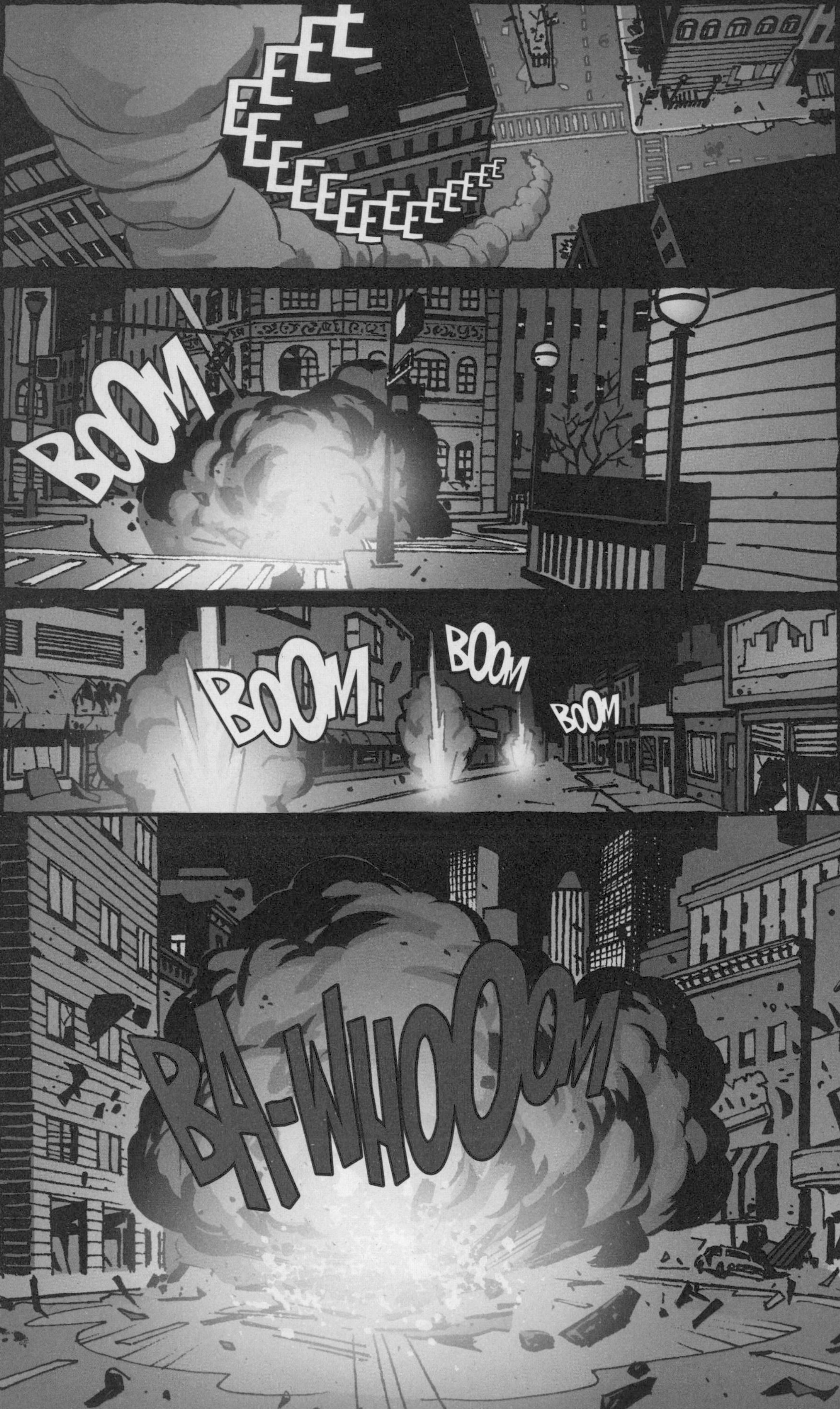
EEEEEEEEEEEEEEEEEE
BOOM
BOOM
BOOM
BOOM
BA-WHOOOOM

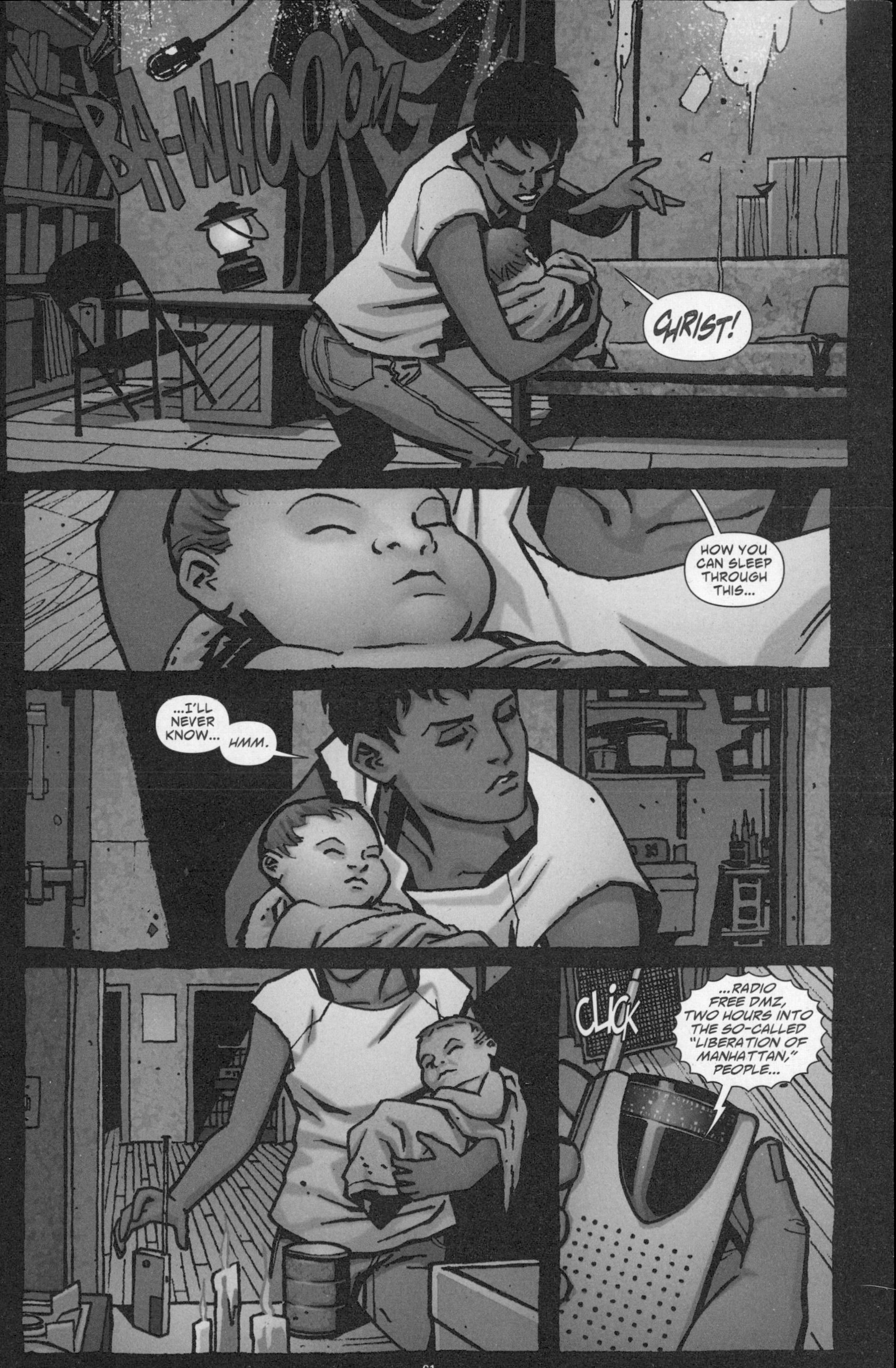
BA-WHOOOOM
CHRIST!
HOW YOU CAN SLEEP THROUGH THIS...
...I'LL NEVER KNOW...
HMM.
CLICK
...RADIO FREE DMZ, TWO HOURS INTO THE SO-CALLED "LIBERATION OF MANHATTAN," PEOPLE...

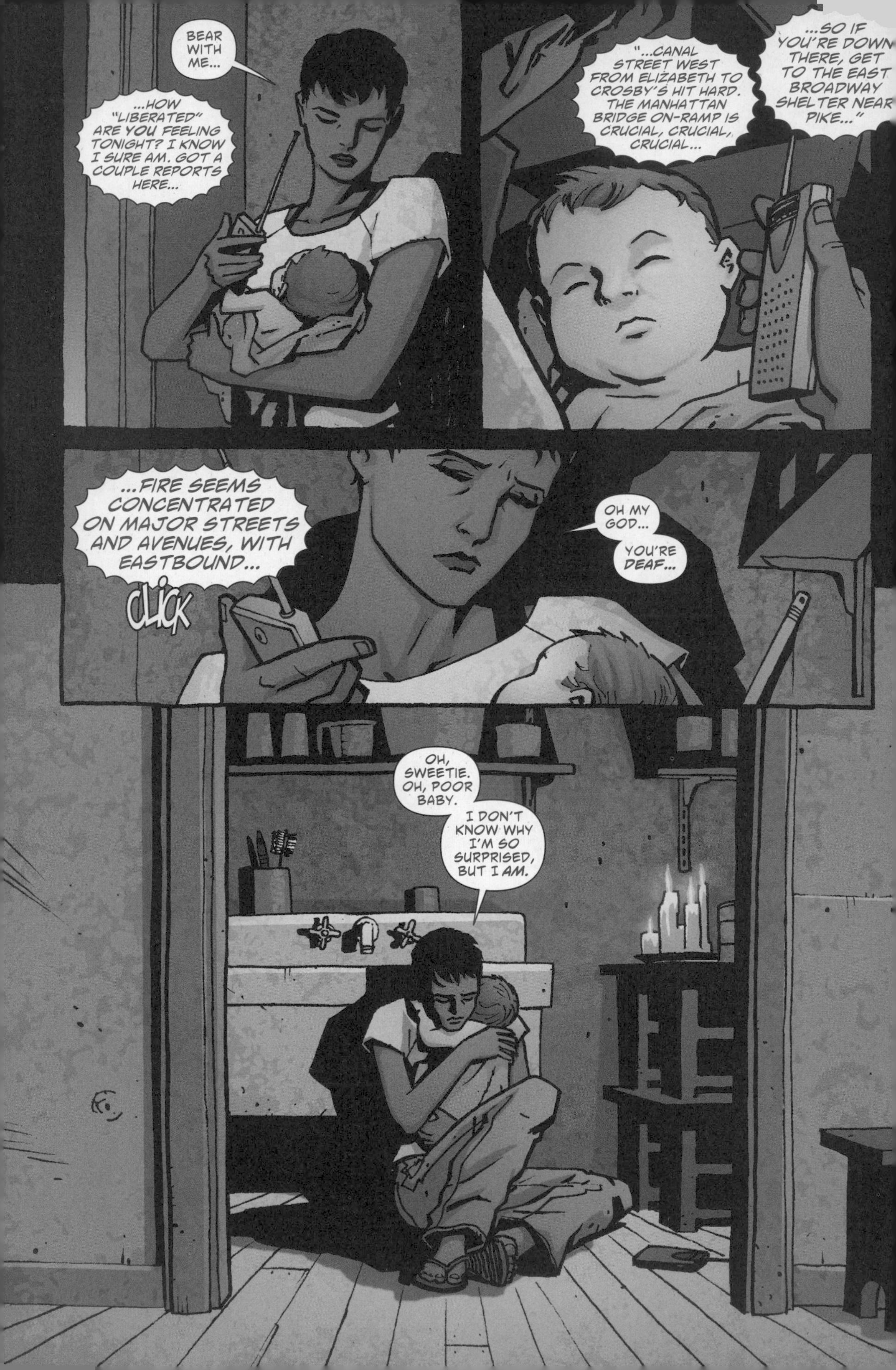
BEAR WITH ME...
...HOW "LIBERATED" ARE YOU FEELING TONIGHT? I KNOW I SURE AM. GOT A COUPLE REPORTS HERE...
"...CANAL STREET WEST FROM ELIZABETH TO CROSBY'S HIT HARD. THE MANHATTAN BRIDGE ON-RAMP IS CRUCIAL, CRUCIAL, CRUCIAL...
...SO IF YOU'RE DOWN THERE, GET TO THE EAST BROADWAY SHELTER NEAR PIKE..."
...FIRE SEEMS CONCENTRATED ON MAJOR STREETS AND AVENUES, WITH EASTBOUND...
CLICK
OH MY GOD...
YOU'RE DEAF...
OH, SWEETIE. OH, POOR BABY.
I DON'T KNOW WHY I'M SO SURPRISED, BUT I AM.

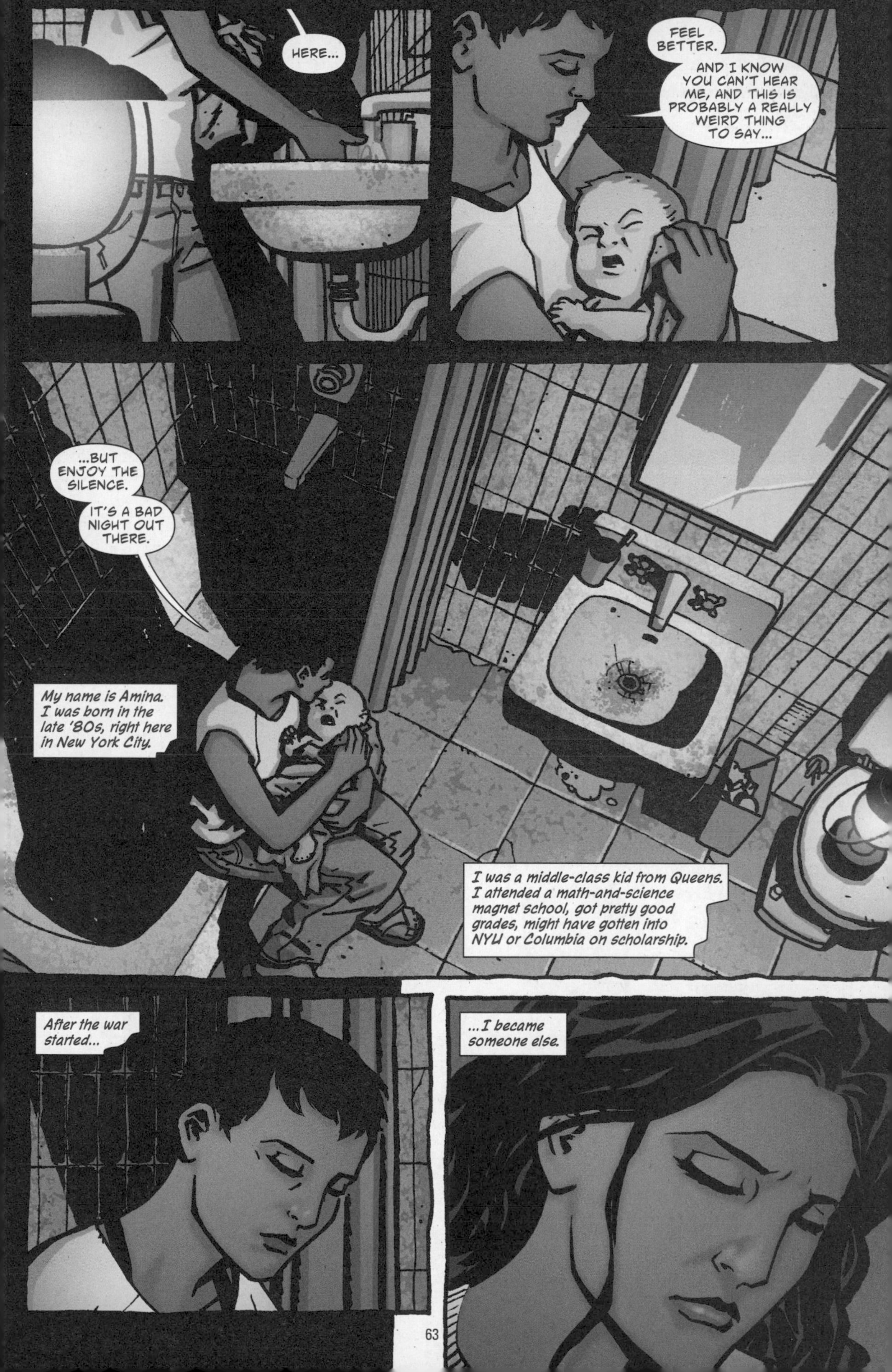
HERE...
FEEL BETTER.
AND I KNOW YOU CAN'T HEAR ME, AND THIS IS PROBABLY A REALLY WEIRD THING TO SAY...
...BUT ENJOY THE SILENCE.
IT'S A BAD NIGHT OUT THERE.
My name is Amina. I was born in the late '80s, right here in New York City.
I was a middle-class kid from Queens. I attended a math-and-science magnet school, got pretty good grades, might have gotten into NYU or Columbia on scholarship.
After the war started...
...I became someone else.

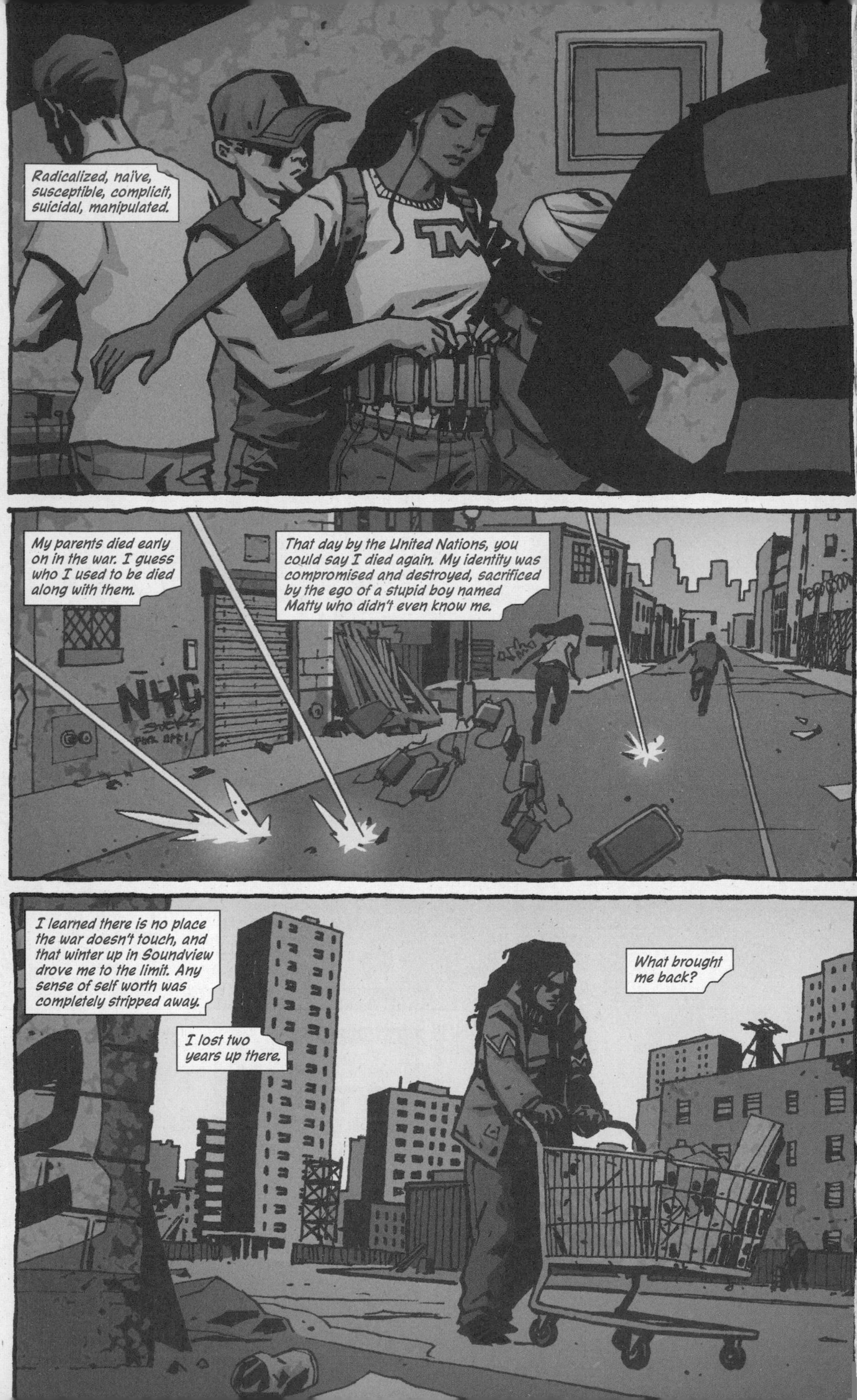
Radicalized, naïve, susceptible, complicit, suicidal, manipulated.
TW
My parents died early on in the war. I guess who I used to be died along with them.
That day by the United Nations, you could say I died again. My identity was compromised and destroyed, sacrificed by the ego of a stupid boy named Matty who didn't even know me.
NYC
I learned there is no place the war doesn't touch, and that winter up in Soundview drove me to the limit. Any sense of self worth was completely stripped away.
I lost two years up there.
What brought me back?

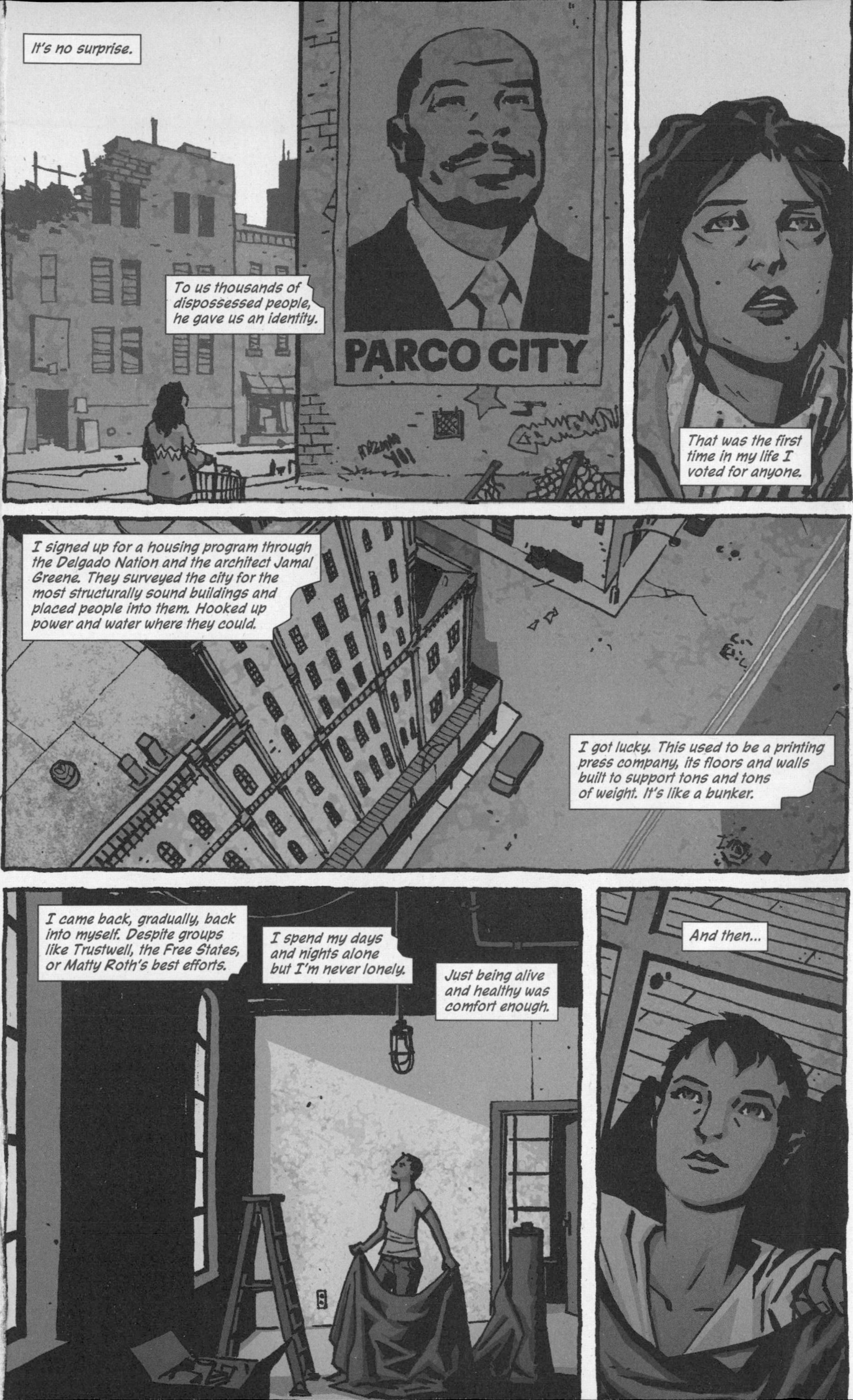

It's no surprise.
To us thousands of dispossessed people, he gave us an identity.
PARCO CITY
That was the first time in my life I voted for anyone.
I signed up for a housing program through the Delgado Nation and the architect Jamal Greene. They surveyed the city for the most structurally sound buildings and placed people into them. Hooked up power and water where they could.
I got lucky. This used to be a printing press company, its floors and walls built to support tons and tons of weight. It's like a bunker.
I came back, gradually, back into myself. Despite groups like Trustwell, the Free States, or Matty Roth's best efforts.
I spend my days and nights alone but I'm never lonely.
Just being alive and healthy was comfort enough.
And then...

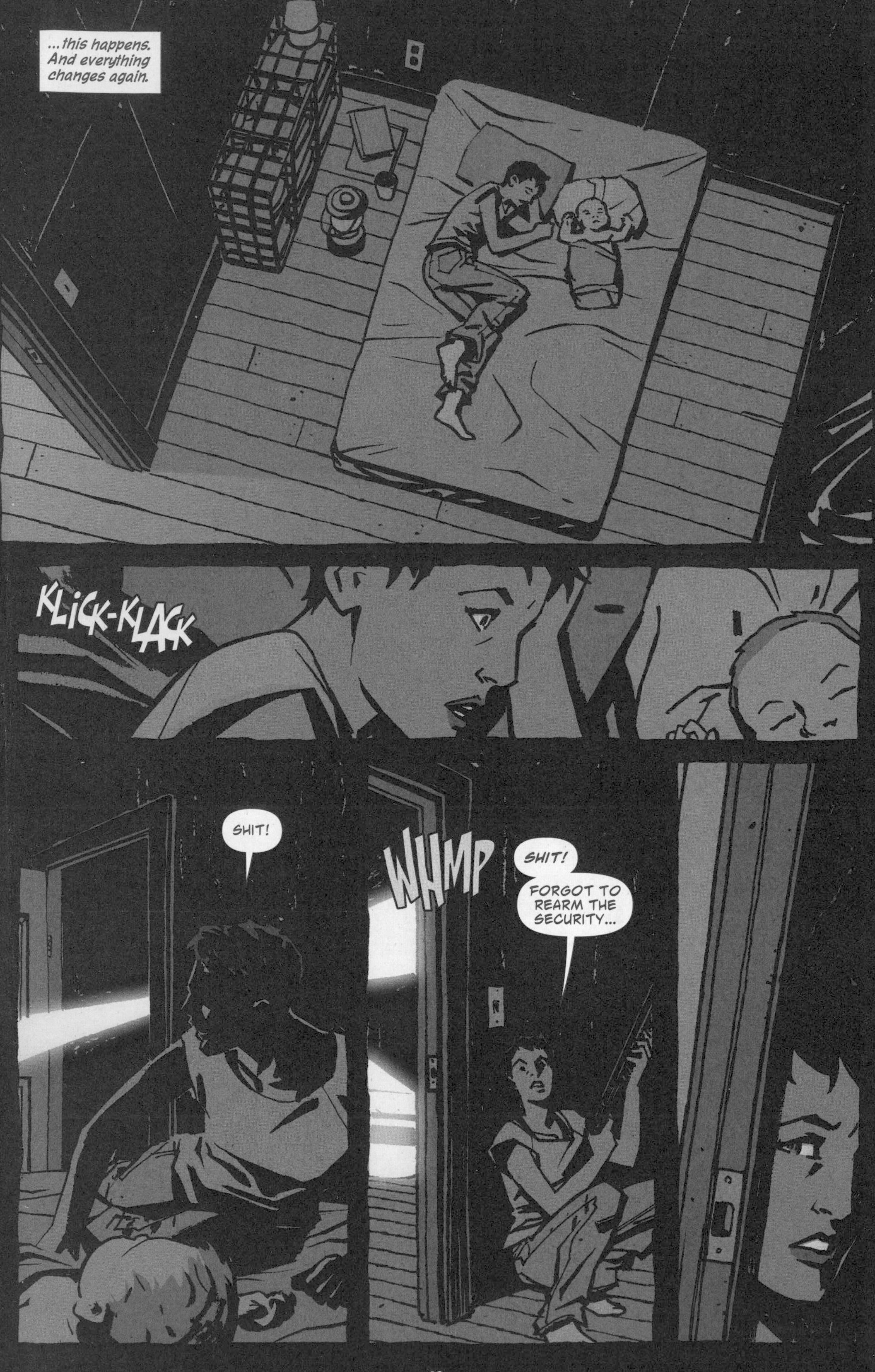
...this happens. And everything changes again.
KLICK-KLACK
SHIT!
WHMP
SHIT!
FORGOT TO REARM THE SECURITY...

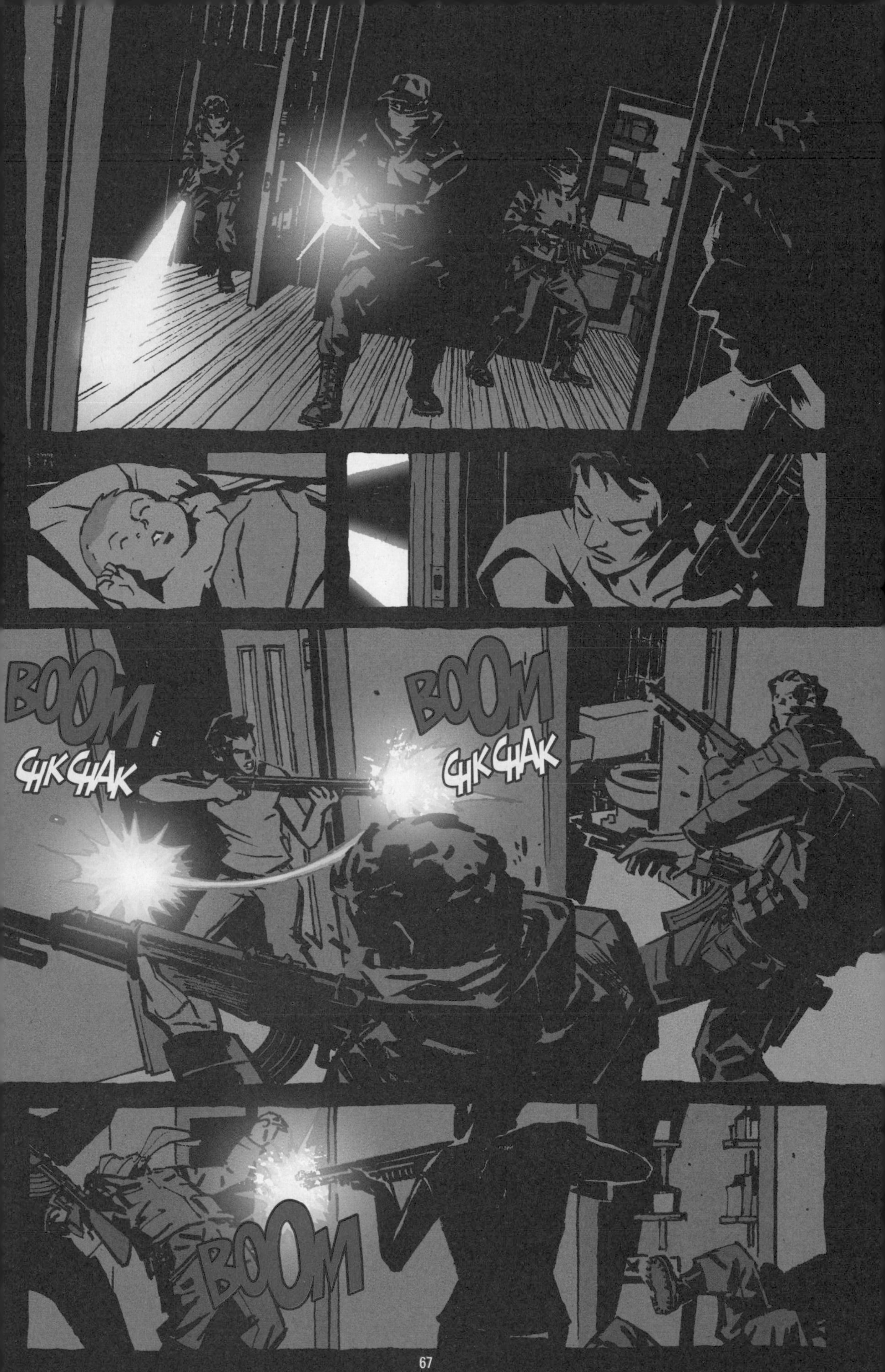
BOOM
CHK CHAK
BOOM
CHK CHAK
BOOM

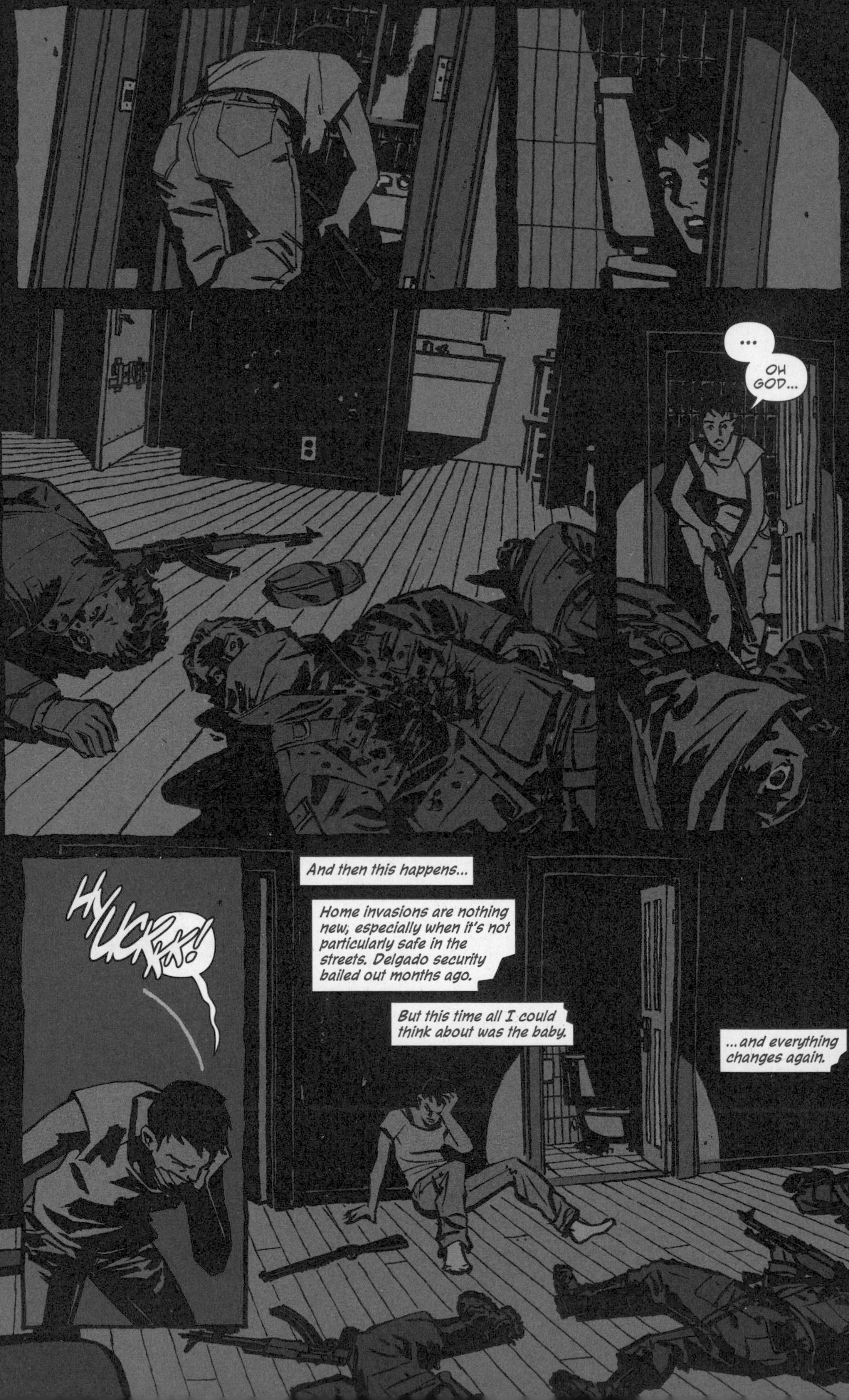
...
OH GOD...
And then this happens...
Home invasions are nothing new, especially when it's not particularly safe in the streets. Delgado security bailed out months ago.
But this time all I could think about was the baby.
HYUCKKK!
...and everything changes again.

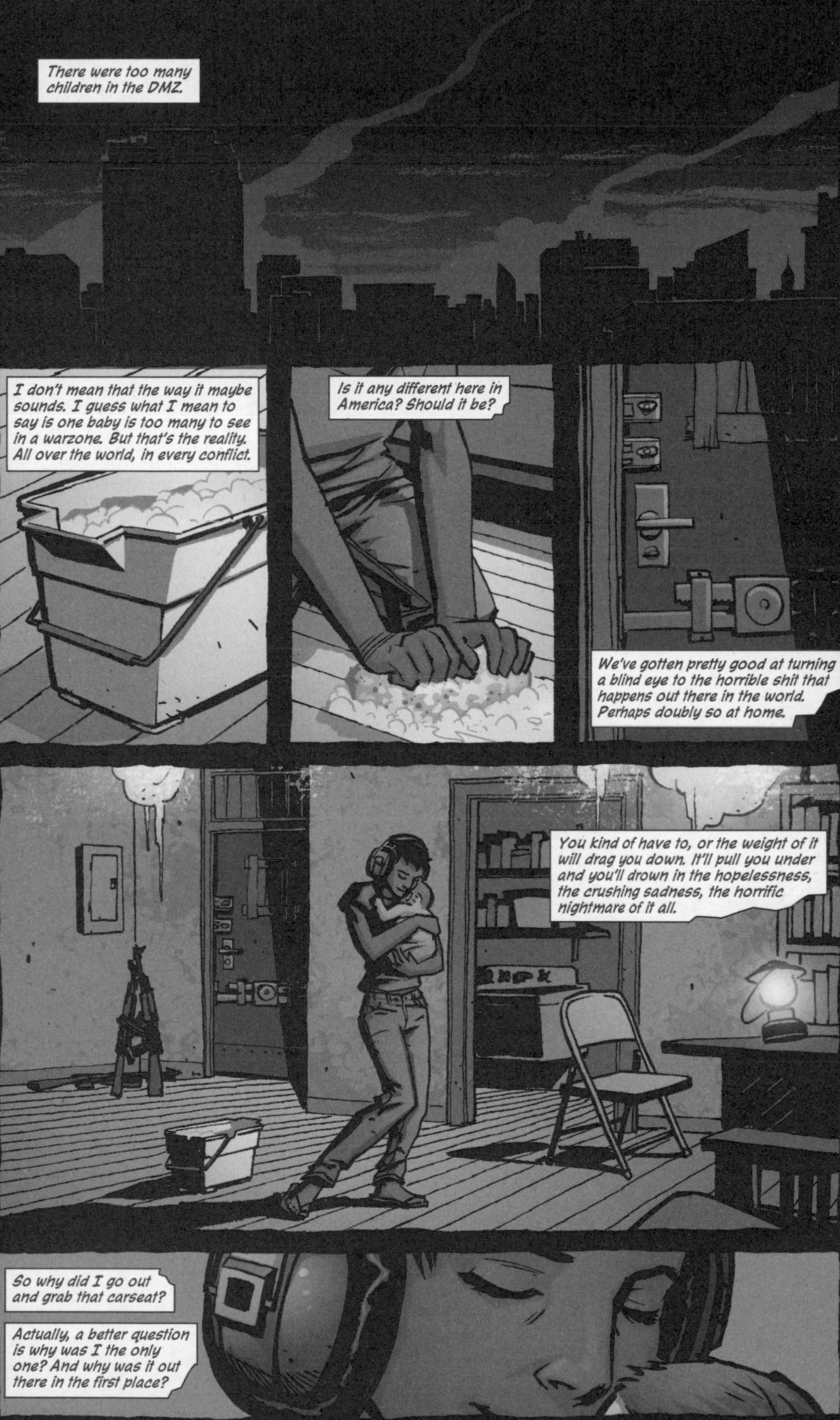
There were too many children in the DMZ.
I don't mean that the way it maybe sounds. I guess what I mean to say is one baby is too many to see in a warzone. But that's the reality. All over the world, in every conflict.
Is it any different here in America? Should it be?
We've gotten pretty good at turning a blind eye to the horrible shit that happens out there in the world. Perhaps doubly so at home.
You kind of have to, or the weight of it will drag you down. It'll pull you under and you'll drown in the hopelessness, the crushing sadness, the horrific nightmare of it all.
So why did I go out and grab that carseat?
Actually, a better question is why was I the only one? And why was it out there in the first place?

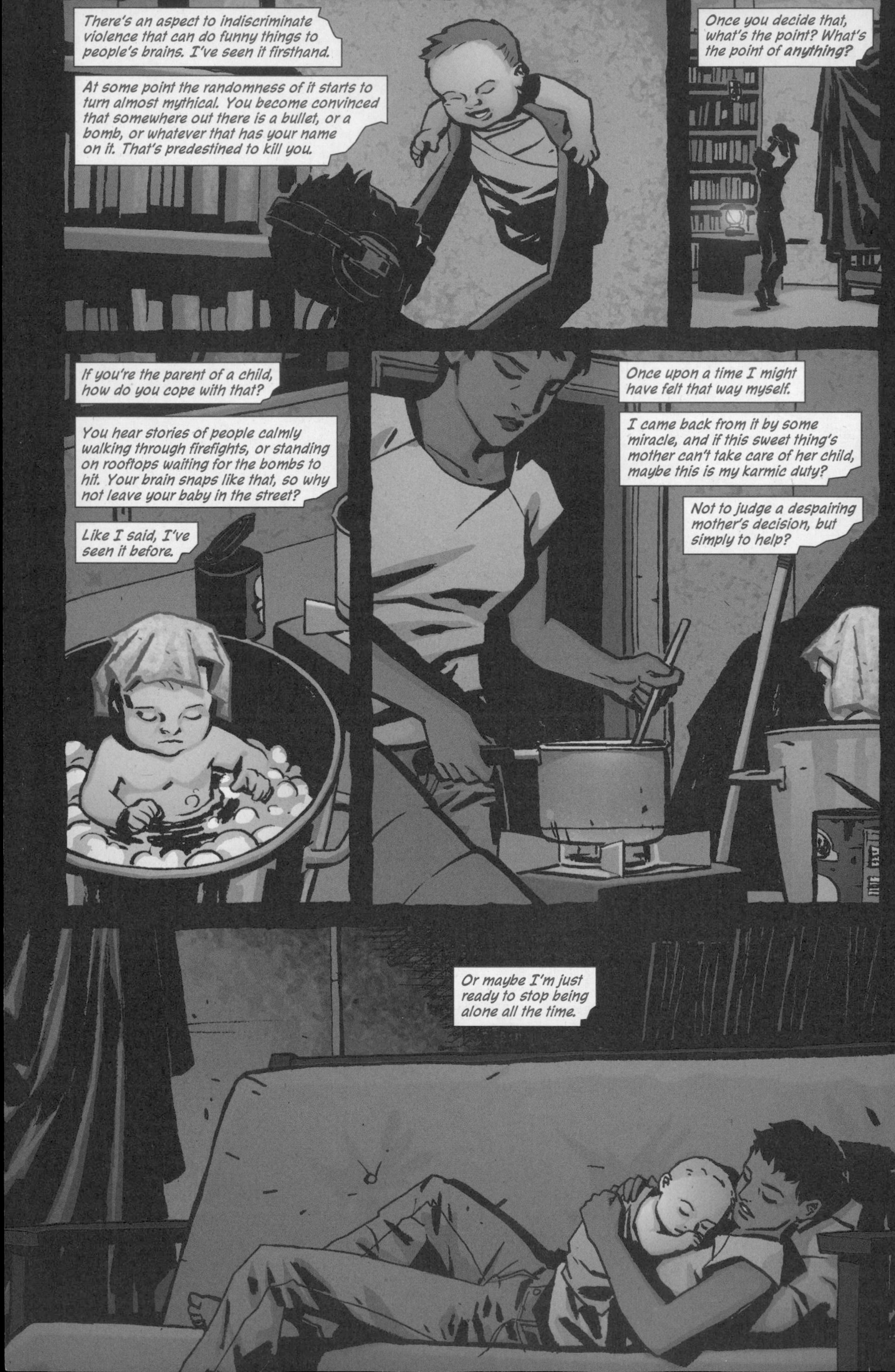
There's an aspect to indiscriminate violence that can do funny things to people's brains. I've seen it firsthand.
At some point the randomness of it starts to turn almost mythical. You become convinced that somewhere out there is a bullet, or a bomb, or whatever that has your name on it. That's predestined to kill you.
Once you decide that, what's the point? What's the point of anything?
If you're the parent of a child, how do you cope with that?
You hear stories of people calmly walking through firefights, or standing on rooftops waiting for the bombs to hit. Your brain snaps like that, so why not leave your baby in the street?
Like I said, I've seen it before.
Once upon a time I might have felt that way myself.
I came back from it by some miracle, and if this sweet thing's mother can't take care of her child, maybe this is my karmic duty?
Not to judge a despairing mother's decision, but simply to help?
Or maybe I'm just ready to stop being alone all the time.

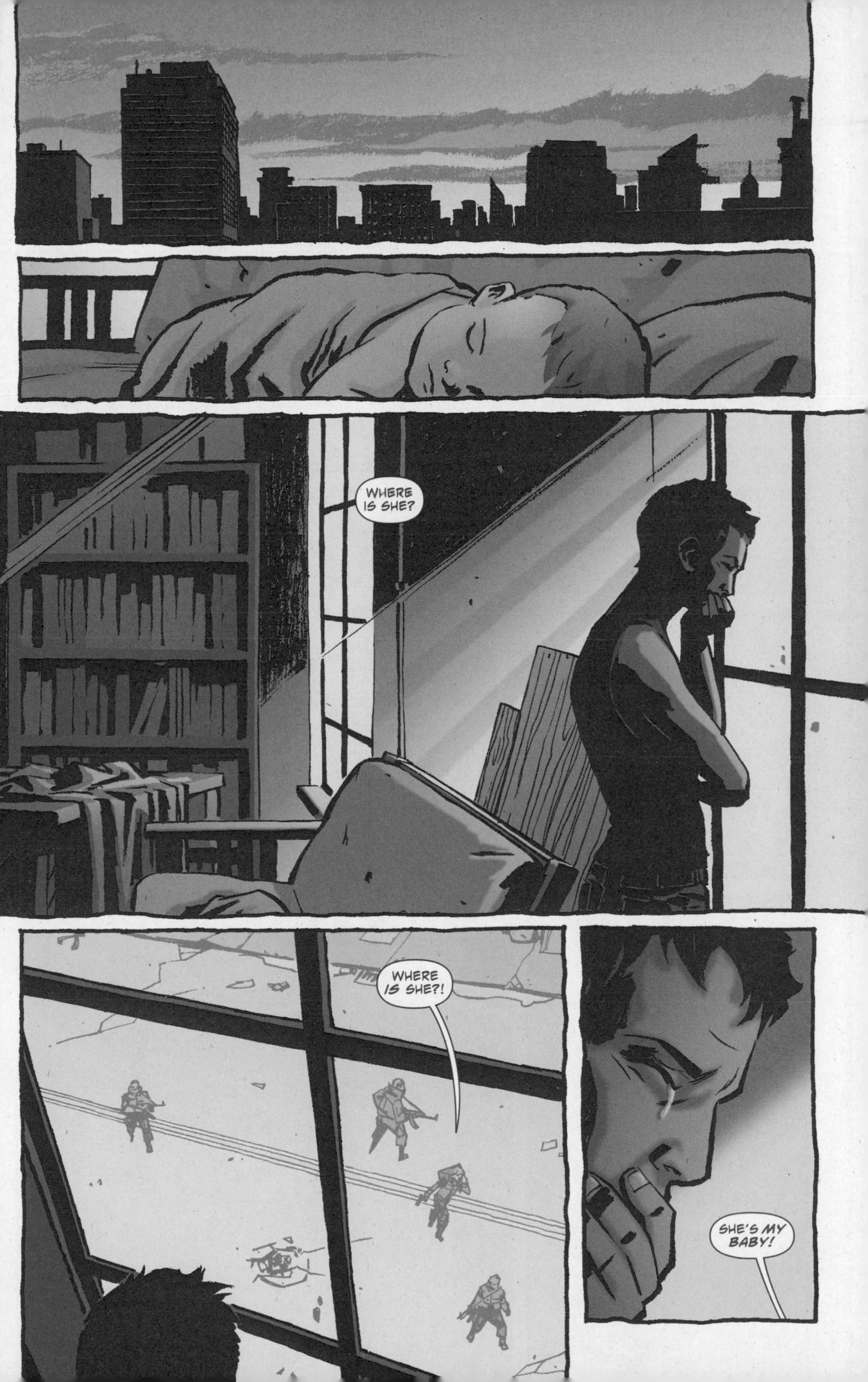
WHERE IS SHE?
WHERE IS SHE?!
SHE'S MY BABY!

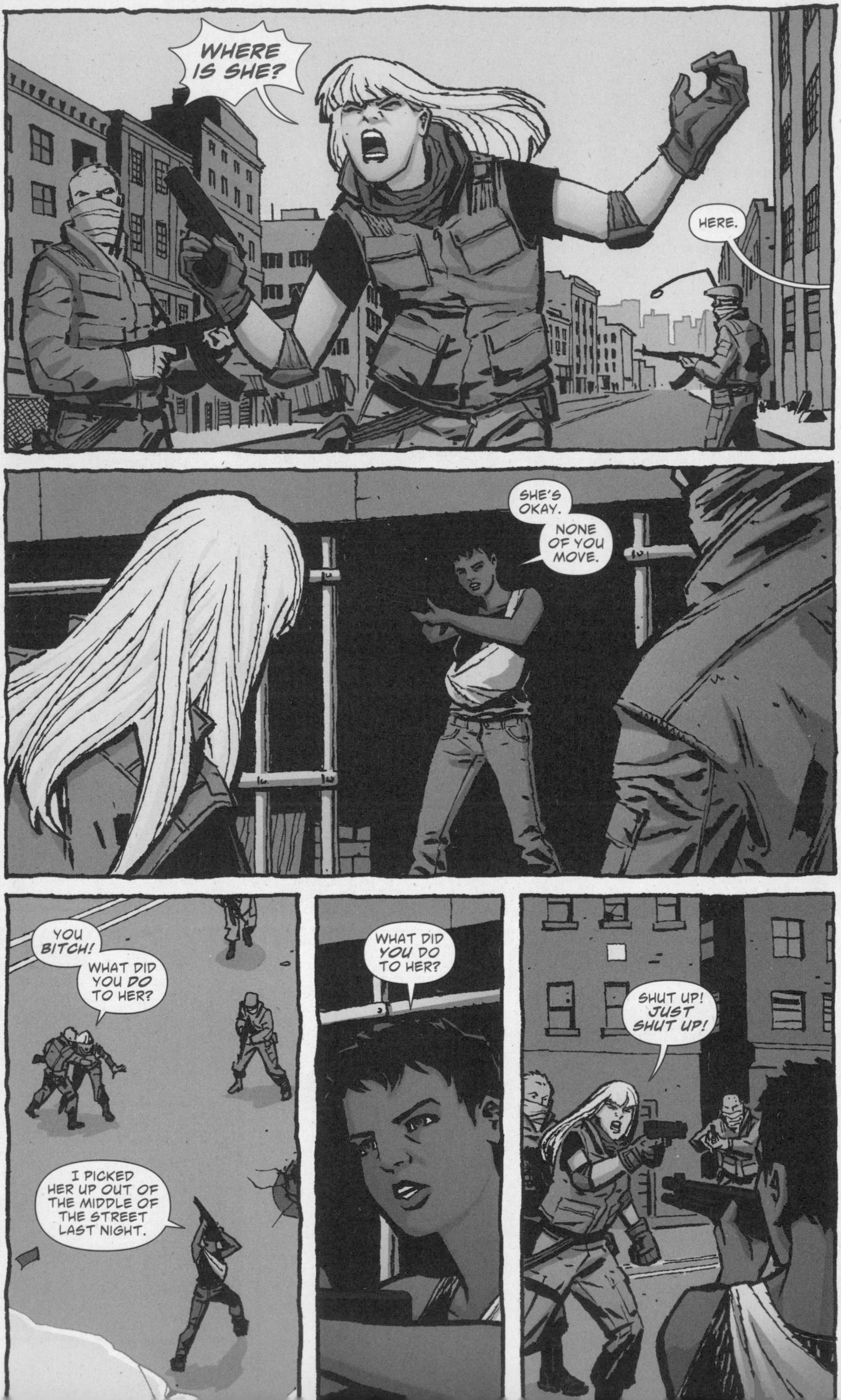
WHERE IS SHE?
HERE.
SHE'S OKAY.
NONE OF YOU MOVE.
YOU BITCH!
WHAT DID YOU DO TO HER?
I PICKED HER UP OUT OF THE MIDDLE OF THE STREET LAST NIGHT.
WHAT DID YOU DO TO HER?
SHUT UP! JUST SHUT UP!

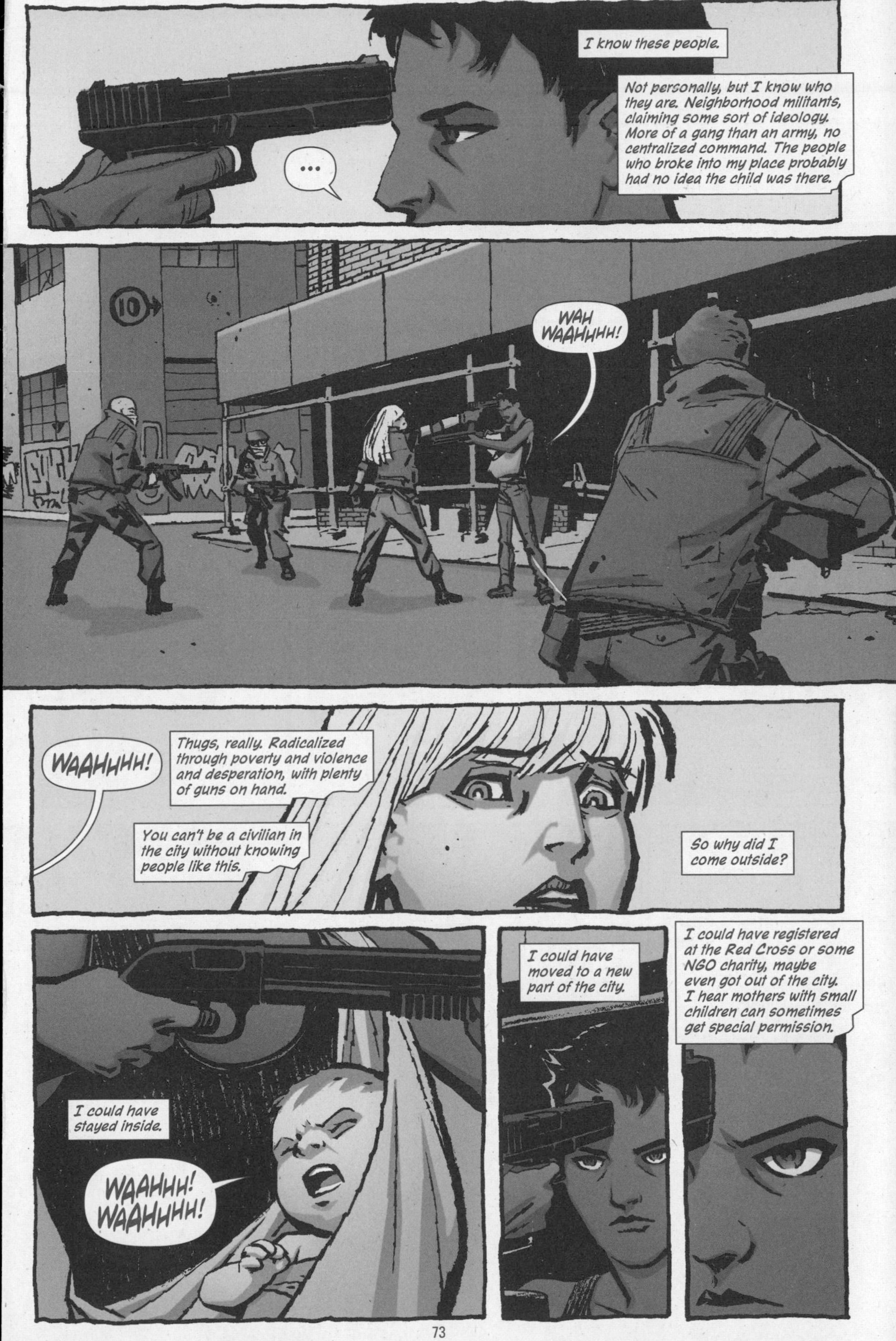

I know these people.
Not personally, but I know who they are. Neighborhood militants, claiming some sort of ideology. More of a gang than an army, no centralized command. The people who broke into my place probably had no idea the child was there.
...
WAH WAAHHHH!
WAAHHHH!
Thugs, really. Radicalized through poverty and violence and desperation, with plenty of guns on hand.
You can't be a civilian in the city without knowing people like this.
So why did I come outside?
I could have stayed inside.
WAAHHH! WAAHHHH!
I could have moved to a new part of the city.
I could have registered at the Red Cross or some NGO charity, maybe even got out of the city. I hear mothers with small children can sometimes get special permission.

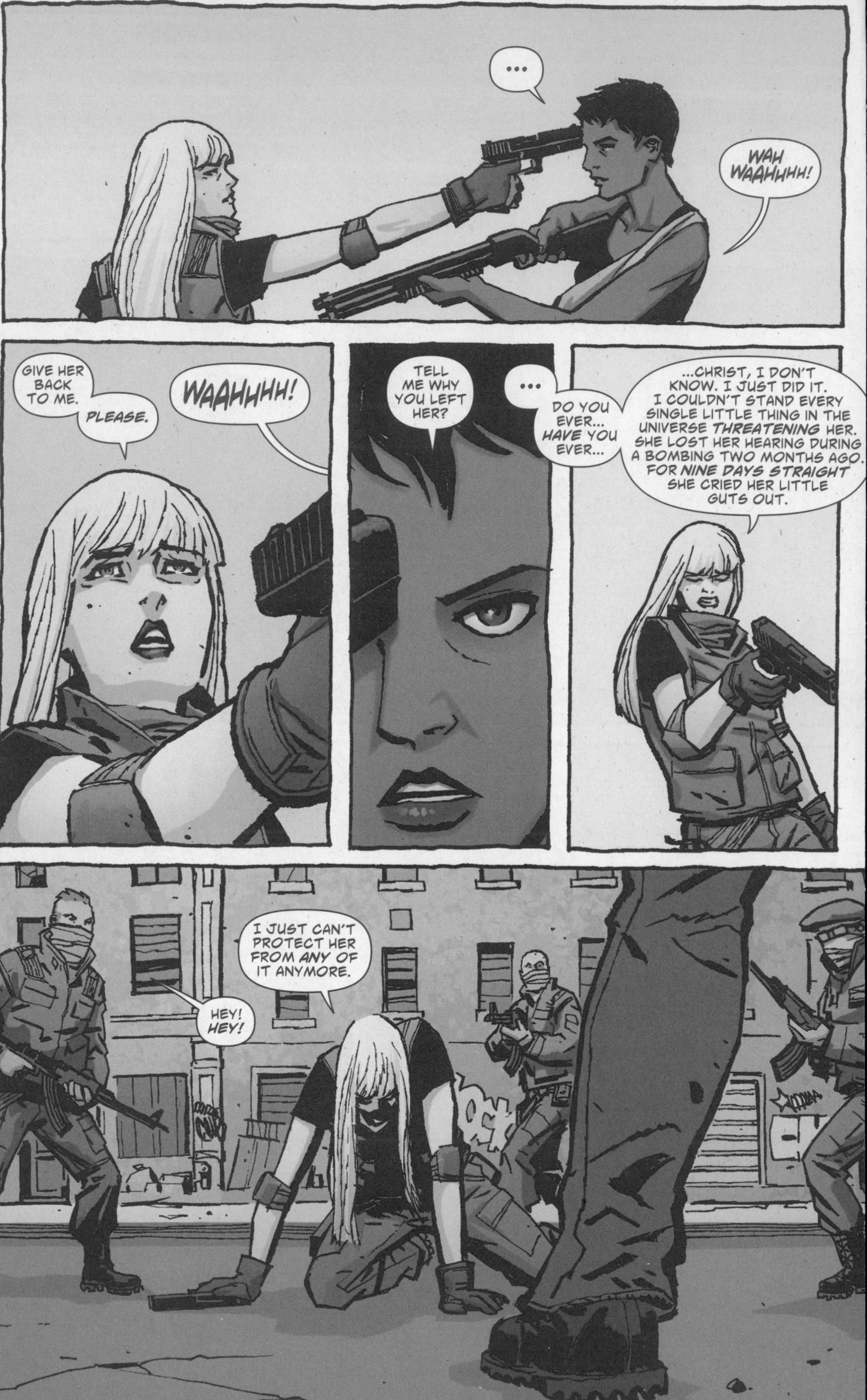
...
WAH WAAHHHH!
GIVE HER BACK TO ME. PLEASE.
WAAHHHH!
TELL ME WHY YOU LEFT HER?
...
DO YOU EVER... HAVE YOU EVER...
...CHRIST, I DON'T KNOW. I JUST DID IT. I COULDN'T STAND EVERY SINGLE LITTLE THING IN THE UNIVERSE THREATENING HER. SHE LOST HER HEARING DURING A BOMBING TWO MONTHS AGO. FOR NINE DAYS STRAIGHT SHE CRIED HER LITTLE GUTS OUT.
I JUST CAN'T PROTECT HER FROM ANY OF IT ANYMORE.
HEY! HEY!

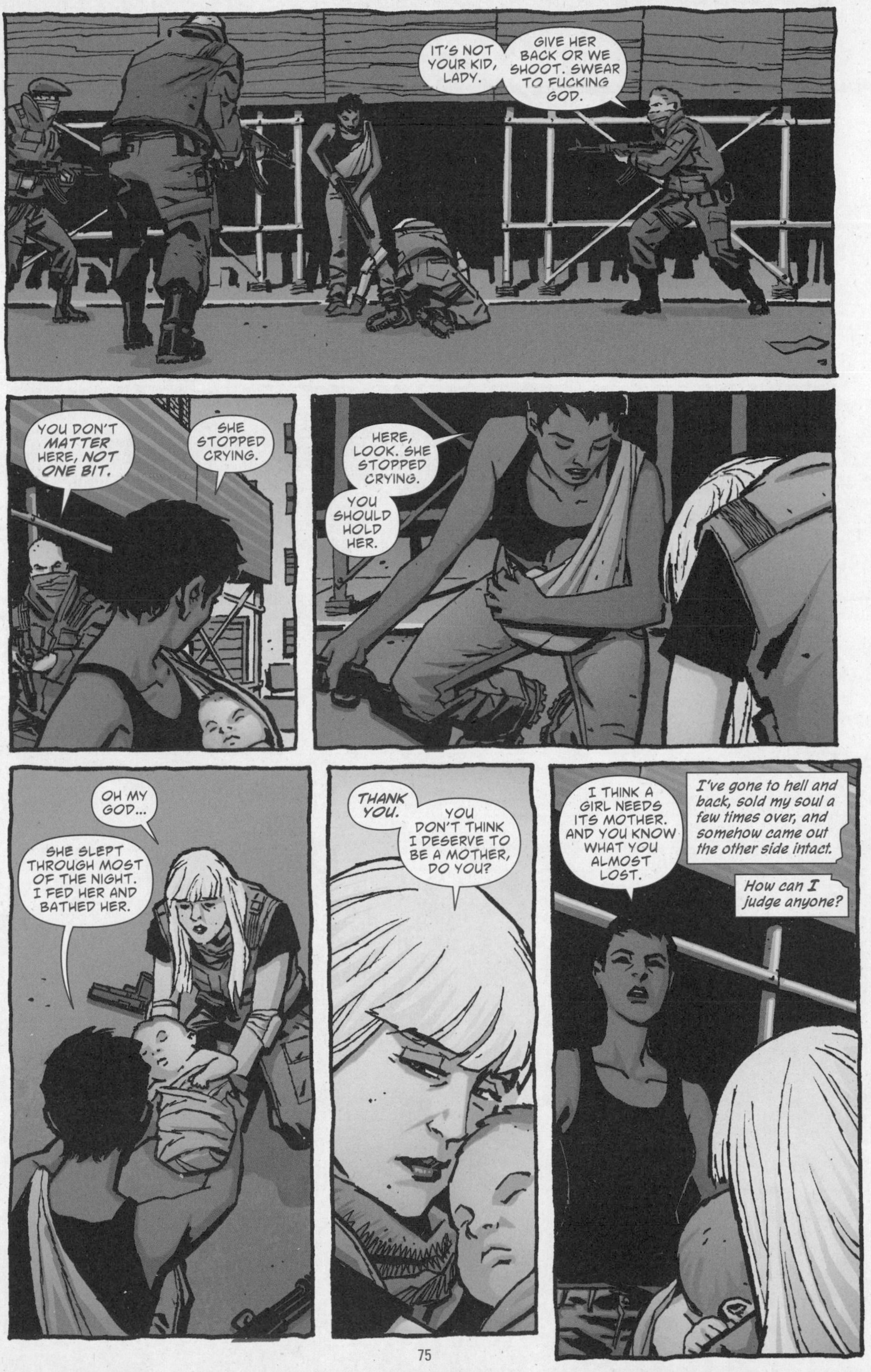
IT'S NOT YOUR KID, LADY.
GIVE HER BACK OR WE SHOOT. SWEAR TO FUCKING GOD.
YOU DON'T *MATTER* HERE, *NOT ONE BIT.*
SHE STOPPED CRYING.
HERE, LOOK. SHE STOPPED CRYING.
YOU SHOULD HOLD HER.
OH MY GOD...
SHE SLEPT THROUGH MOST OF THE NIGHT. I FED HER AND BATHED HER.
THANK YOU.
YOU DON'T THINK I DESERVE TO BE A MOTHER, DO YOU?
I THINK A GIRL NEEDS ITS MOTHER. AND YOU KNOW WHAT YOU ALMOST LOST.
I've gone to hell and back, sold my soul a few times over, and somehow came out the other side intact.
*How can **I** judge anyone?*

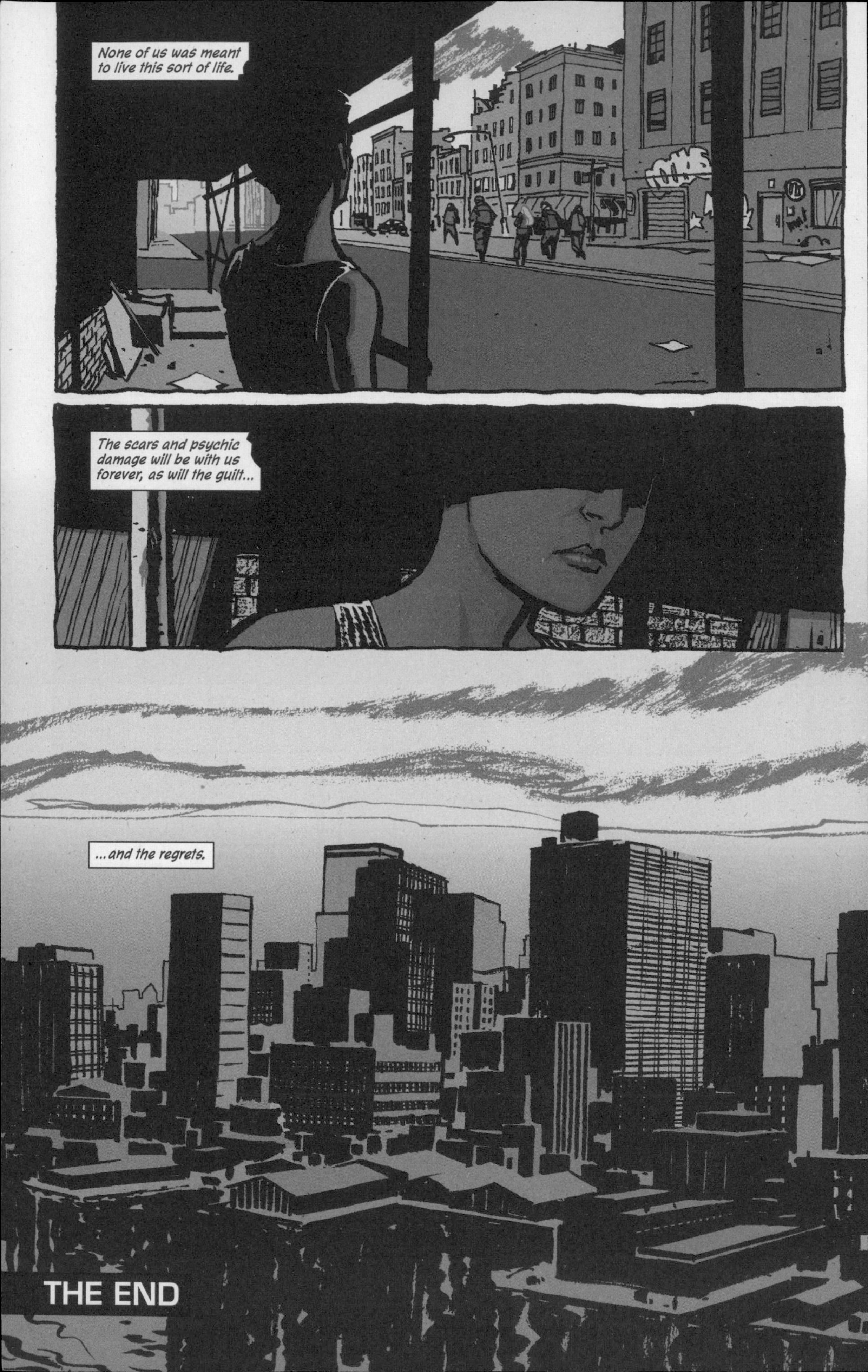
None of us was meant to live this sort of life.
The scars and psychic damage will be with us forever, as will the guilt...
...and the regrets.
THE END

A DECADE ON THE WALL

JPL

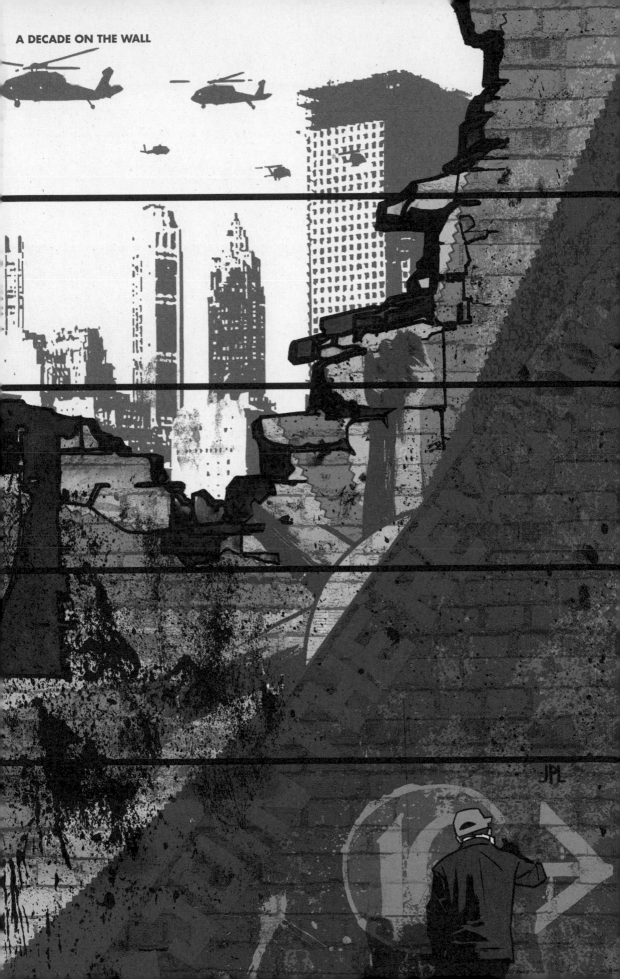

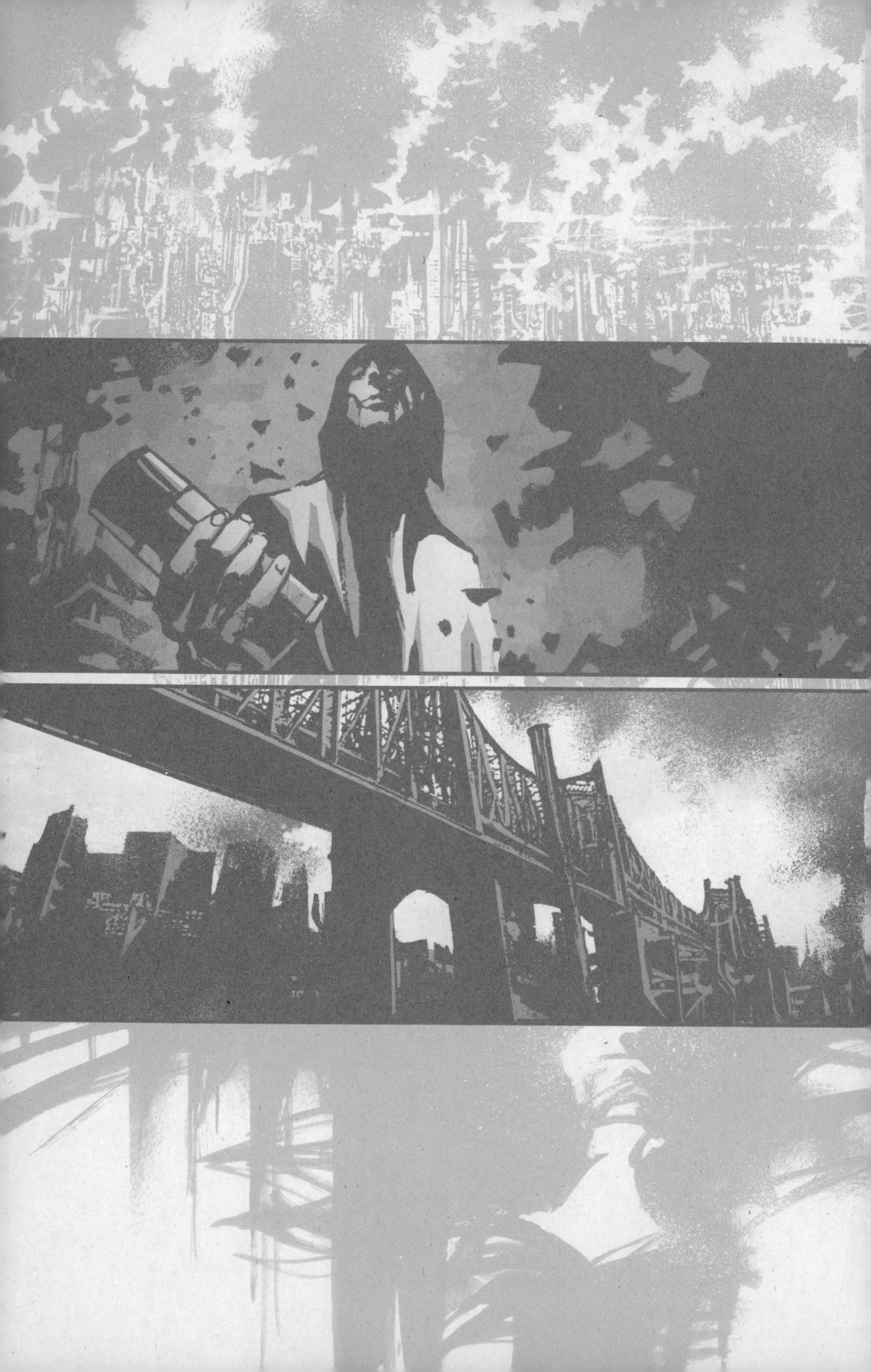

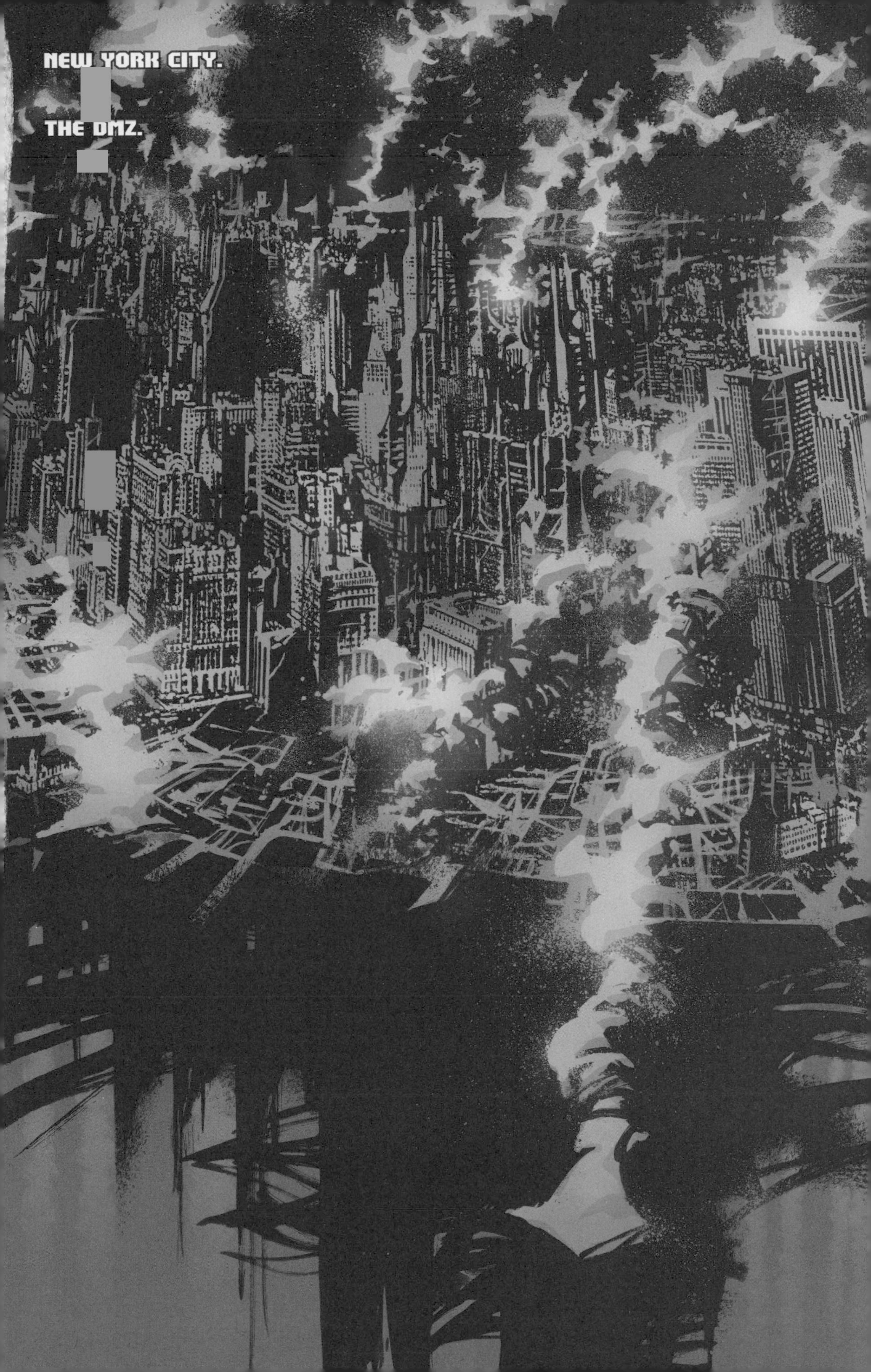
NEW YORK CITY.
THE DMZ.

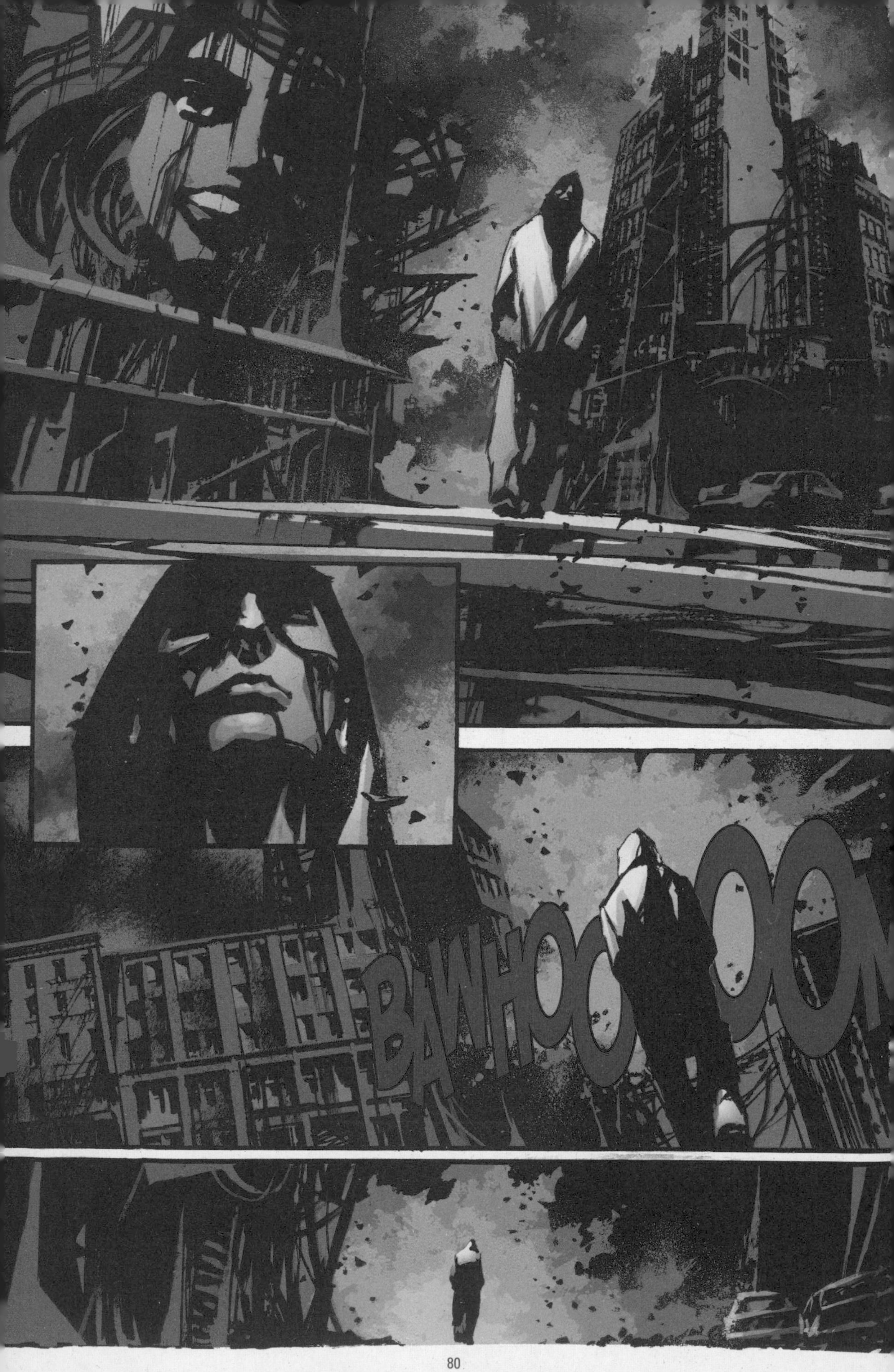
BAWHOOOOOOM

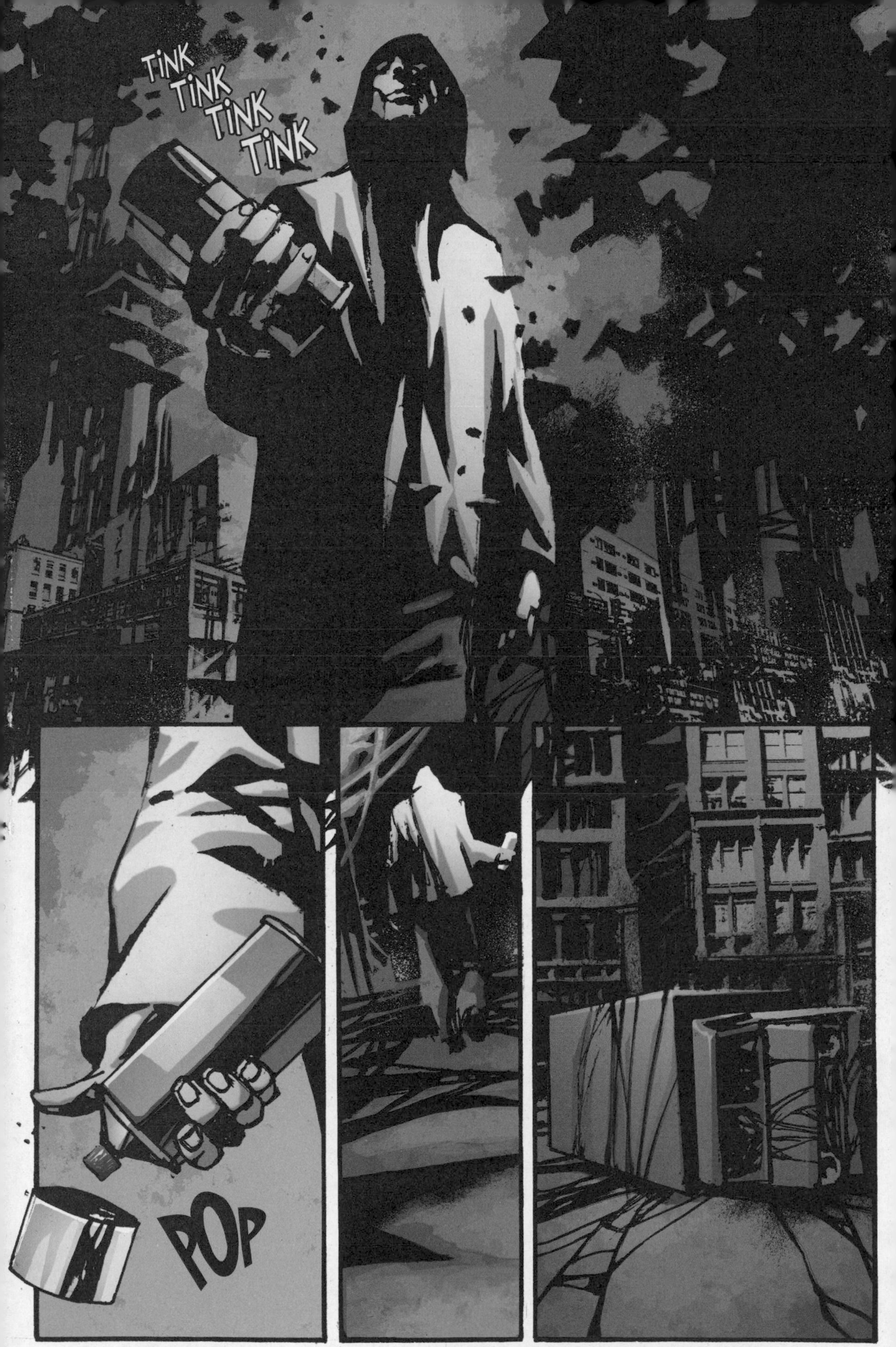
TINK
TINK
TINK
TINK
POP

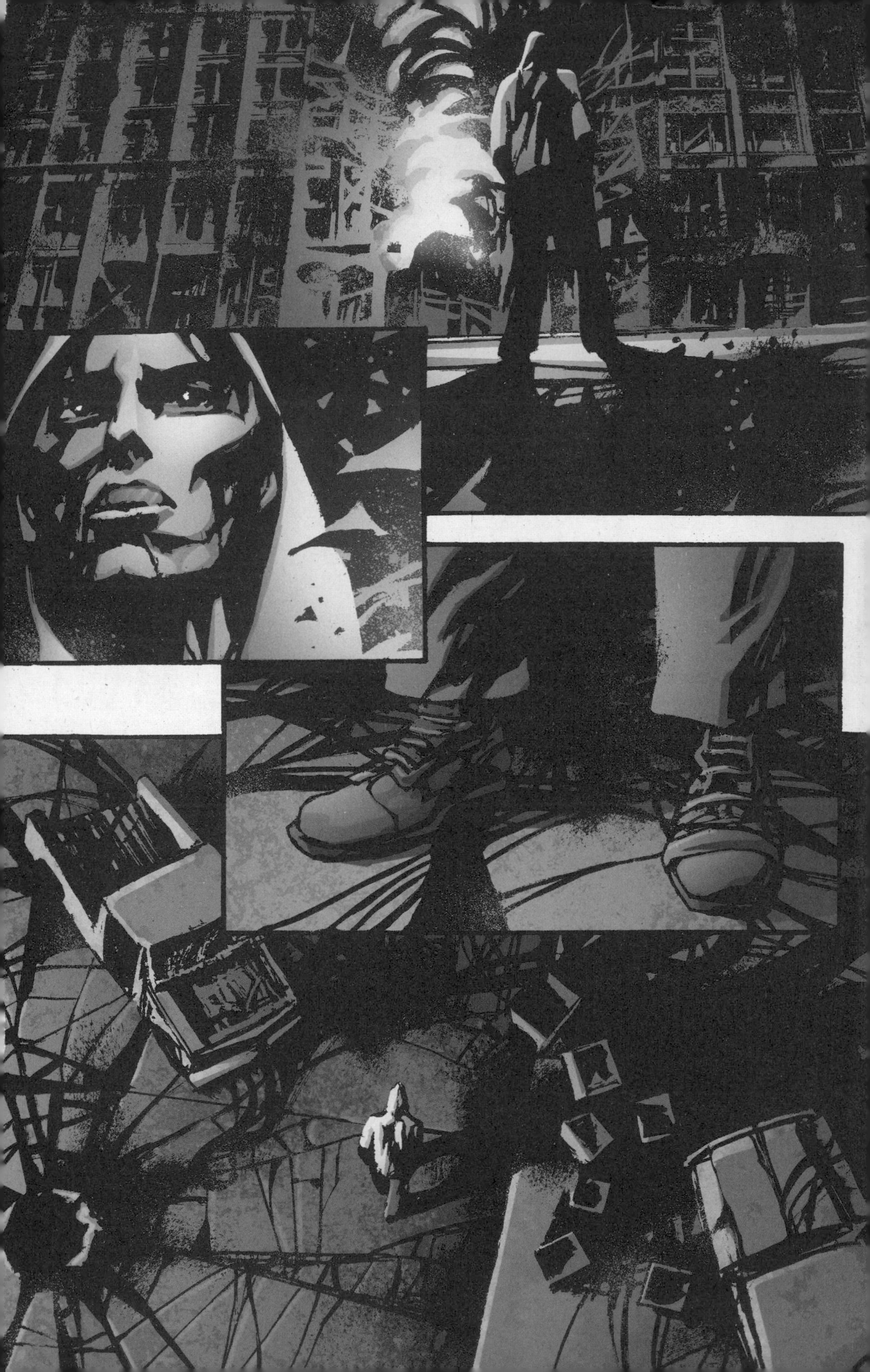

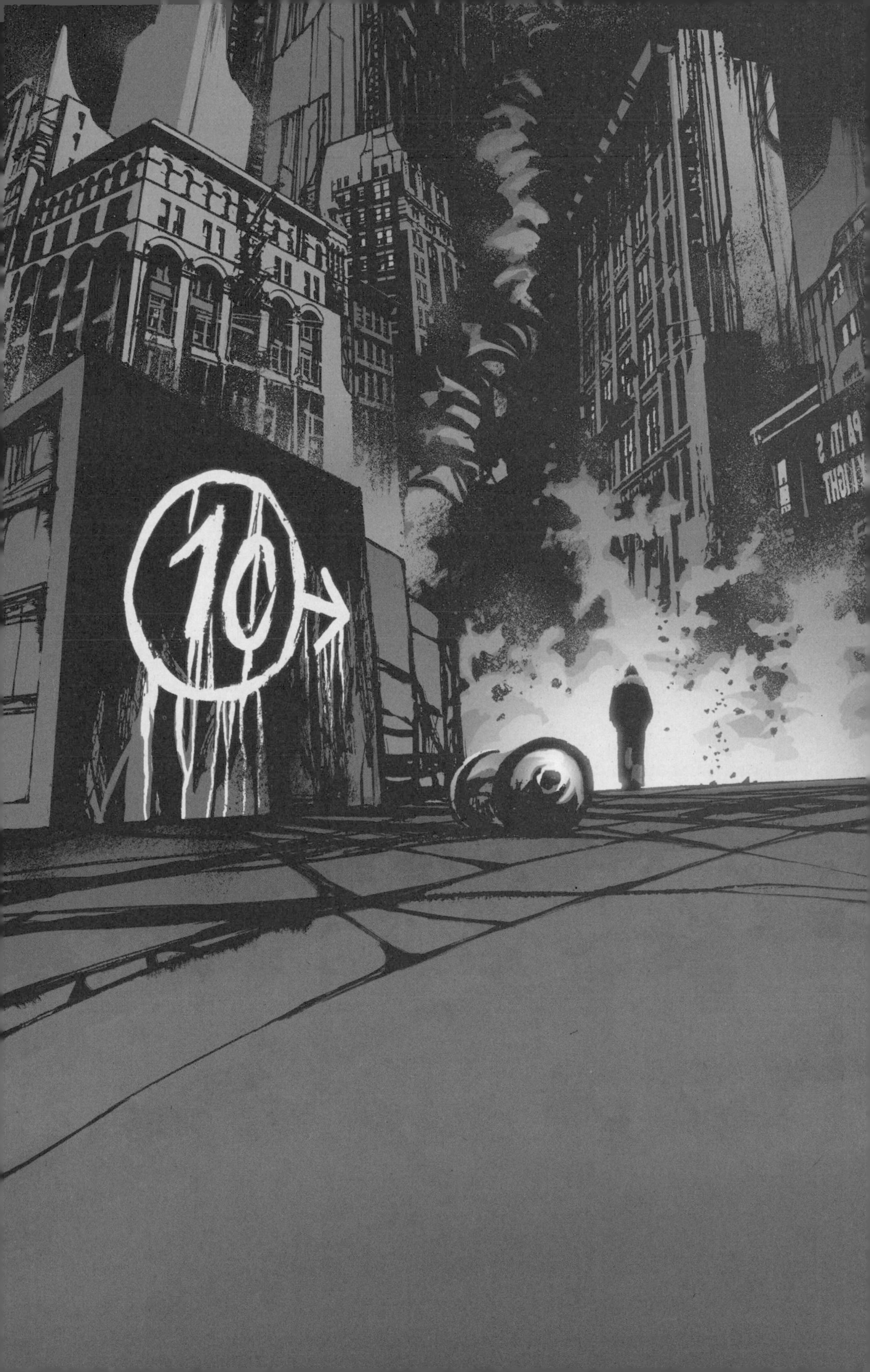
1¢

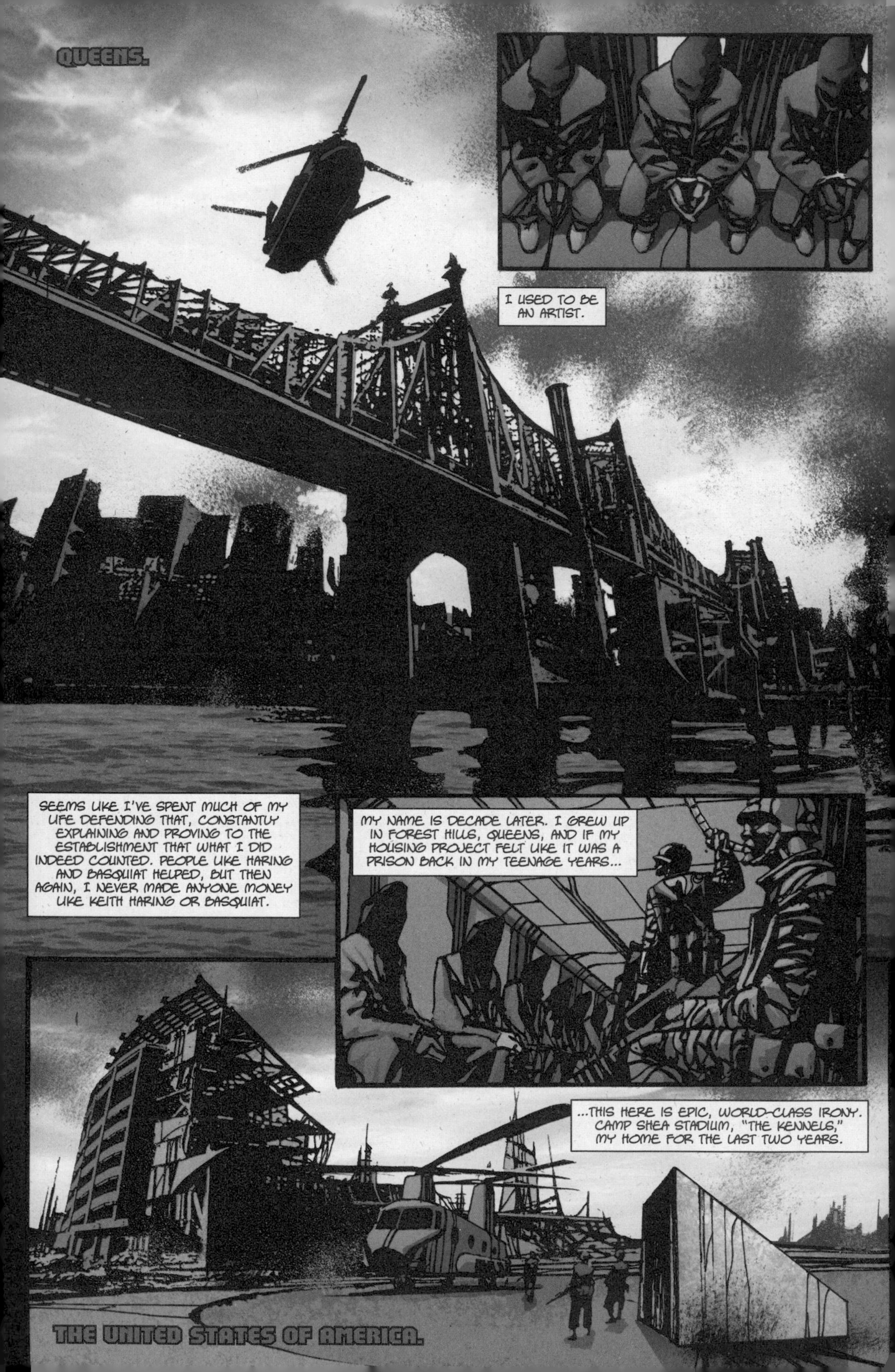
QUEENS.
I USED TO BE AN ARTIST.
SEEMS LIKE I'VE SPENT MUCH OF MY LIFE DEFENDING THAT, CONSTANTLY EXPLAINING AND PROVING TO THE ESTABLISHMENT THAT WHAT I DID INDEED COUNTED. PEOPLE LIKE HARING AND BASQUIAT HELPED, BUT THEN AGAIN, I NEVER MADE ANYONE MONEY LIKE KEITH HARING OR BASQUIAT.
MY NAME IS DECADE LATER. I GREW UP IN FOREST HILLS, QUEENS, AND IF MY HOUSING PROJECT FELT LIKE IT WAS A PRISON BACK IN MY TEENAGE YEARS...
...THIS HERE IS EPIC, WORLD-CLASS IRONY. CAMP SHEA STADIUM, "THE KENNELS," MY HOME FOR THE LAST TWO YEARS.
THE UNITED STATES OF AMERICA.

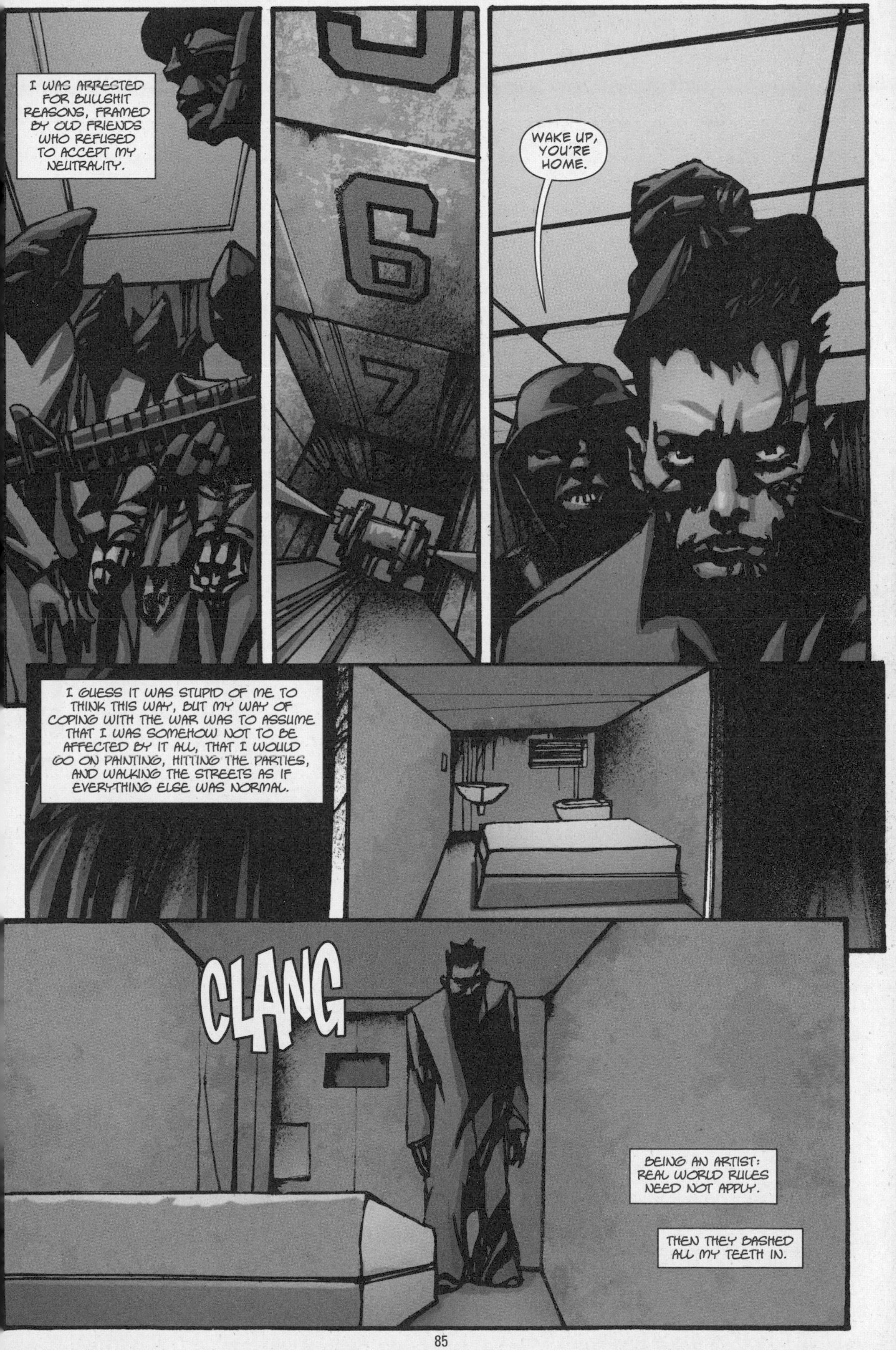

I WAS ARRESTED FOR BULLSHIT REASONS, FRAMED BY OLD FRIENDS WHO REFUSED TO ACCEPT MY NEUTRALITY.
6
7
WAKE UP, YOU'RE HOME.
I GUESS IT WAS STUPID OF ME TO THINK THIS WAY, BUT MY WAY OF COPING WITH THE WAR WAS TO ASSUME THAT I WAS SOMEHOW NOT TO BE AFFECTED BY IT ALL, THAT I WOULD GO ON PAINTING, HITTING THE PARTIES, AND WALKING THE STREETS AS IF EVERYTHING ELSE WAS NORMAL.
CLANG
BEING AN ARTIST: REAL WORLD RULES NEED NOT APPLY.
THEN THEY BASHED ALL MY TEETH IN.

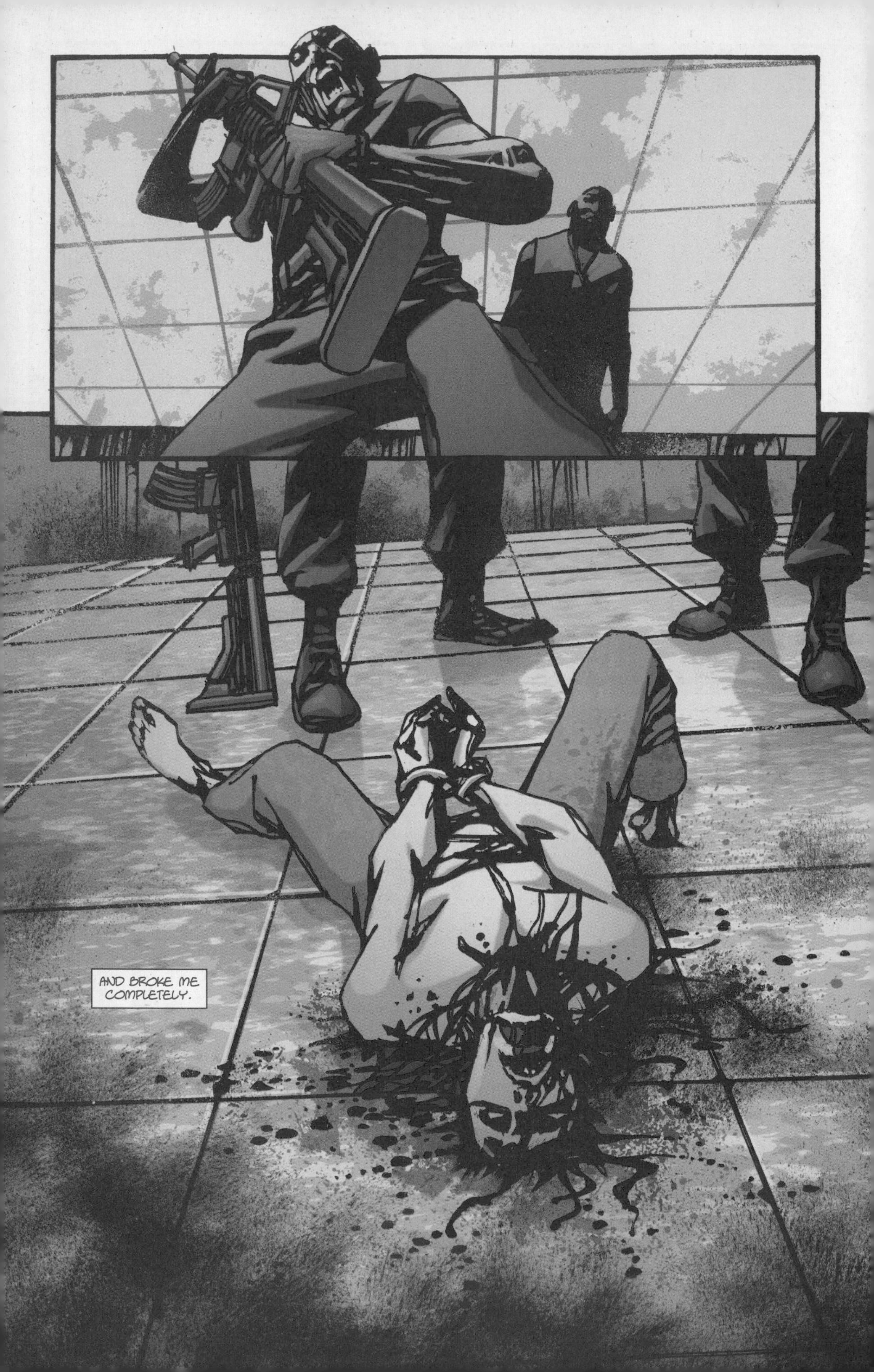
AND BROKE ME COMPLETELY.

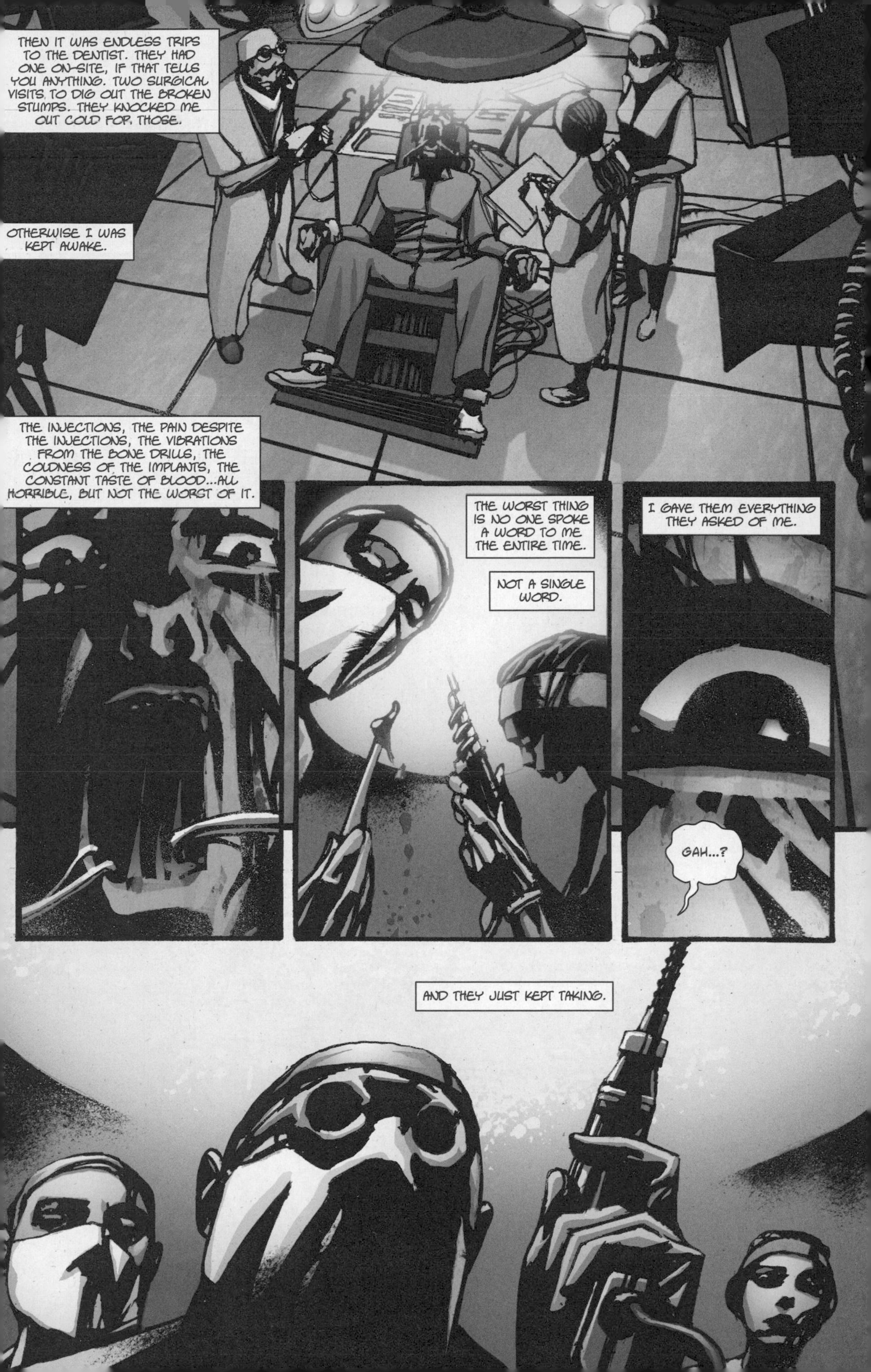
THEN IT WAS ENDLESS TRIPS TO THE DENTIST. THEY HAD ONE ON-SITE, IF THAT TELLS YOU ANYTHING. TWO SURGICAL VISITS TO DIG OUT THE BROKEN STUMPS. THEY KNOCKED ME OUT COLD FOR THOSE.
OTHERWISE I WAS KEPT AWAKE.
THE INJECTIONS, THE PAIN DESPITE THE INJECTIONS, THE VIBRATIONS FROM THE BONE DRILLS, THE COLDNESS OF THE IMPLANTS, THE CONSTANT TASTE OF BLOOD...ALL HORRIBLE, BUT NOT THE WORST OF IT.
THE WORST THING IS NO ONE SPOKE A WORD TO ME THE ENTIRE TIME.
NOT A SINGLE WORD.
I GAVE THEM EVERYTHING THEY ASKED OF ME.
GAH...?
AND THEY JUST KEPT TAKING.

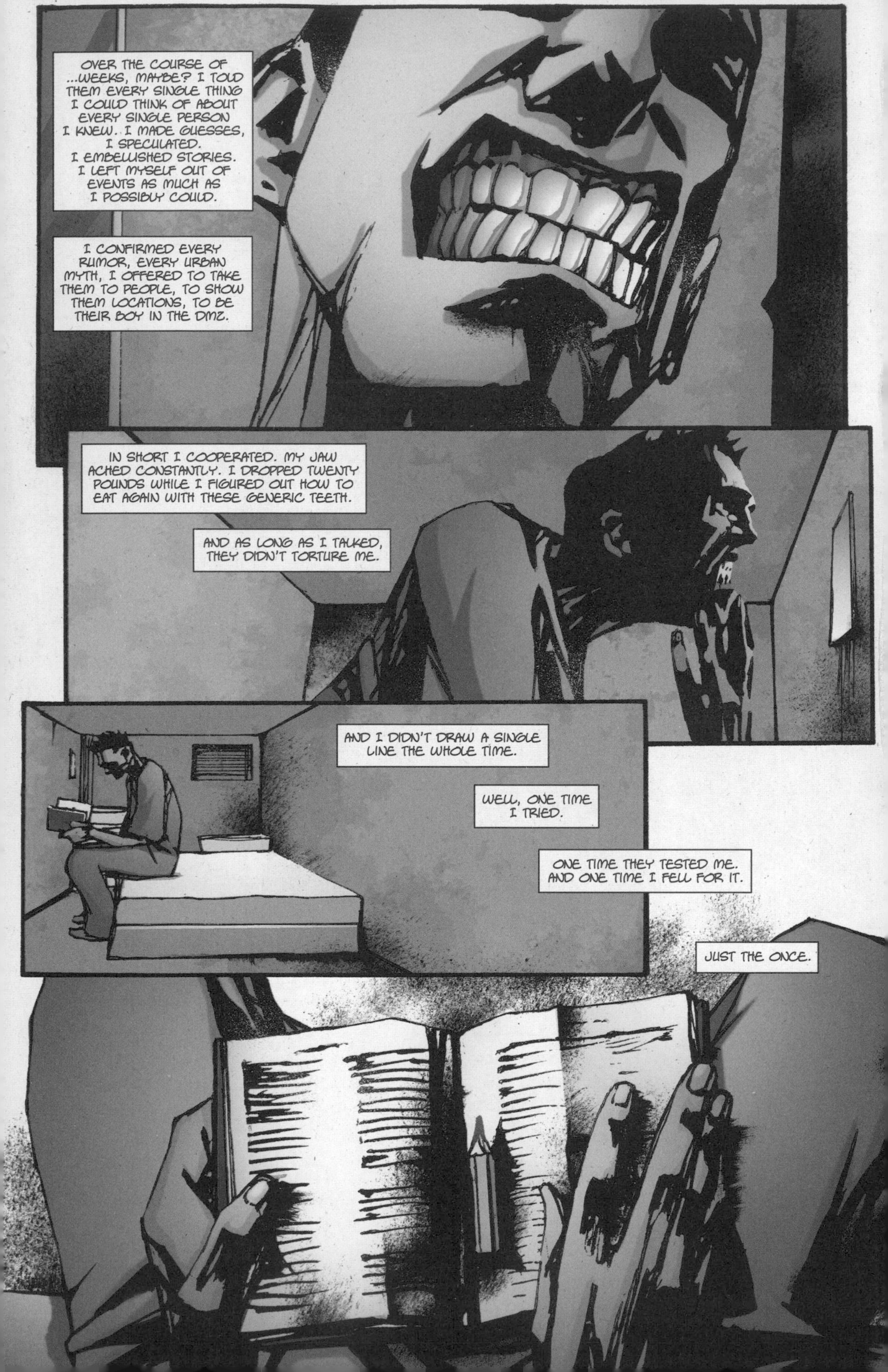
OVER THE COURSE OF ...WEEKS, MAYBE? I TOLD THEM EVERY SINGLE THING I COULD THINK OF ABOUT EVERY SINGLE PERSON I KNEW. I MADE GUESSES, I SPECULATED. I EMBELLISHED STORIES. I LEFT MYSELF OUT OF EVENTS AS MUCH AS I POSSIBLY COULD.
I CONFIRMED EVERY RUMOR, EVERY URBAN MYTH, I OFFERED TO TAKE THEM TO PEOPLE, TO SHOW THEM LOCATIONS, TO BE THEIR BOY IN THE DMZ.
IN SHORT I COOPERATED. MY JAW ACHED CONSTANTLY. I DROPPED TWENTY POUNDS WHILE I FIGURED OUT HOW TO EAT AGAIN WITH THESE GENERIC TEETH.
AND AS LONG AS I TALKED, THEY DIDN'T TORTURE ME.
AND I DIDN'T DRAW A SINGLE LINE THE WHOLE TIME.
WELL, ONE TIME I TRIED.
ONE TIME THEY TESTED ME. AND ONE TIME I FELL FOR IT.
JUST THE ONCE.

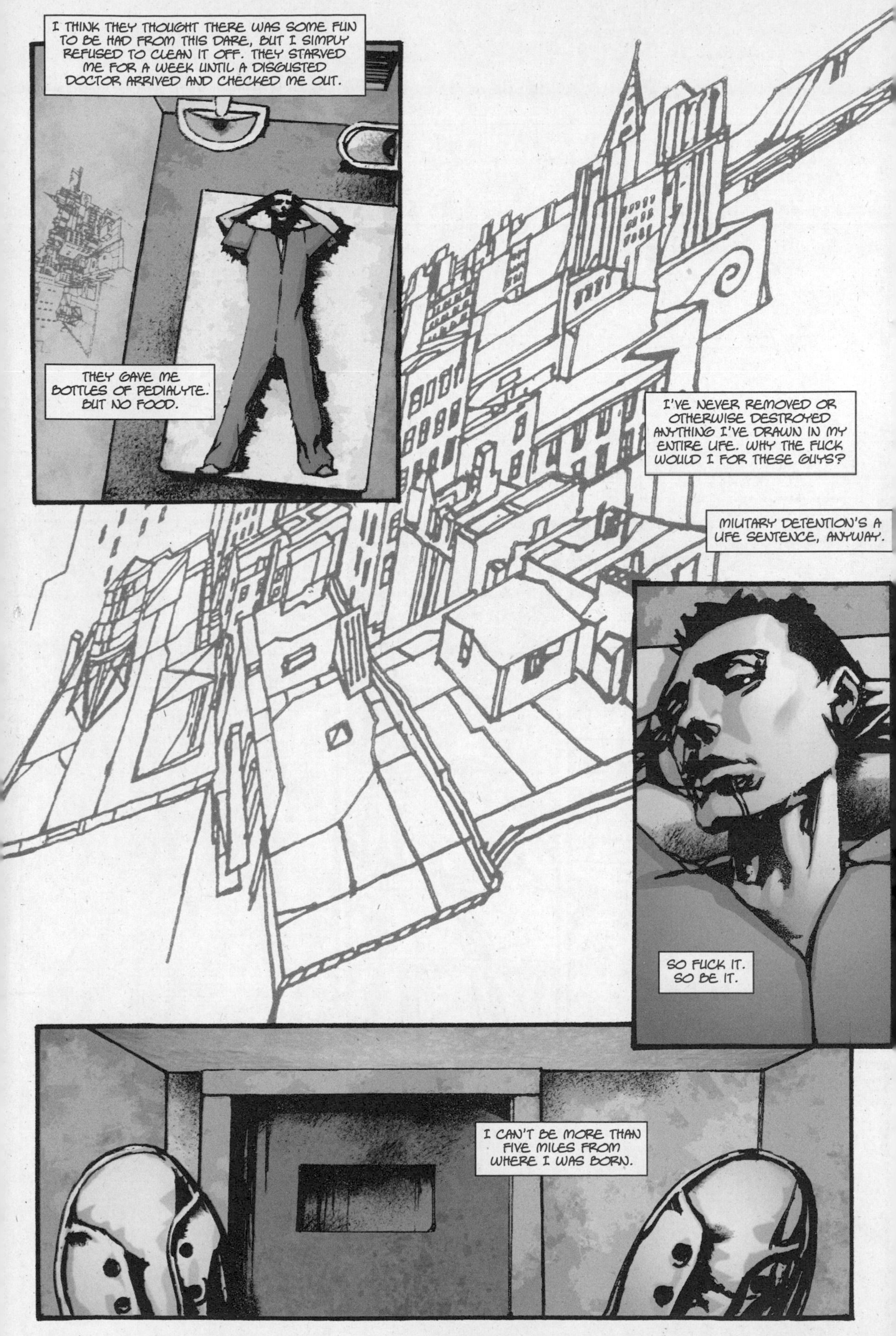
I THINK THEY THOUGHT THERE WAS SOME FUN TO BE HAD FROM THIS DARE, BUT I SIMPLY REFUSED TO CLEAN IT OFF. THEY STARVED ME FOR A WEEK UNTIL A DISGUSTED DOCTOR ARRIVED AND CHECKED ME OUT.
THEY GAVE ME BOTTLES OF PEDIALYTE. BUT NO FOOD.
I'VE NEVER REMOVED OR OTHERWISE DESTROYED ANYTHING I'VE DRAWN IN MY ENTIRE LIFE. WHY THE FUCK WOULD I FOR THESE GUYS?
MILITARY DETENTION'S A LIFE SENTENCE, ANYWAY.
SO FUCK IT. SO BE IT.
I CAN'T BE MORE THAN FIVE MILES FROM WHERE I WAS BORN.

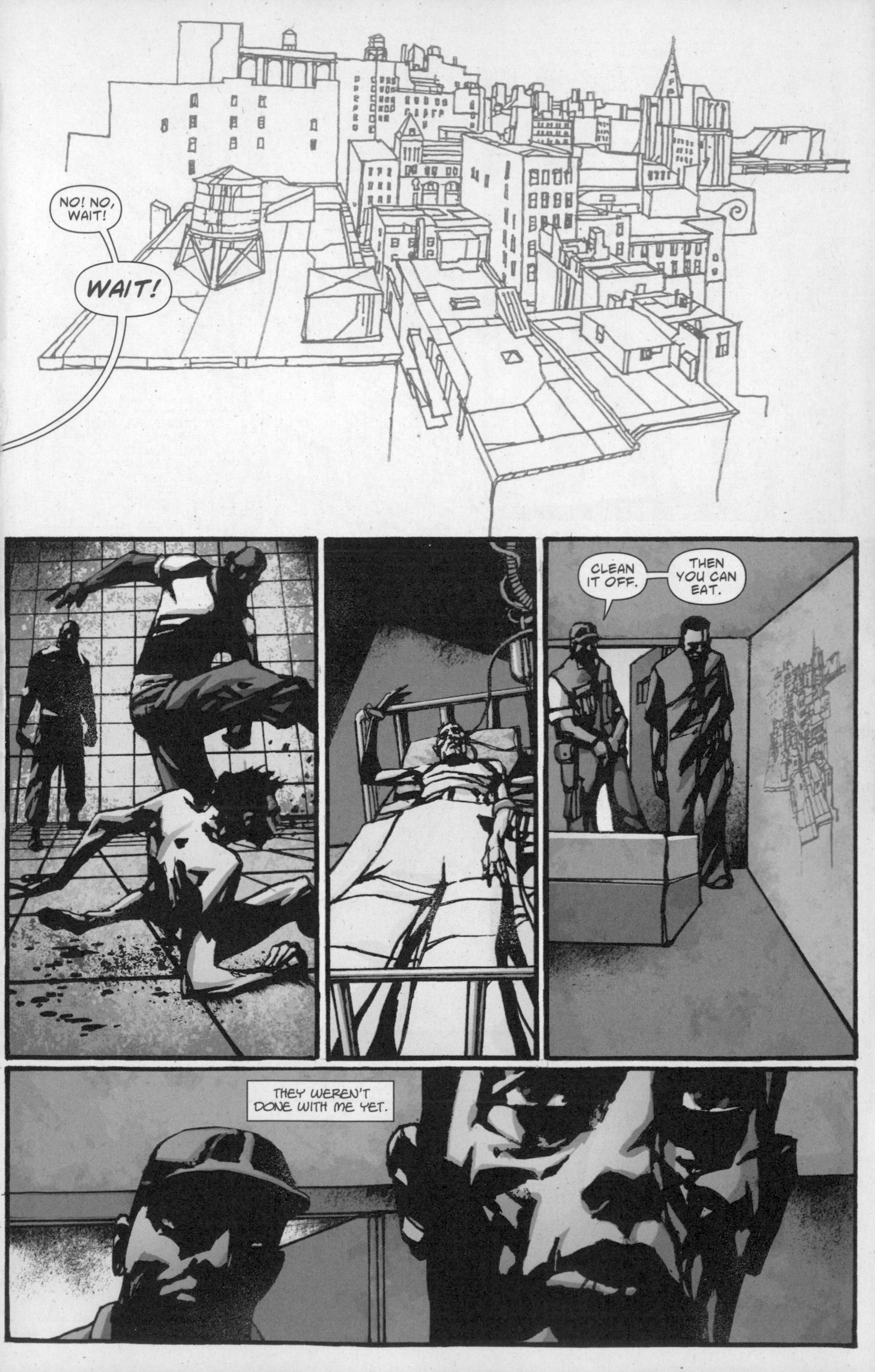
NO! NO, WAIT!
WAIT!
CLEAN IT OFF.
THEN YOU CAN EAT.
THEY WEREN'T DONE WITH ME YET.

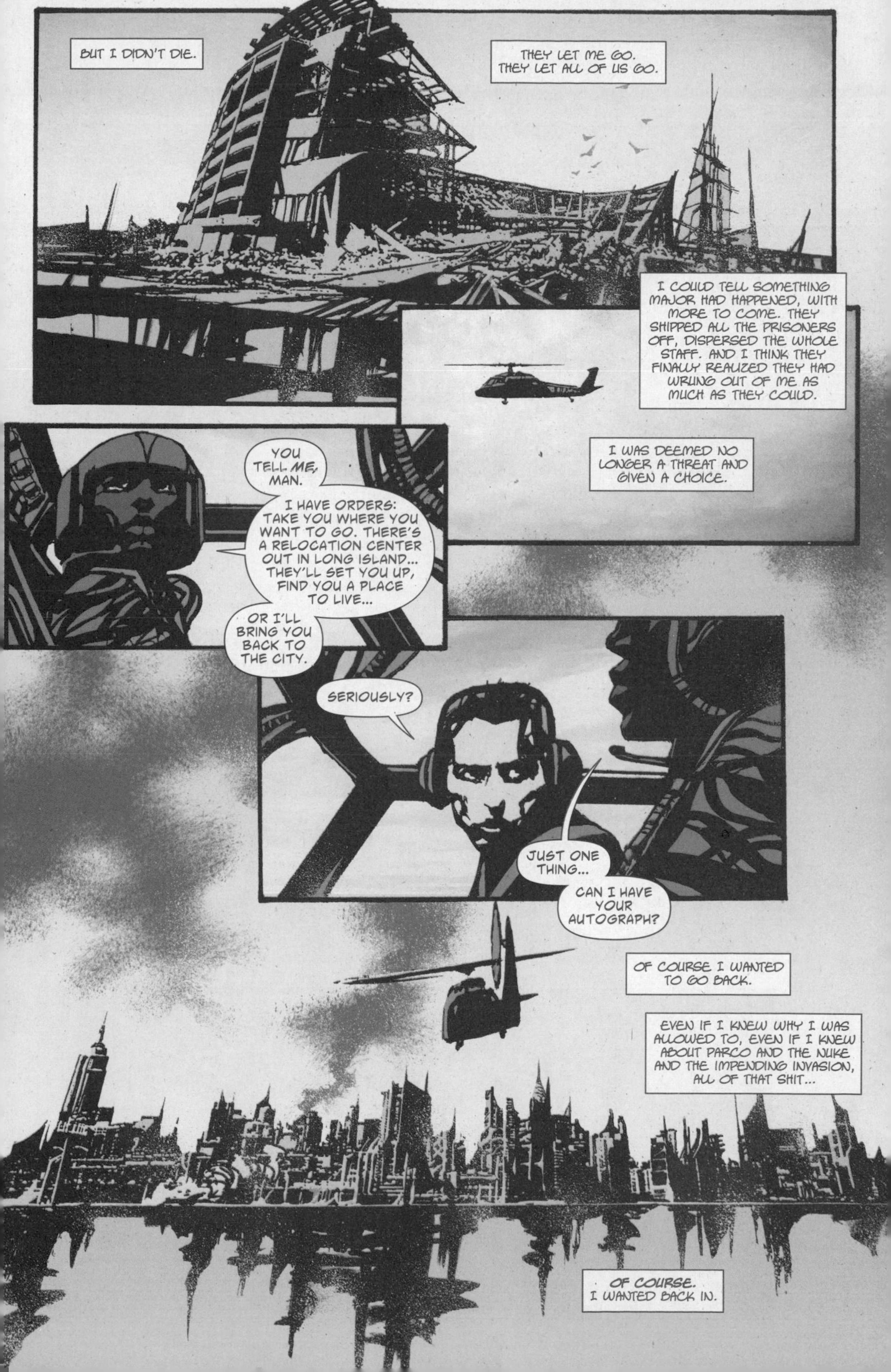

BUT I DIDN'T DIE.
THEY LET ME GO. THEY LET ALL OF US GO.
I COULD TELL SOMETHING MAJOR HAD HAPPENED, WITH MORE TO COME. THEY SHIPPED ALL THE PRISONERS OFF, DISPERSED THE WHOLE STAFF. AND I THINK THEY FINALLY REALIZED THEY HAD WRUNG OUT OF ME AS MUCH AS THEY COULD.
I WAS DEEMED NO LONGER A THREAT AND GIVEN A CHOICE.
YOU TELL ME, MAN.
I HAVE ORDERS: TAKE YOU WHERE YOU WANT TO GO. THERE'S A RELOCATION CENTER OUT IN LONG ISLAND... THEY'LL SET YOU UP, FIND YOU A PLACE TO LIVE...
OR I'LL BRING YOU BACK TO THE CITY.
SERIOUSLY?
JUST ONE THING...
CAN I HAVE YOUR AUTOGRAPH?
OF COURSE I WANTED TO GO BACK.
EVEN IF I KNEW WHY I WAS ALLOWED TO, EVEN IF I KNEW ABOUT PARCO AND THE NUKE AND THE IMPENDING INVASION, ALL OF THAT SHIT...
OF COURSE. I WANTED BACK IN.

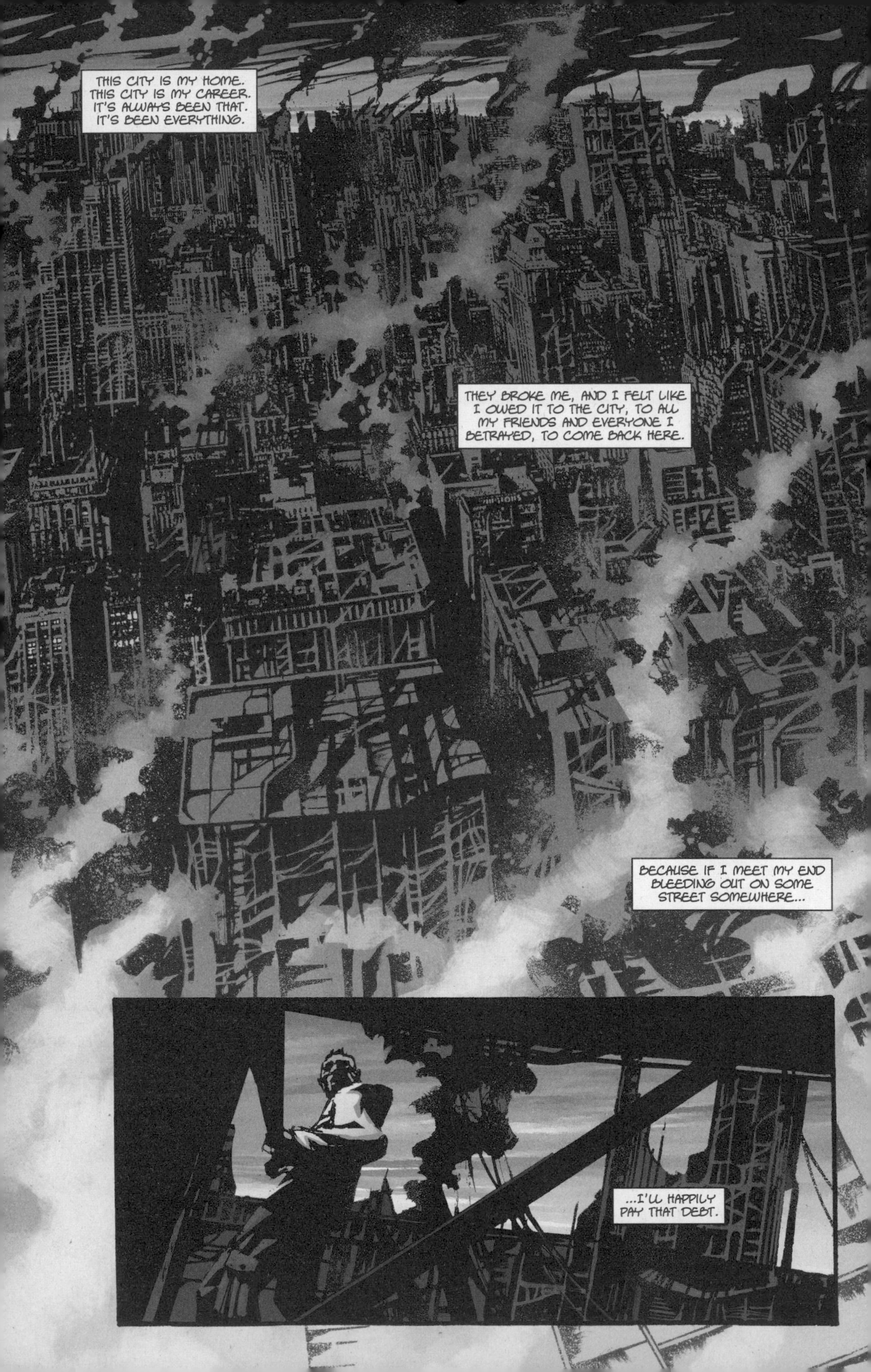
THIS CITY IS MY HOME. THIS CITY IS MY CAREER. IT'S ALWAYS BEEN THAT. IT'S BEEN EVERYTHING.
THEY BROKE ME, AND I FELT LIKE I OWED IT TO THE CITY, TO ALL MY FRIENDS AND EVERYONE I BETRAYED, TO COME BACK HERE.
BECAUSE IF I MEET MY END BLEEDING OUT ON SOME STREET SOMEWHERE...
...I'LL HAPPILY PAY THAT DEBT.

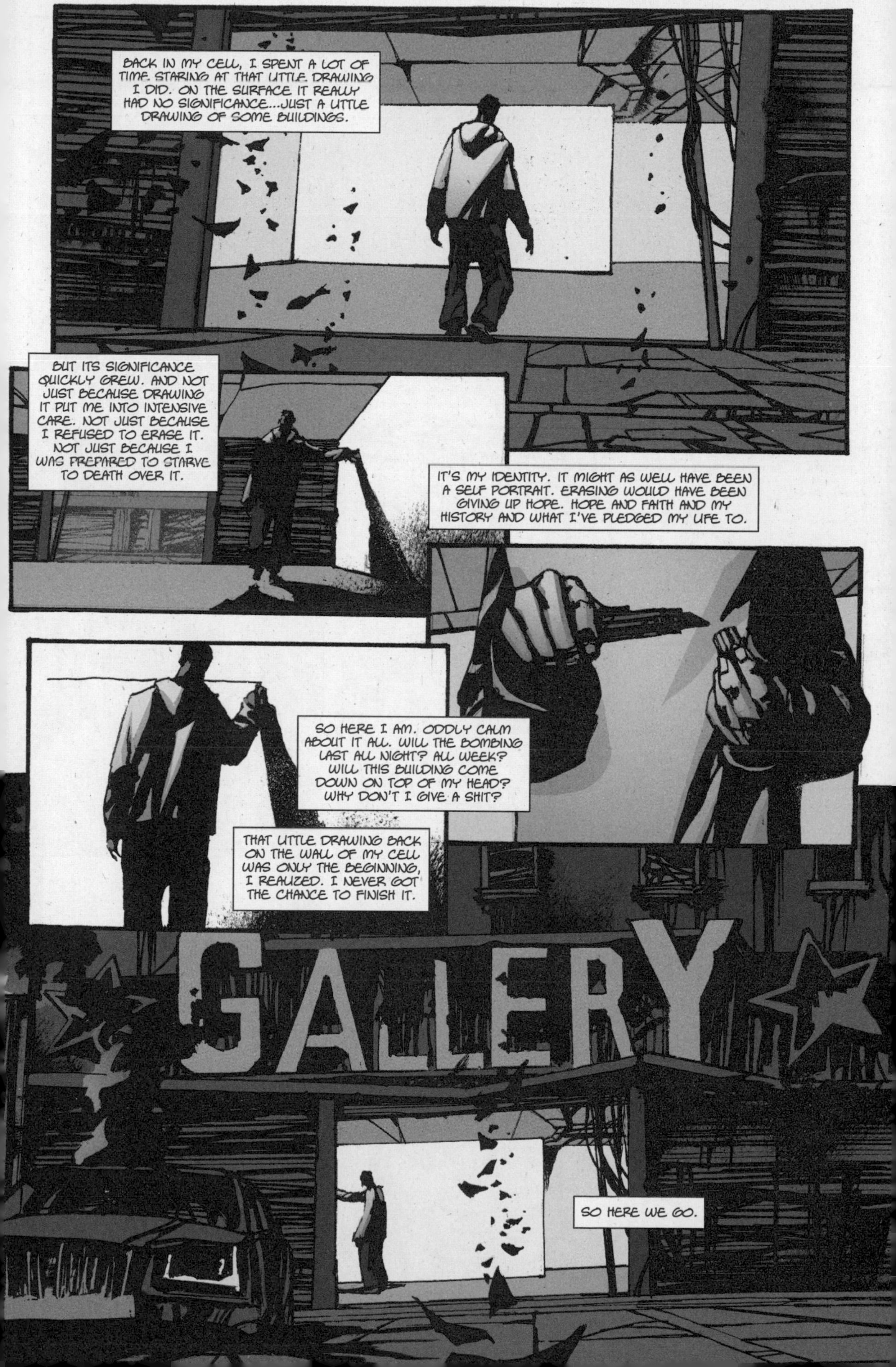
BACK IN MY CELL, I SPENT A LOT OF TIME STARING AT THAT LITTLE DRAWING I DID. ON THE SURFACE IT REALLY HAD NO SIGNIFICANCE...JUST A LITTLE DRAWING OF SOME BUILDINGS.
BUT ITS SIGNIFICANCE QUICKLY GREW. AND NOT JUST BECAUSE DRAWING IT PUT ME INTO INTENSIVE CARE. NOT JUST BECAUSE I REFUSED TO ERASE IT. NOT JUST BECAUSE I WAS PREPARED TO STARVE TO DEATH OVER IT.
IT'S MY IDENTITY. IT MIGHT AS WELL HAVE BEEN A SELF PORTRAIT. ERASING WOULD HAVE BEEN GIVING UP HOPE. HOPE AND FAITH AND MY HISTORY AND WHAT I'VE PLEDGED MY LIFE TO.
SO HERE I AM. ODDLY CALM ABOUT IT ALL. WILL THE BOMBING LAST ALL NIGHT? ALL WEEK? WILL THIS BUILDING COME DOWN ON TOP OF MY HEAD? WHY DON'T I GIVE A SHIT?
THAT LITTLE DRAWING BACK ON THE WALL OF MY CELL WAS ONLY THE BEGINNING, I REALIZED. I NEVER GOT THE CHANCE TO FINISH IT.
GALLERY
SO HERE WE GO.

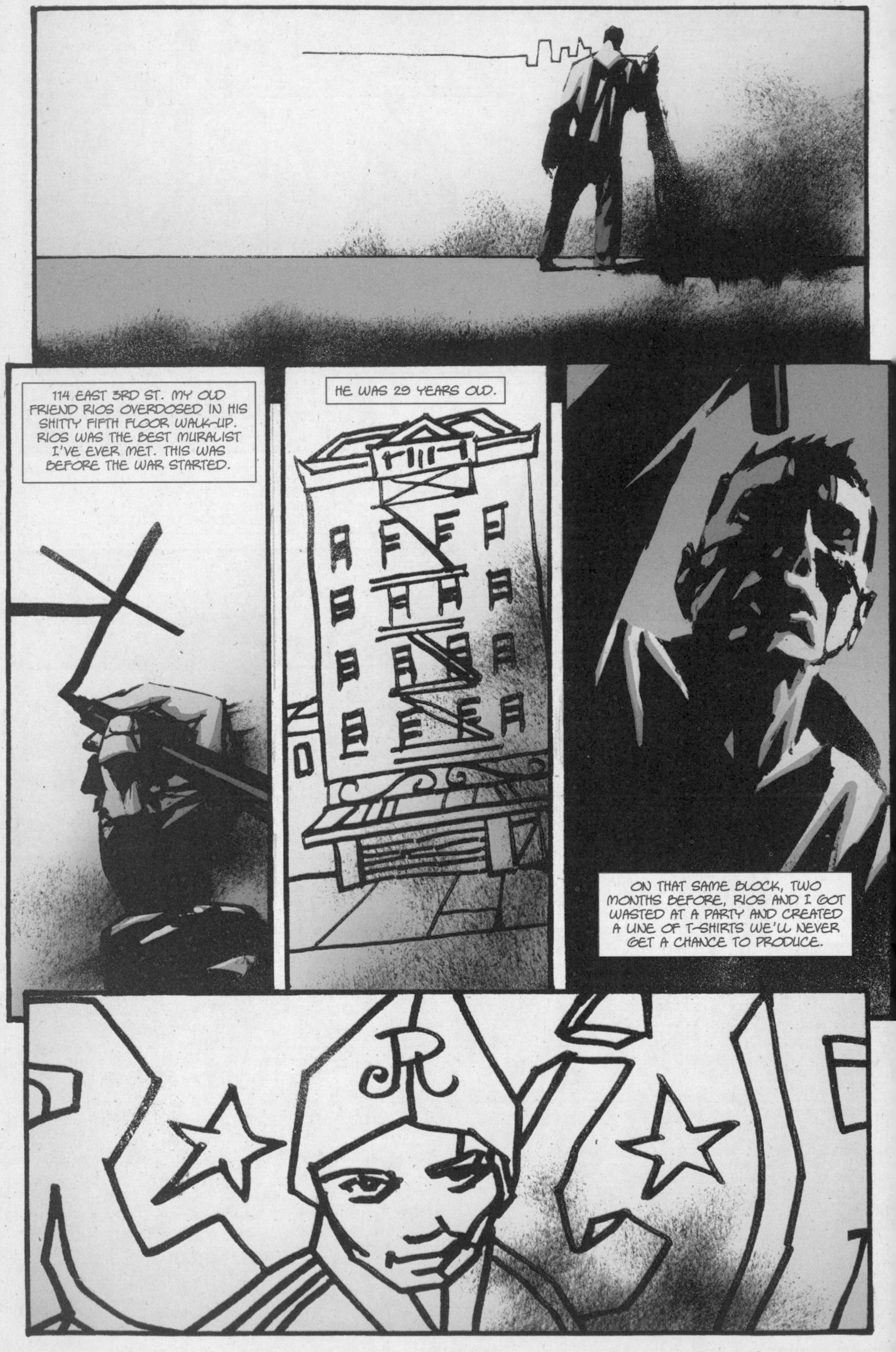
114 EAST 3RD ST. MY OLD FRIEND RIOS OVERDOSED IN HIS SHITTY FIFTH FLOOR WALK-UP. RIOS WAS THE BEST MURALIST I'VE EVER MET. THIS WAS BEFORE THE WAR STARTED.
HE WAS 29 YEARS OLD.
ON THAT SAME BLOCK, TWO MONTHS BEFORE, RIOS AND I GOT WASTED AT A PARTY AND CREATED A LINE OF T-SHIRTS WE'LL NEVER GET A CHANCE TO PRODUCE.

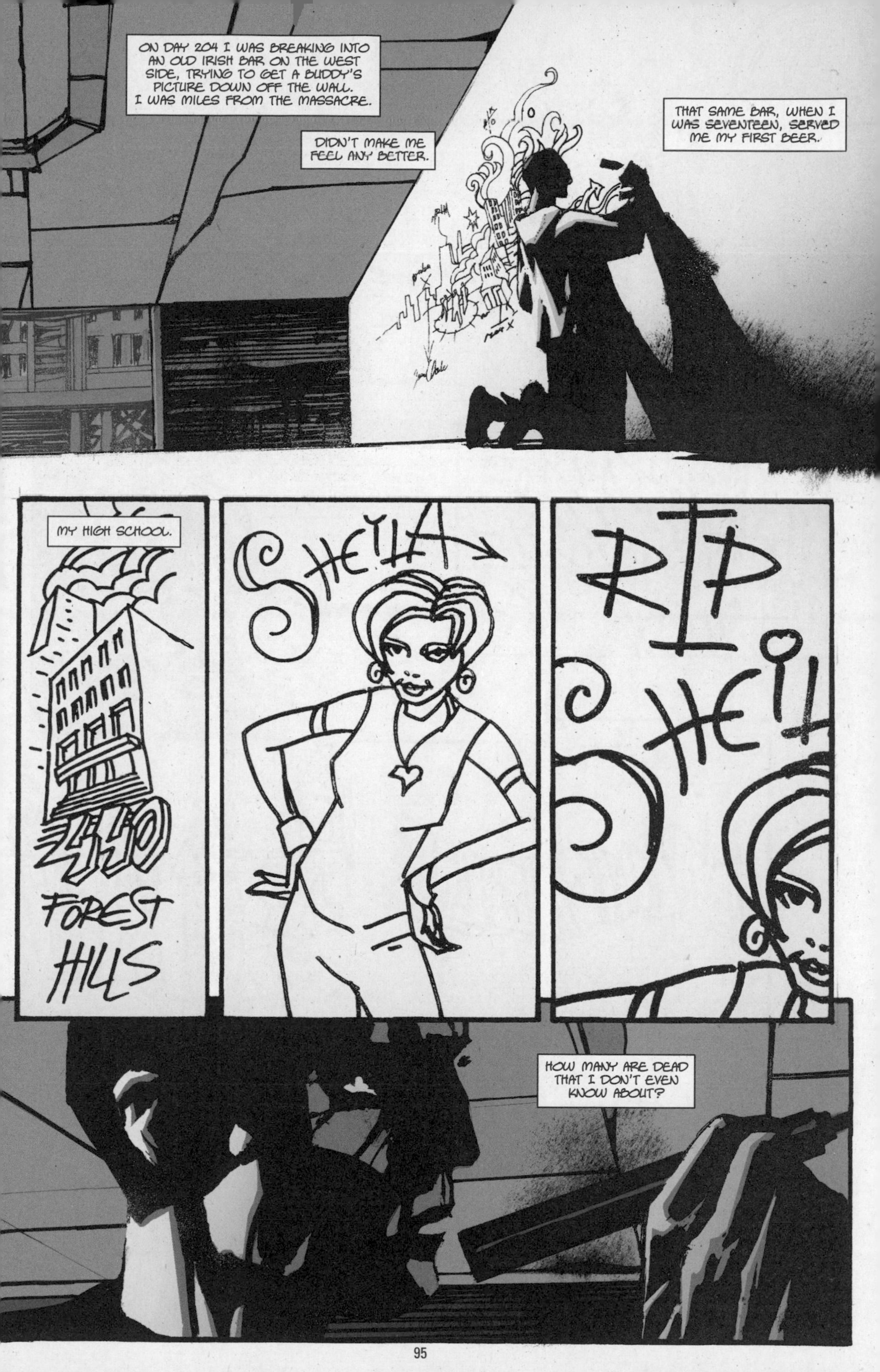
ON DAY 204 I WAS BREAKING INTO AN OLD IRISH BAR ON THE WEST SIDE, TRYING TO GET A BUDDY'S PICTURE DOWN OFF THE WALL. I WAS MILES FROM THE MASSACRE.
DIDN'T MAKE ME FEEL ANY BETTER.
THAT SAME BAR, WHEN I WAS SEVENTEEN, SERVED ME MY FIRST BEER.
MY HIGH SCHOOL.
FOREST HILLS
SHEILA
RIP
HOW MANY ARE DEAD THAT I DON'T EVEN KNOW ABOUT?

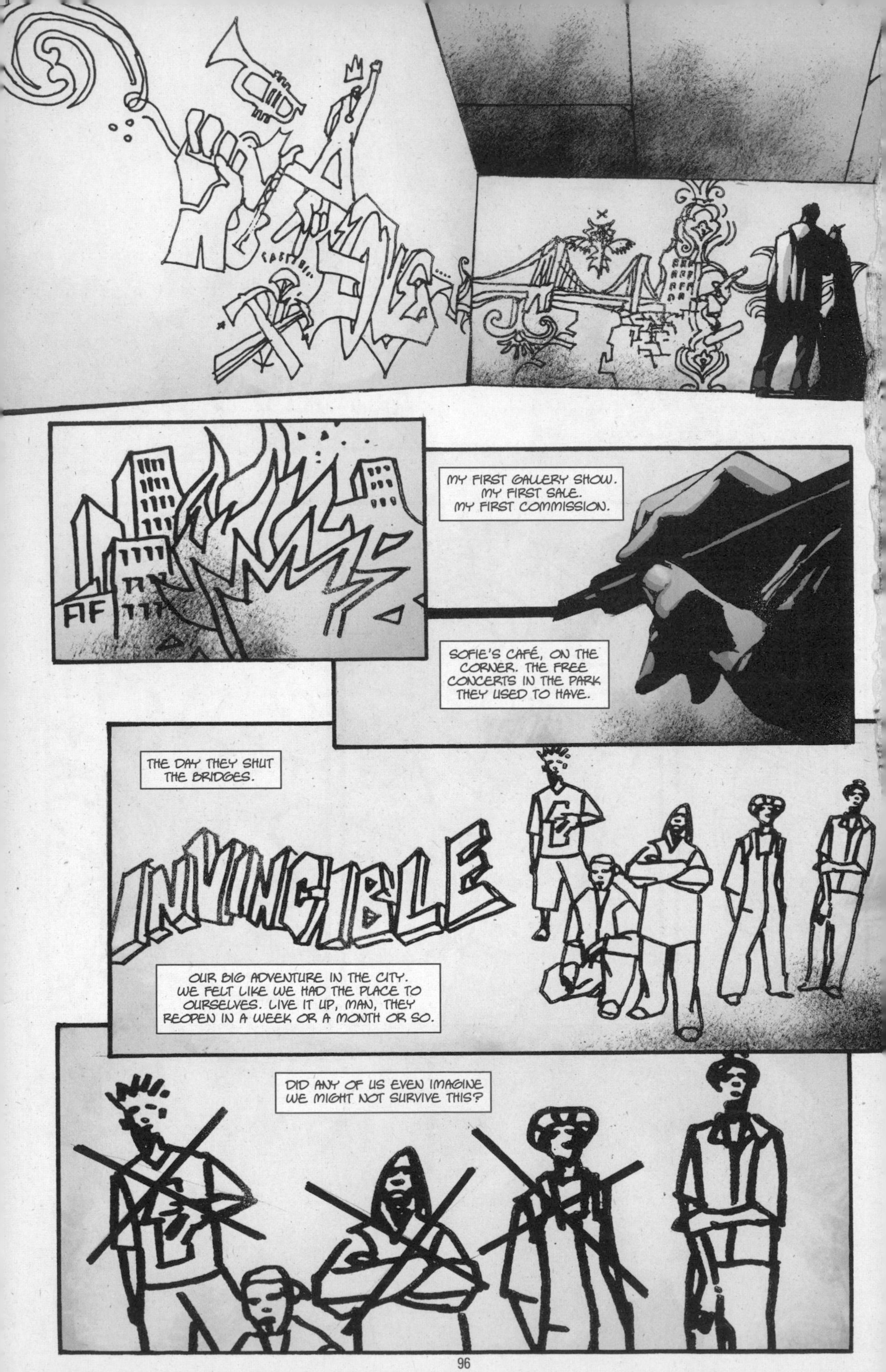
MY FIRST GALLERY SHOW. MY FIRST SALE. MY FIRST COMMISSION.
SOFIE'S CAFÉ, ON THE CORNER. THE FREE CONCERTS IN THE PARK THEY USED TO HAVE.
THE DAY THEY SHUT THE BRIDGES.
INVINCIBLE
OUR BIG ADVENTURE IN THE CITY. WE FELT LIKE WE HAD THE PLACE TO OURSELVES. LIVE IT UP, MAN, THEY REOPEN IN A WEEK OR A MONTH OR SO.
DID ANY OF US EVEN IMAGINE WE MIGHT NOT SURVIVE THIS?

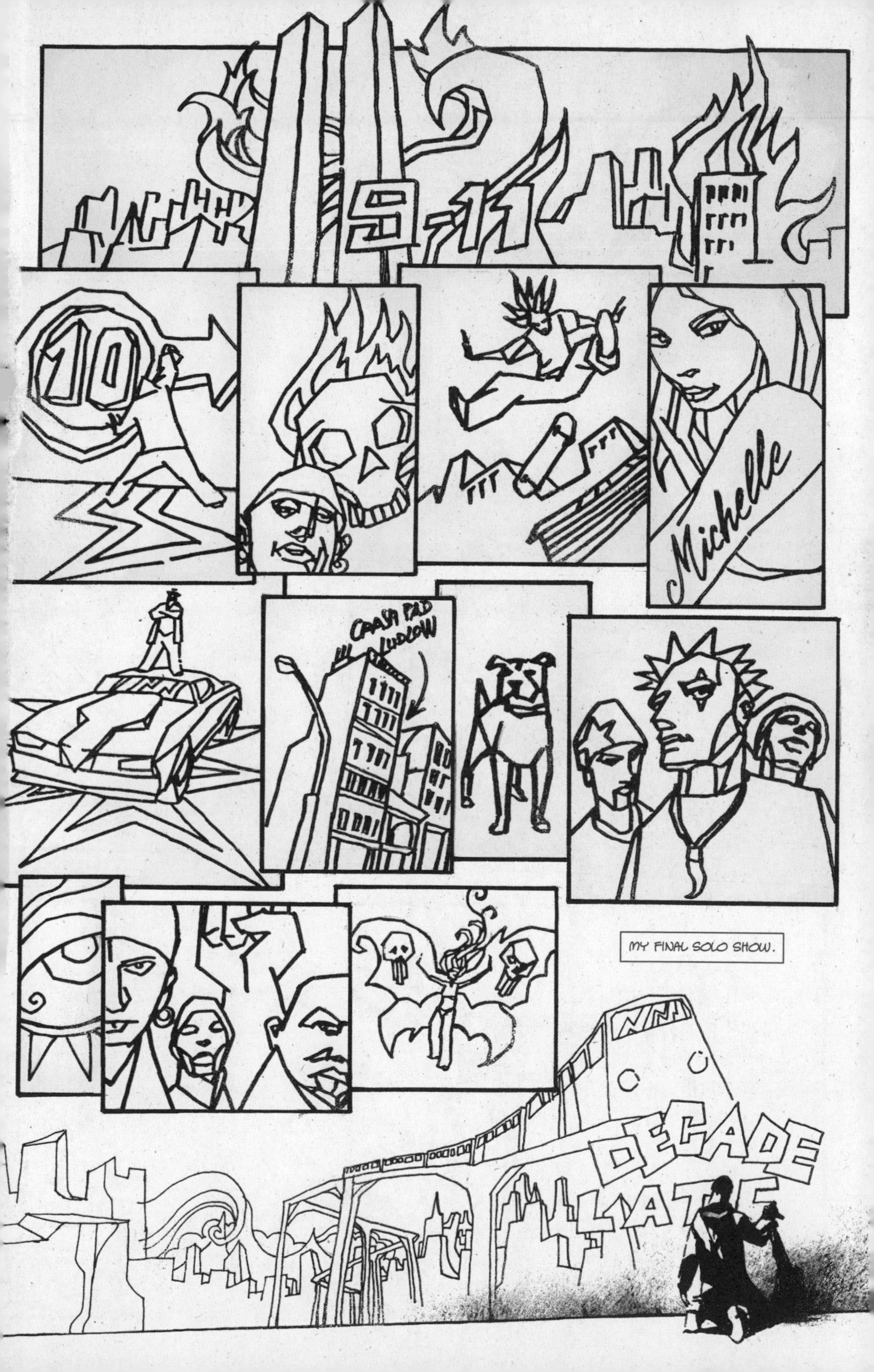
9-11
10
Michelle
CRASH PAD
LUDLOW
MY FINAL SOLO SHOW.
DECADE
LATE

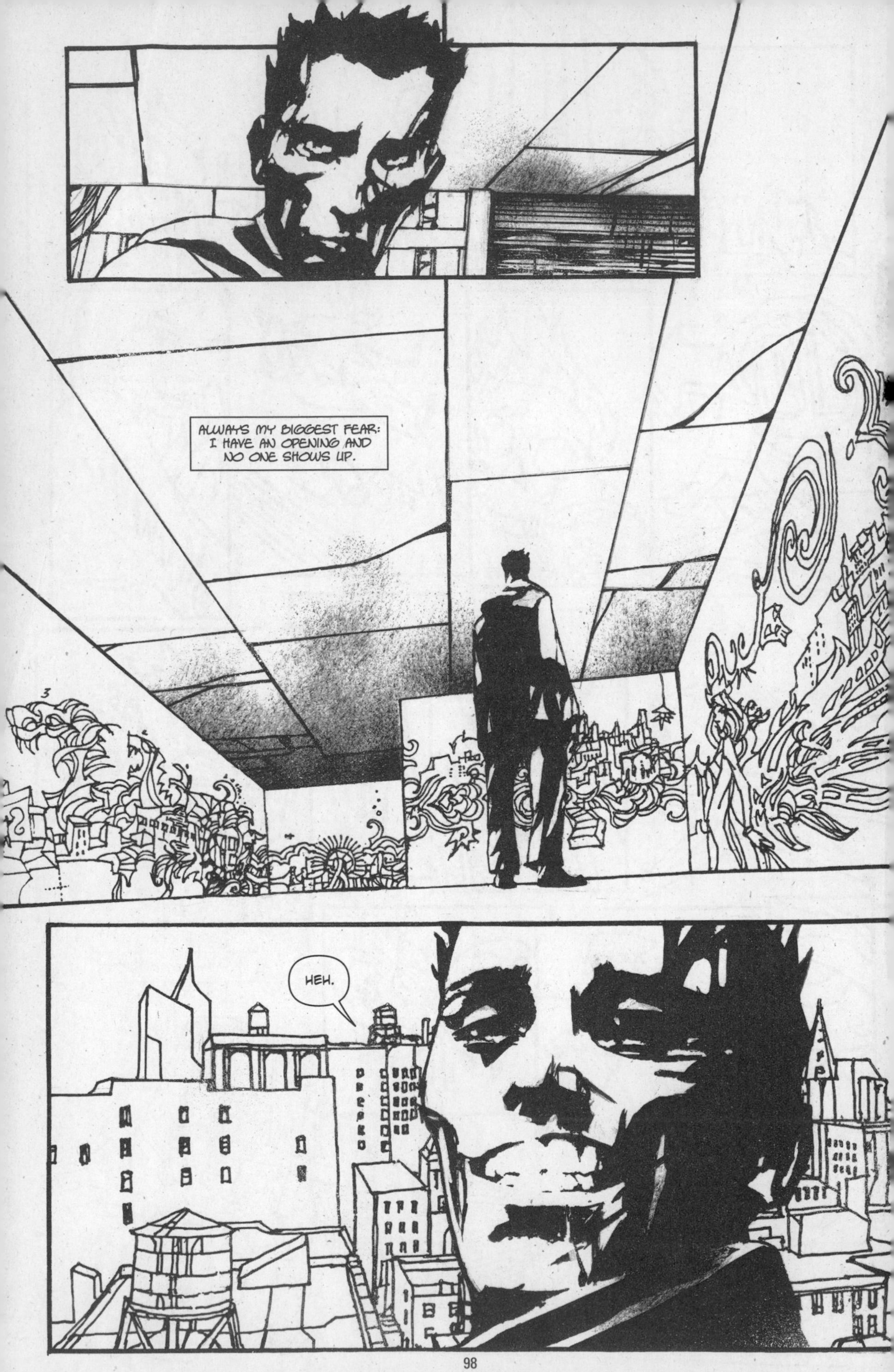
ALWAYS MY BIGGEST FEAR:
I HAVE AN OPENING AND
NO ONE SHOWS UP.
HEH.

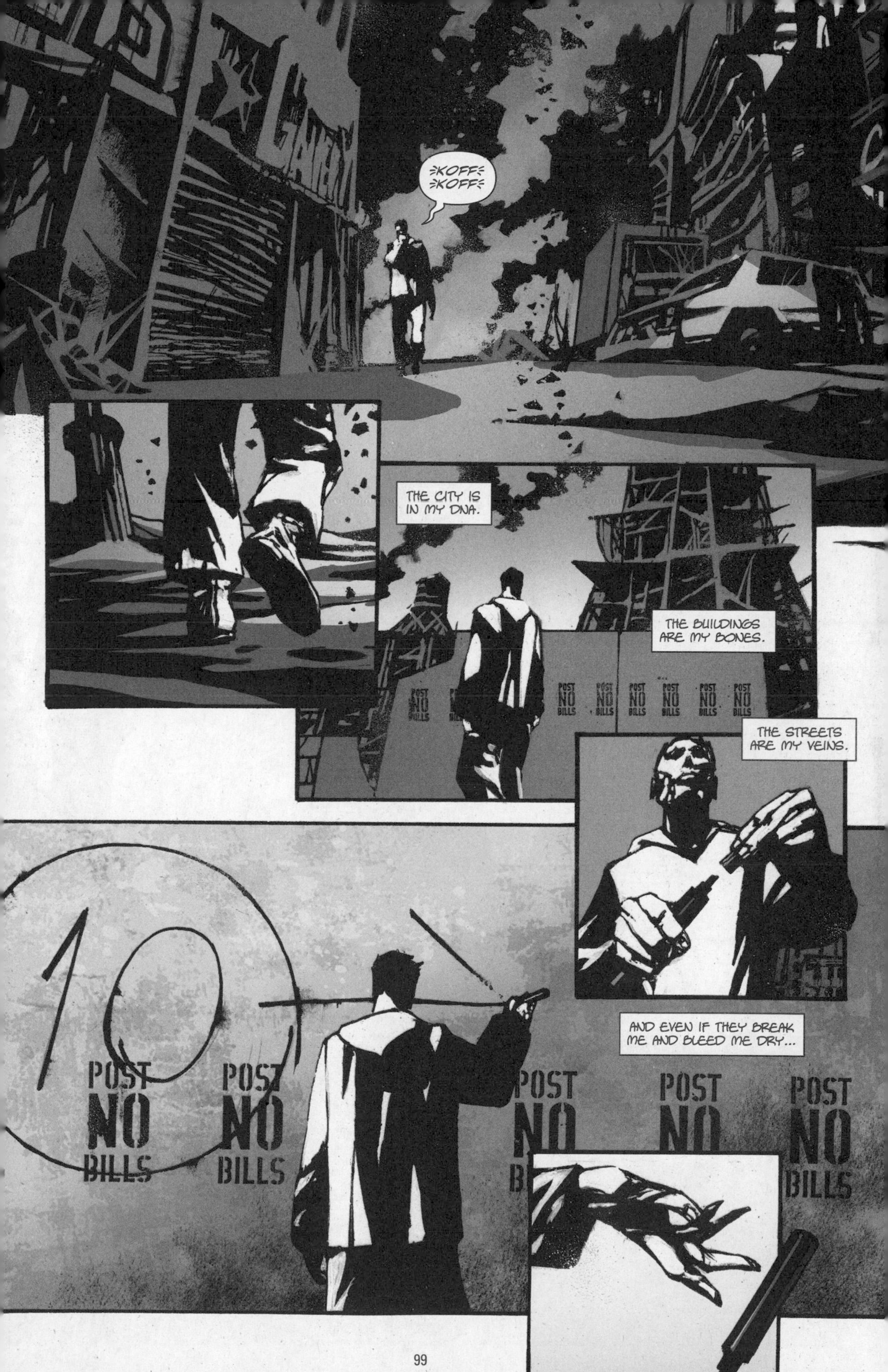

KOFF KOFF
THE CITY IS IN MY DNA.
THE BUILDINGS ARE MY BONES.
POST NO BILLS
THE STREETS ARE MY VEINS.
AND EVEN IF THEY BREAK ME AND BLEED ME DRY...
10
POST NO BILLS
POST NO BILLS
POST NO BILLS

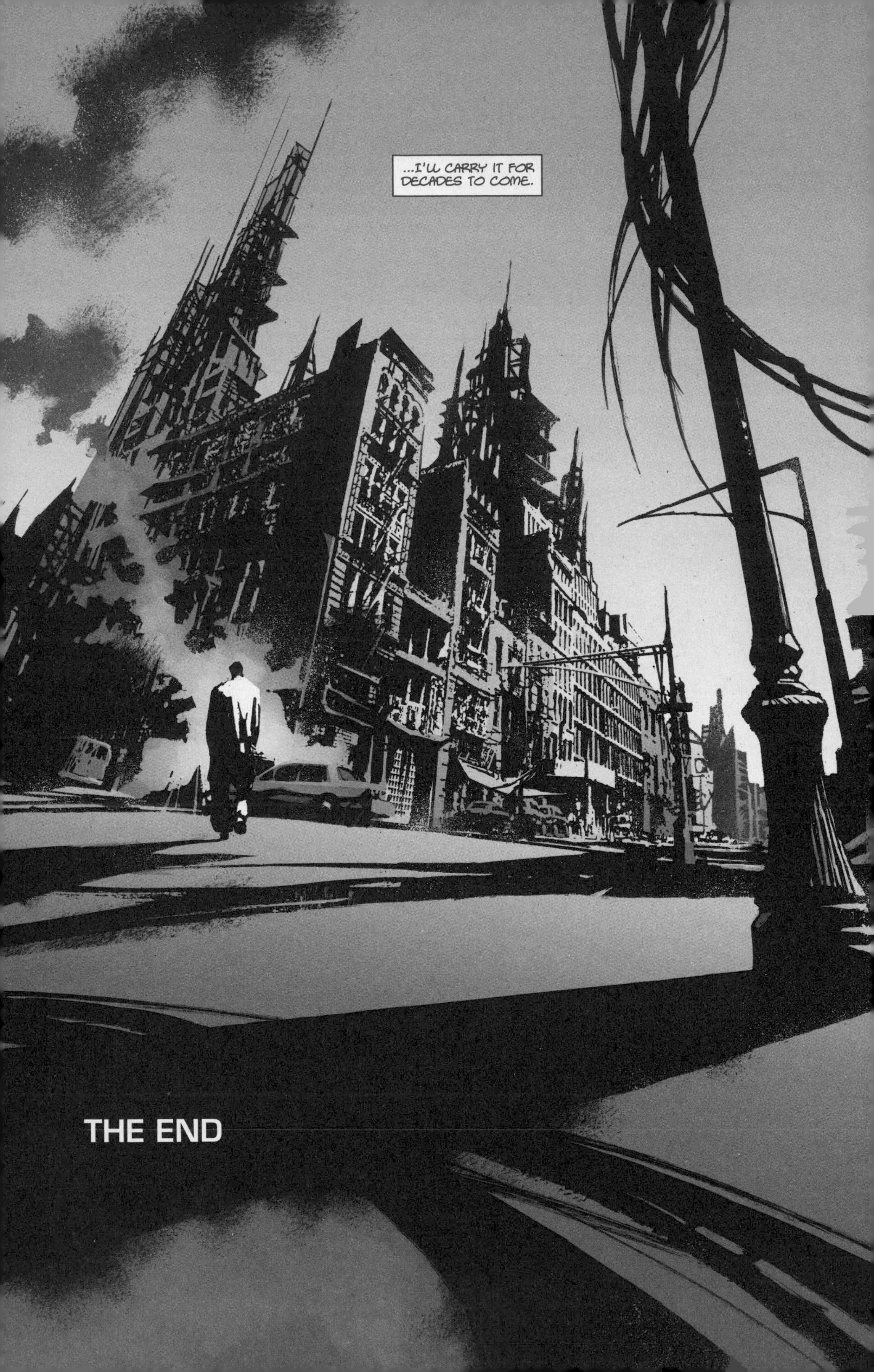
...I'LL CARRY IT FOR DECADES TO COME.
THE END

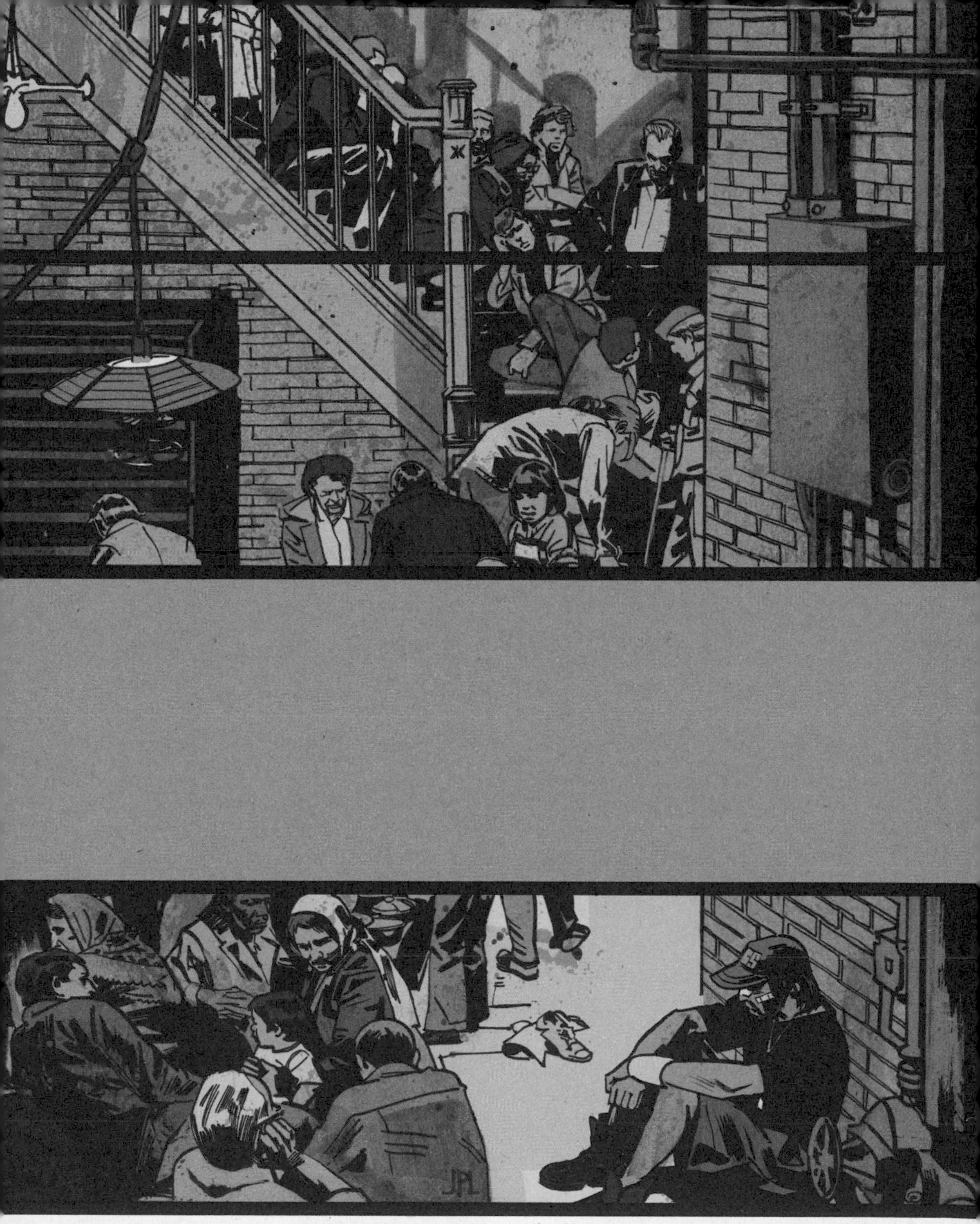

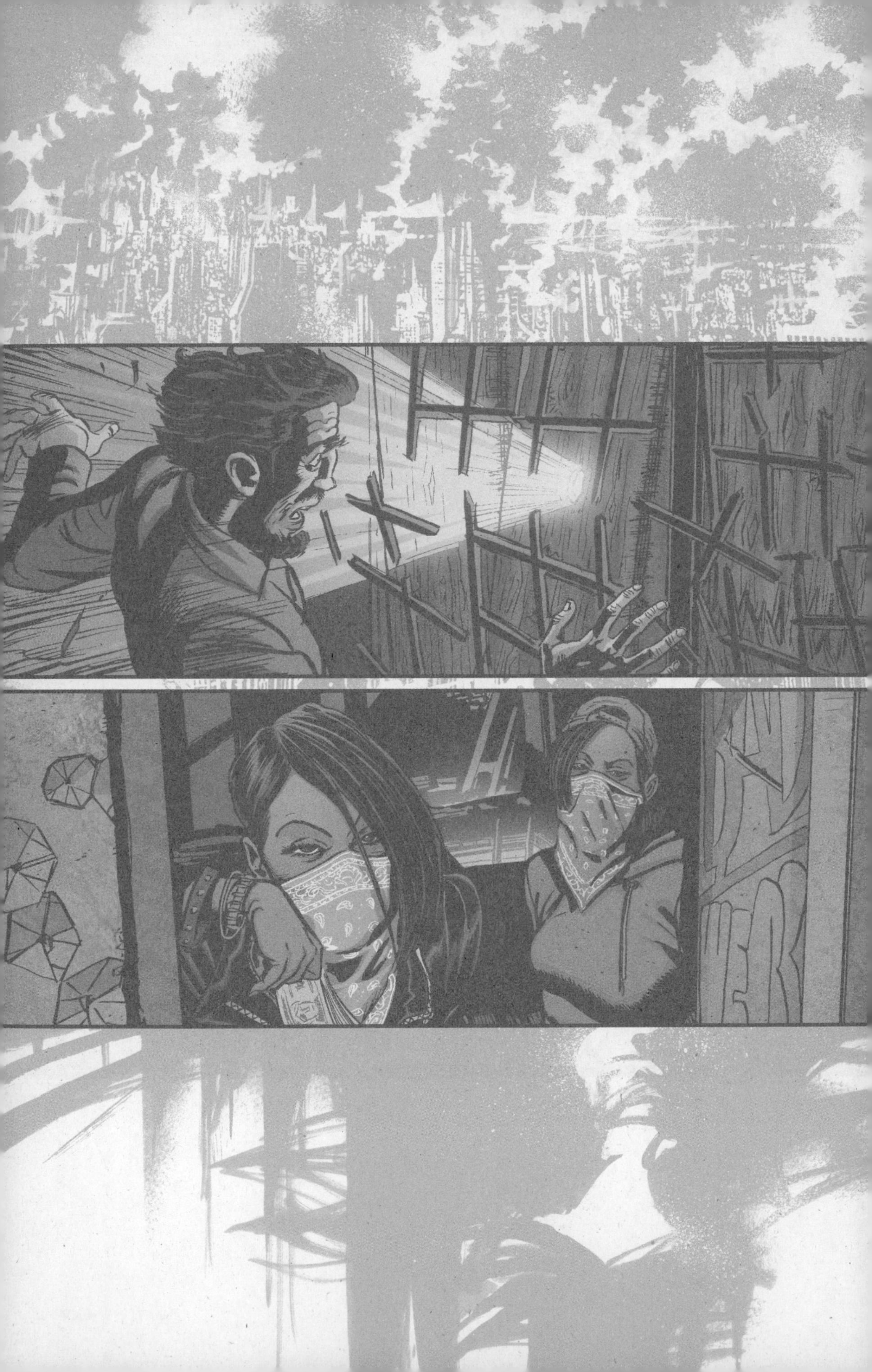

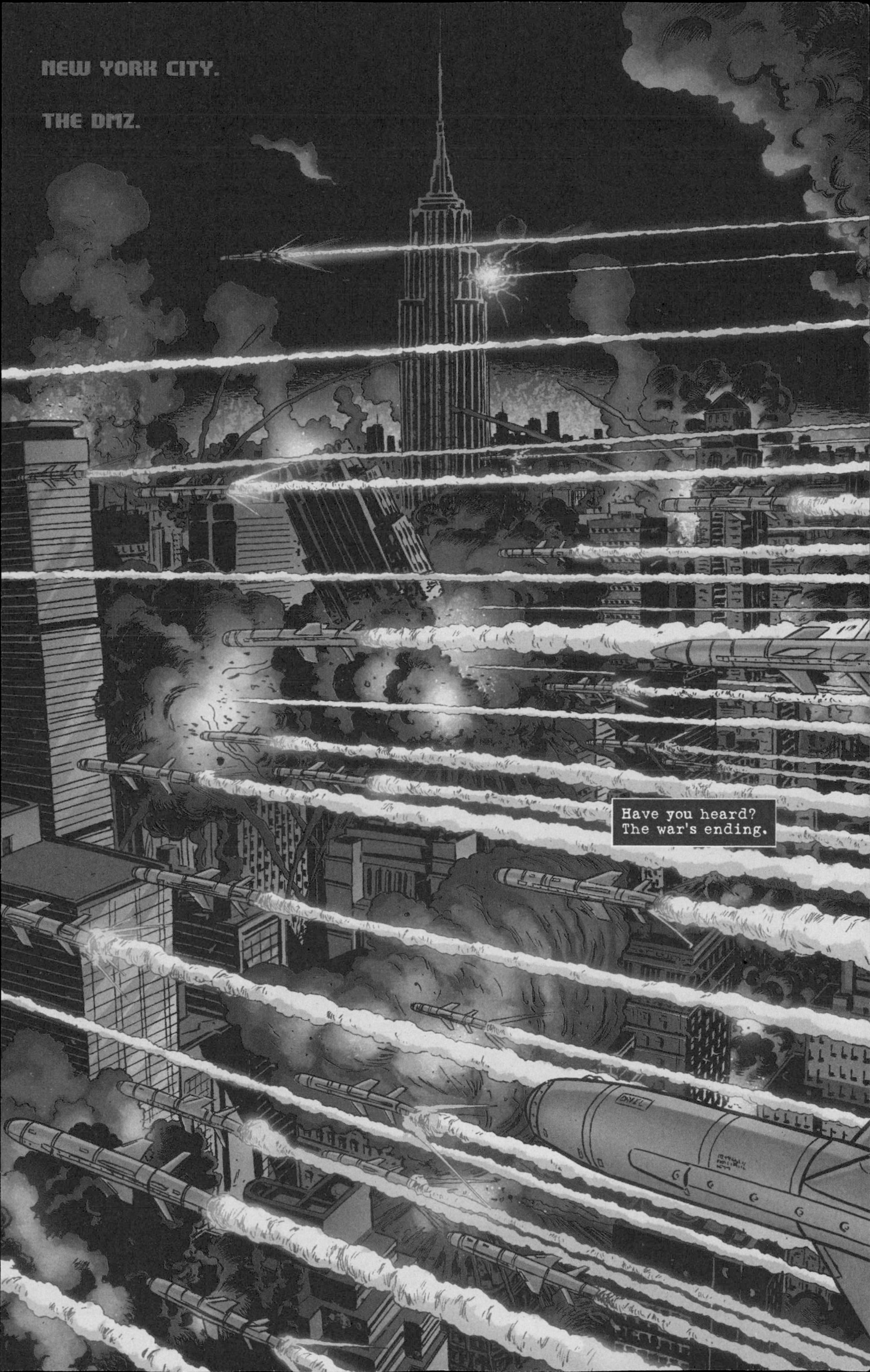
NEW YORK CITY.
THE DMZ.
Have you heard? The war's ending.

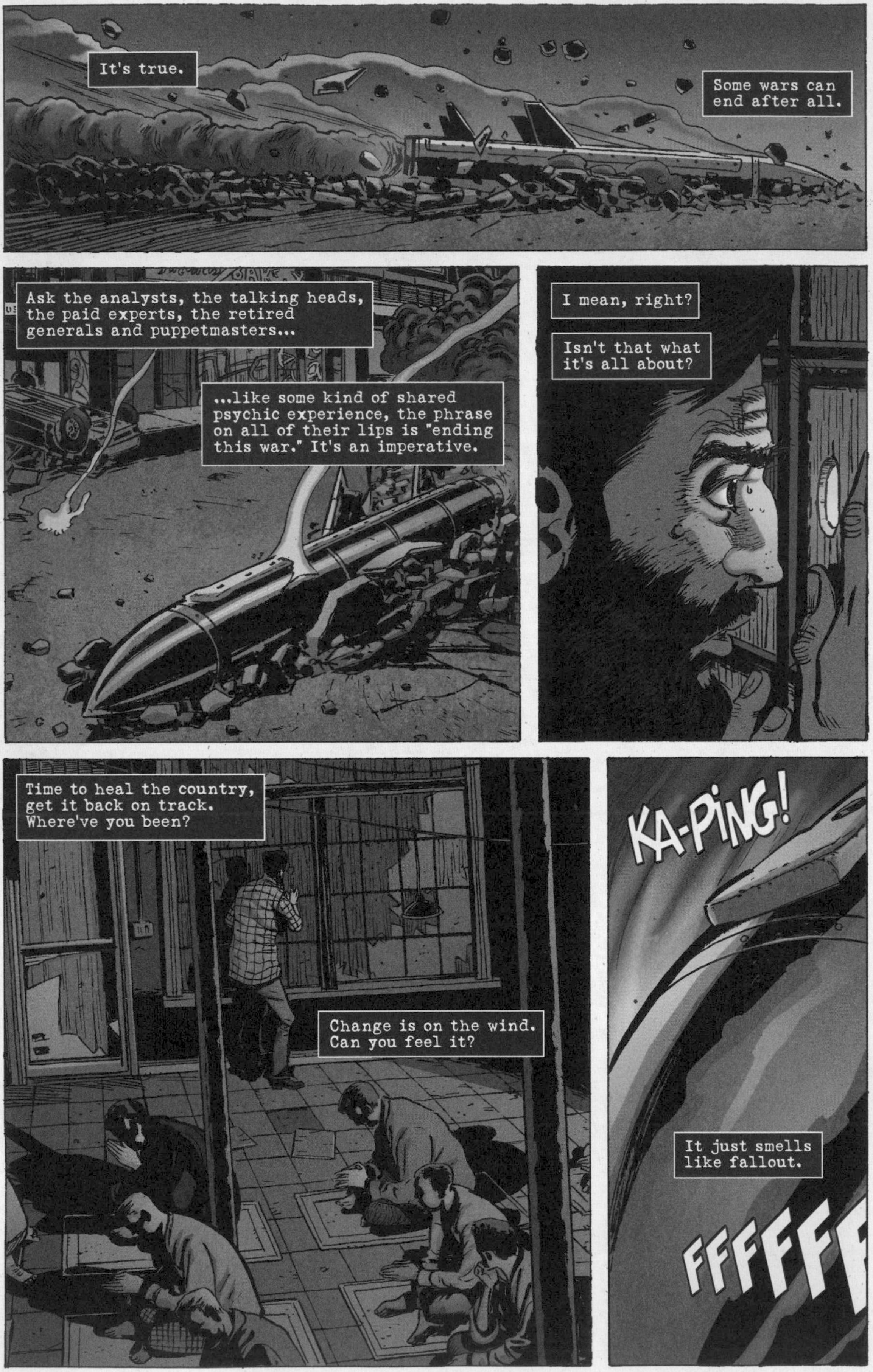
It's true.
Some wars can end after all.
Ask the analysts, the talking heads, the paid experts, the retired generals and puppetmasters...
...like some kind of shared psychic experience, the phrase on all of their lips is "ending this war." It's an imperative.
I mean, right?
Isn't that what it's all about?
Time to heal the country, get it back on track. Where've you been?
Change is on the wind. Can you feel it?
KA-PING!
It just smells like fallout.
FFFFF

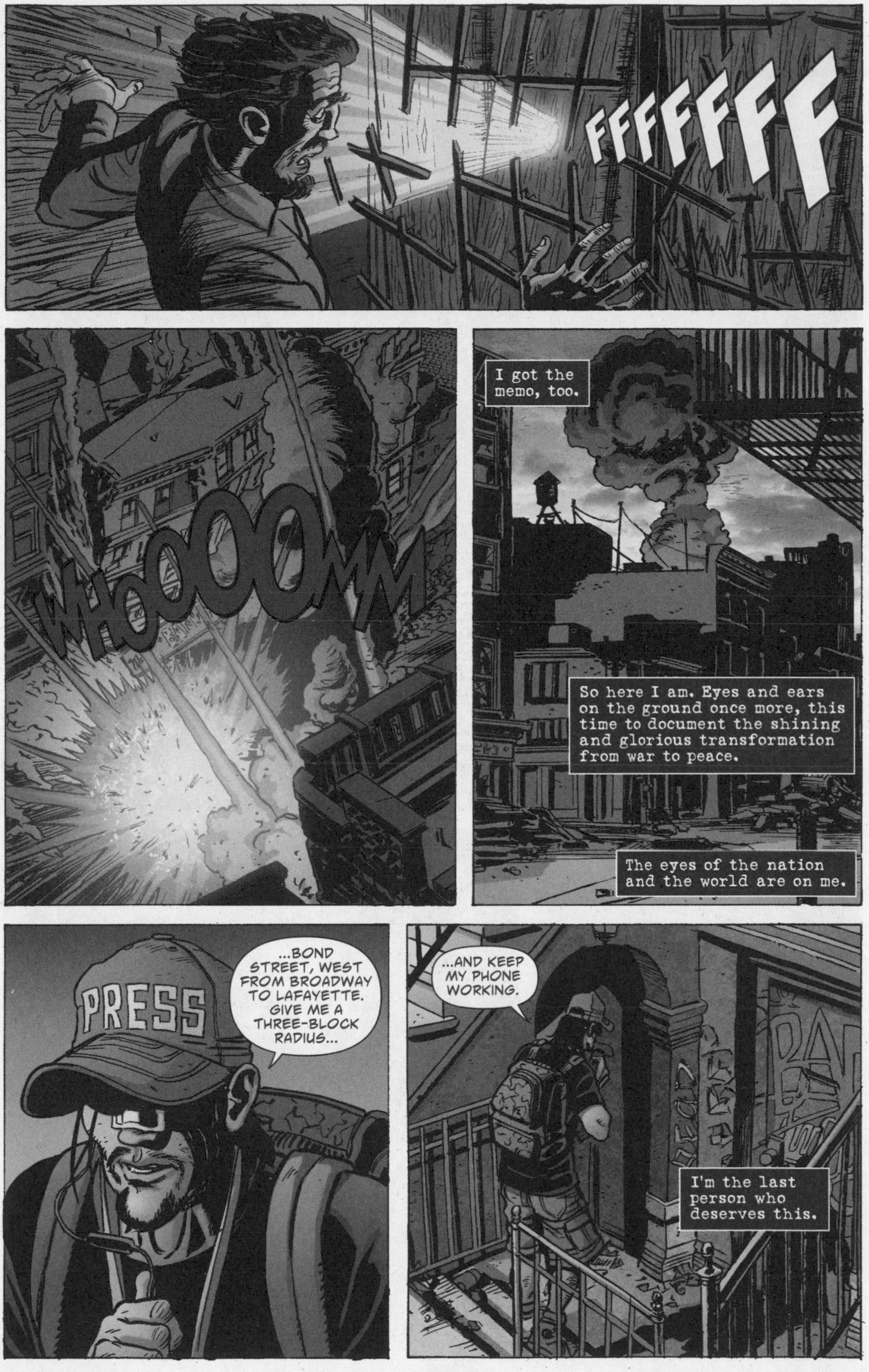
FFFFFF
WHOOOOMM
I got the memo, too.
So here I am. Eyes and ears on the ground once more, this time to document the shining and glorious transformation from war to peace.
The eyes of the nation and the world are on me.
PRESS
...BOND STREET, WEST FROM BROADWAY TO LAFAYETTE. GIVE ME A THREE-BLOCK RADIUS...
...AND KEEP MY PHONE WORKING.
I'm the last person who deserves this.

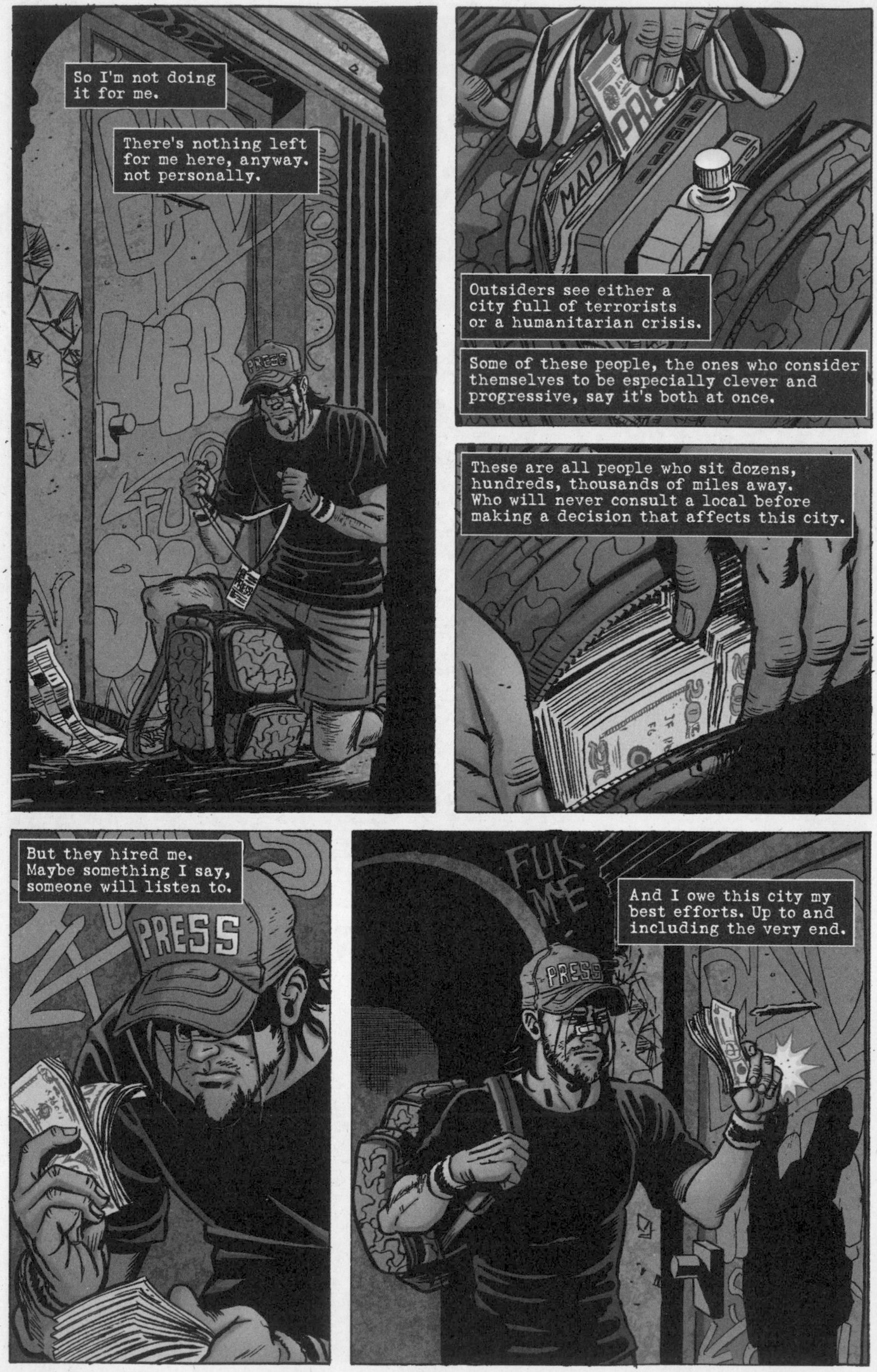
So I'm not doing it for me.
There's nothing left for me here, anyway. not personally.
PRESS
MAP
Outsiders see either a city full of terrorists or a humanitarian crisis.
Some of these people, the ones who consider themselves to be especially clever and progressive, say it's both at once.
These are all people who sit dozens, hundreds, thousands of miles away. Who will never consult a local before making a decision that affects this city.
But they hired me. Maybe something I say, someone will listen to.
PRESS
FUK ME
And I owe this city my best efforts. Up to and including the very end.
PRESS

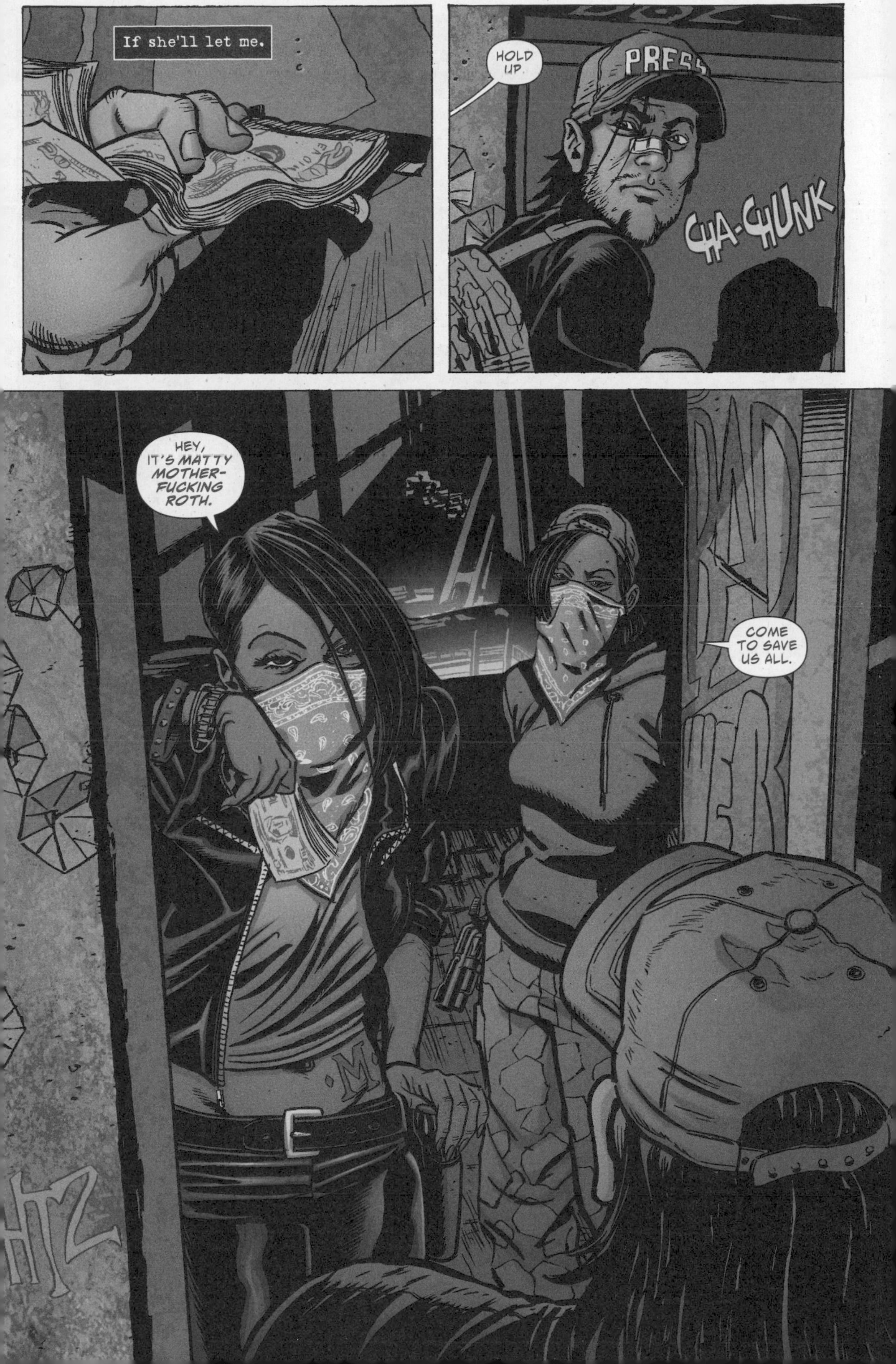
If she'll let me.
HOLD UP.
CHA-CHUNK
HEY, IT'S MATTY MOTHER-FUCKING ROTH.
COME TO SAVE US ALL.

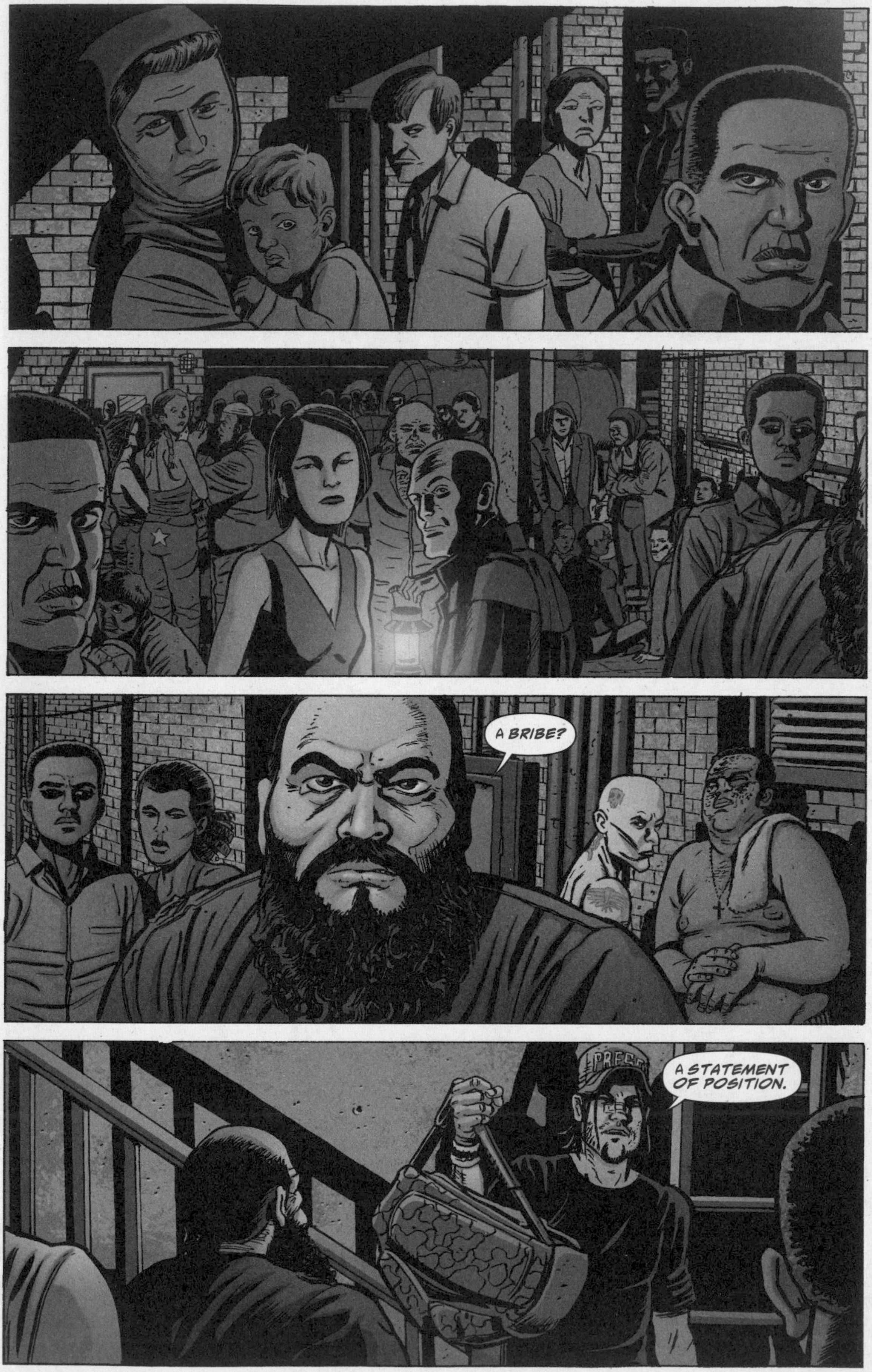
A BRIBE?
A STATEMENT OF POSITION.

WHAT IS IT?

A LIBERTY NEWS MEDIA KIT--LAPTOP, BROADCAST SOFTWARE, SOME MAPS. AND MY PRESS BADGE.

THERE'S LIKE TWENTY GRAND IN CASH IN HERE!

THAT TOO.

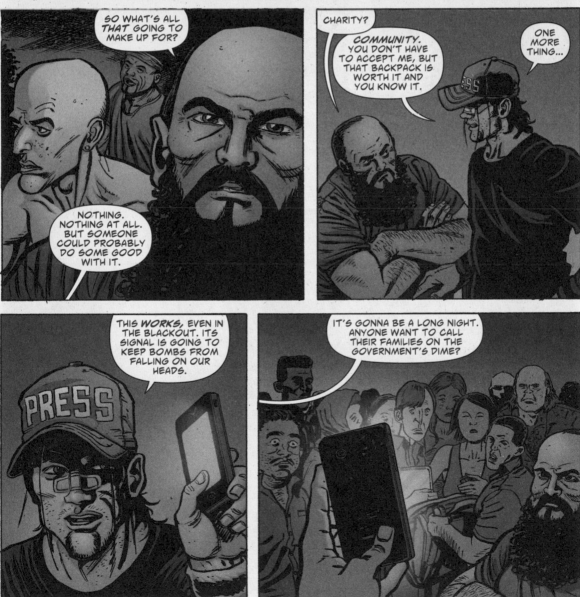

SO WHAT'S ALL THAT GOING TO MAKE UP FOR?

NOTHING. NOTHING AT ALL. BUT SOMEONE COULD PROBABLY DO SOME GOOD WITH IT.

CHARITY?

COMMUNITY. YOU DON'T HAVE TO ACCEPT ME, BUT THAT BACKPACK IS WORTH IT AND YOU KNOW IT.

ONE MORE THING...

THIS WORKS, EVEN IN THE BLACKOUT. ITS SIGNAL IS GOING TO KEEP BOMBS FROM FALLING ON OUR HEADS.

IT'S GONNA BE A LONG NIGHT. ANYONE WANT TO CALL THEIR FAMILIES ON THE GOVERNMENT'S DIME?

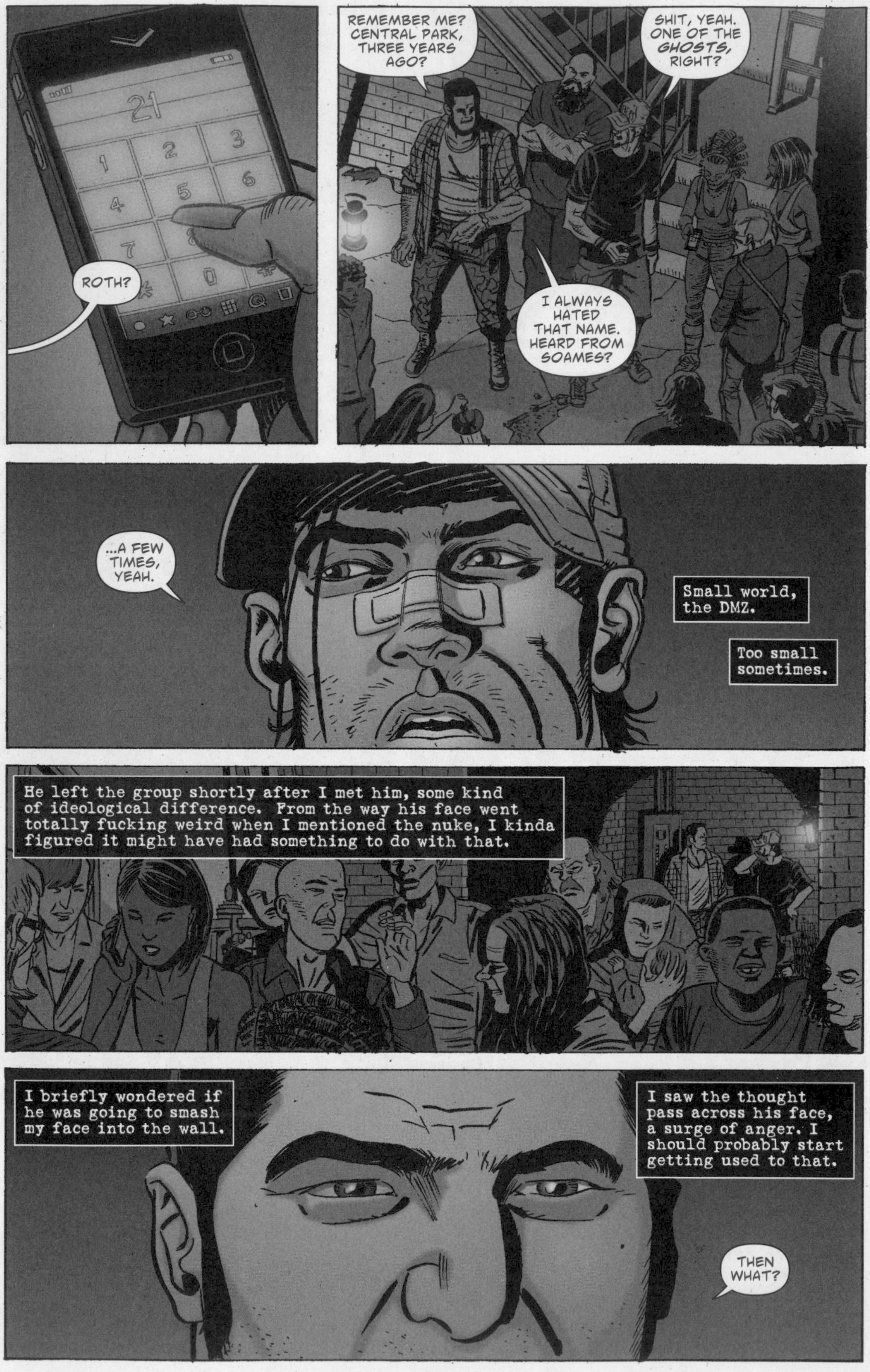
ROTH?
REMEMBER ME? CENTRAL PARK, THREE YEARS AGO?
SHIT, YEAH. ONE OF THE GHOSTS, RIGHT?
I ALWAYS HATED THAT NAME. HEARD FROM SOAMES?
...A FEW TIMES, YEAH.
Small world, the DMZ.
Too small sometimes.
He left the group shortly after I met him, some kind of ideological difference. From the way his face went totally fucking weird when I mentioned the nuke, I kinda figured it might have had something to do with that.
I briefly wondered if he was going to smash my face into the wall.
I saw the thought pass across his face, a surge of anger. I should probably start getting used to that.
THEN WHAT?

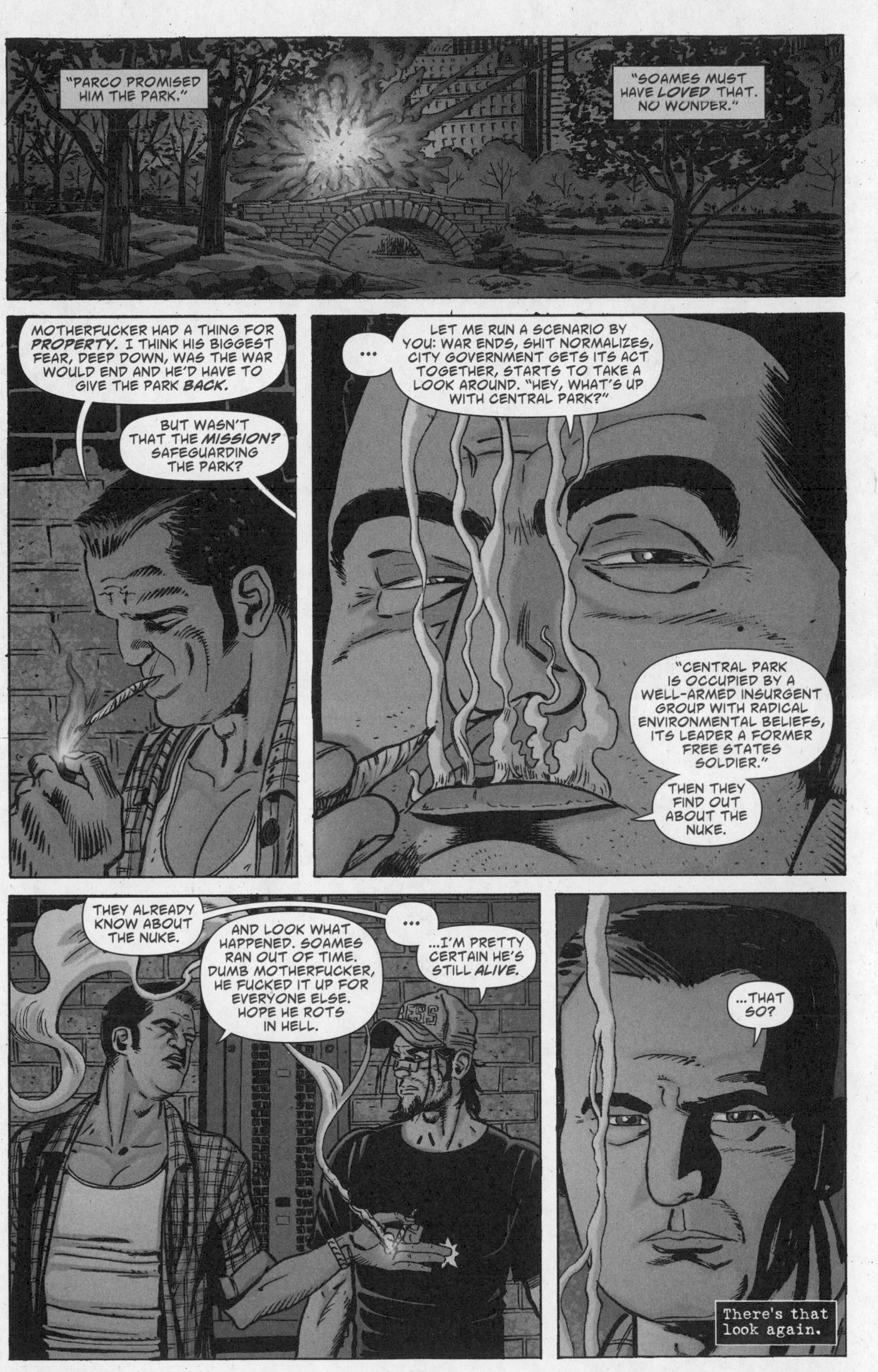
"PARCO PROMISED HIM THE PARK."
"SOAMES MUST HAVE LOVED THAT. NO WONDER."
MOTHERFUCKER HAD A THING FOR PROPERTY. I THINK HIS BIGGEST FEAR, DEEP DOWN, WAS THE WAR WOULD END AND HE'D HAVE TO GIVE THE PARK BACK.
BUT WASN'T THAT THE MISSION? SAFEGUARDING THE PARK?
...
LET ME RUN A SCENARIO BY YOU: WAR ENDS, SHIT NORMALIZES, CITY GOVERNMENT GETS ITS ACT TOGETHER, STARTS TO TAKE A LOOK AROUND. "HEY, WHAT'S UP WITH CENTRAL PARK?"
"CENTRAL PARK IS OCCUPIED BY A WELL-ARMED INSURGENT GROUP WITH RADICAL ENVIRONMENTAL BELIEFS, ITS LEADER A FORMER FREE STATES SOLDIER."
THEN THEY FIND OUT ABOUT THE NUKE.
THEY ALREADY KNOW ABOUT THE NUKE.
AND LOOK WHAT HAPPENED. SOAMES RAN OUT OF TIME. DUMB MOTHERFUCKER, HE FUCKED IT UP FOR EVERYONE ELSE. HOPE HE ROTS IN HELL.
...
...I'M PRETTY CERTAIN HE'S STILL ALIVE.
...THAT SO?
There's that look again.

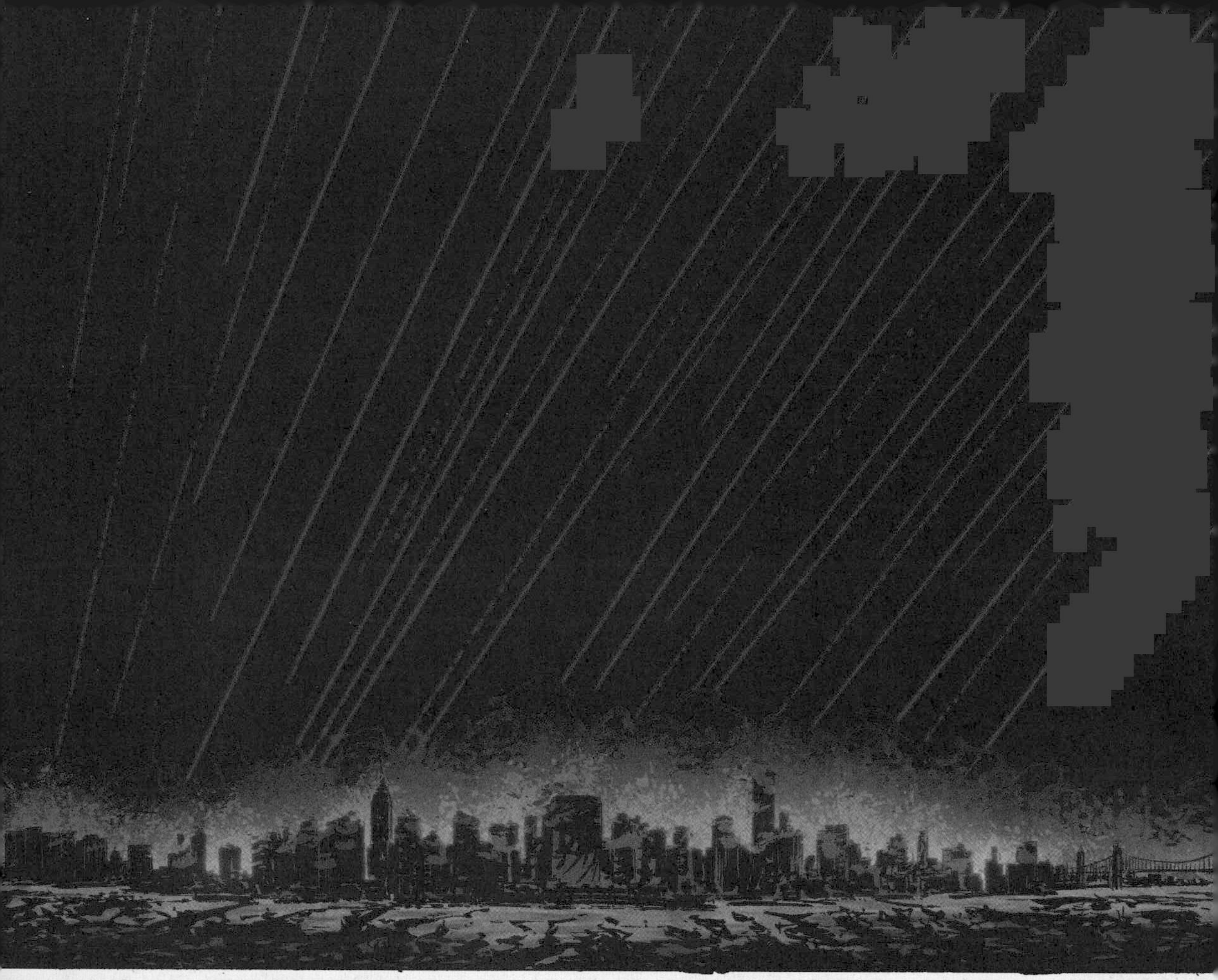

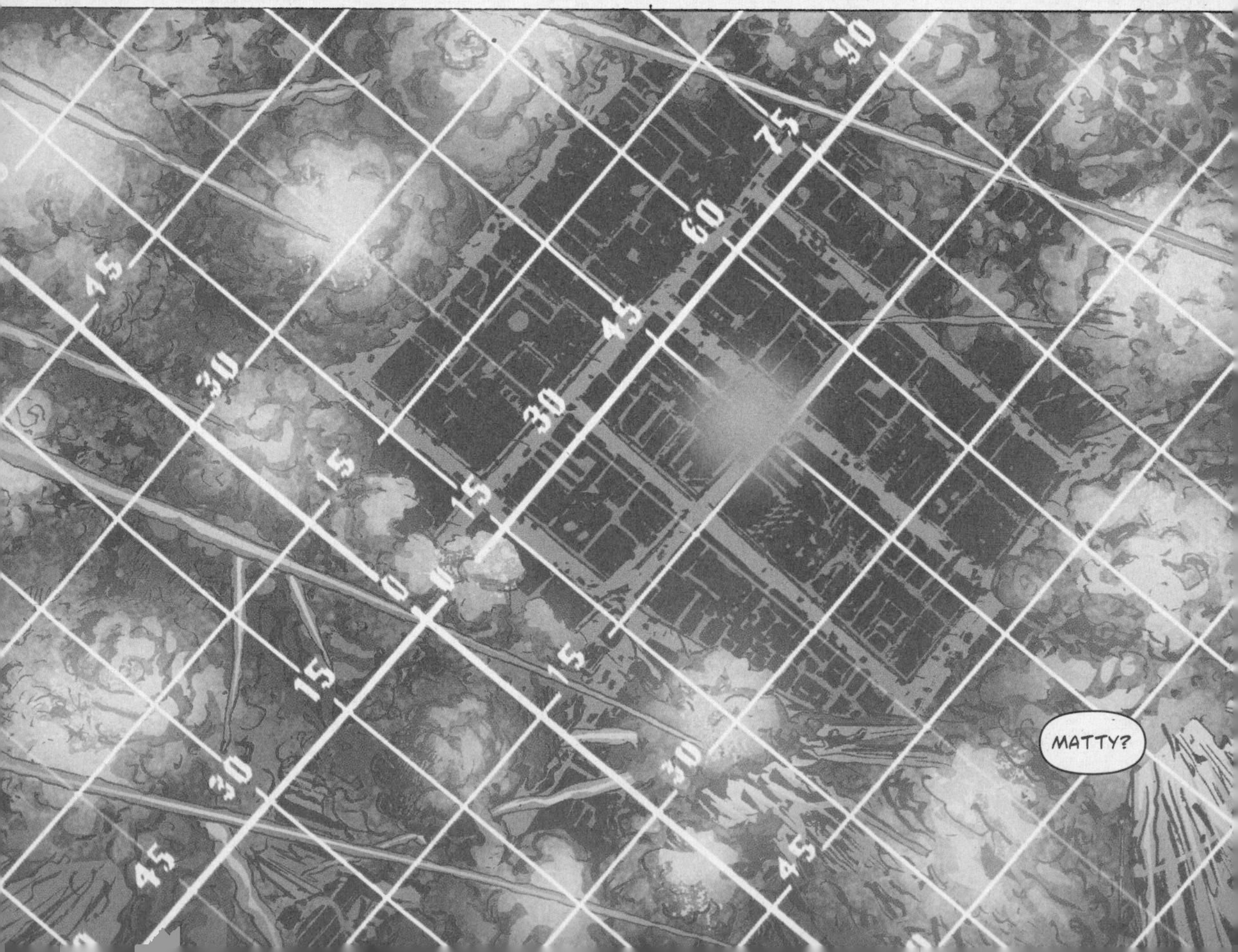
MATTY?

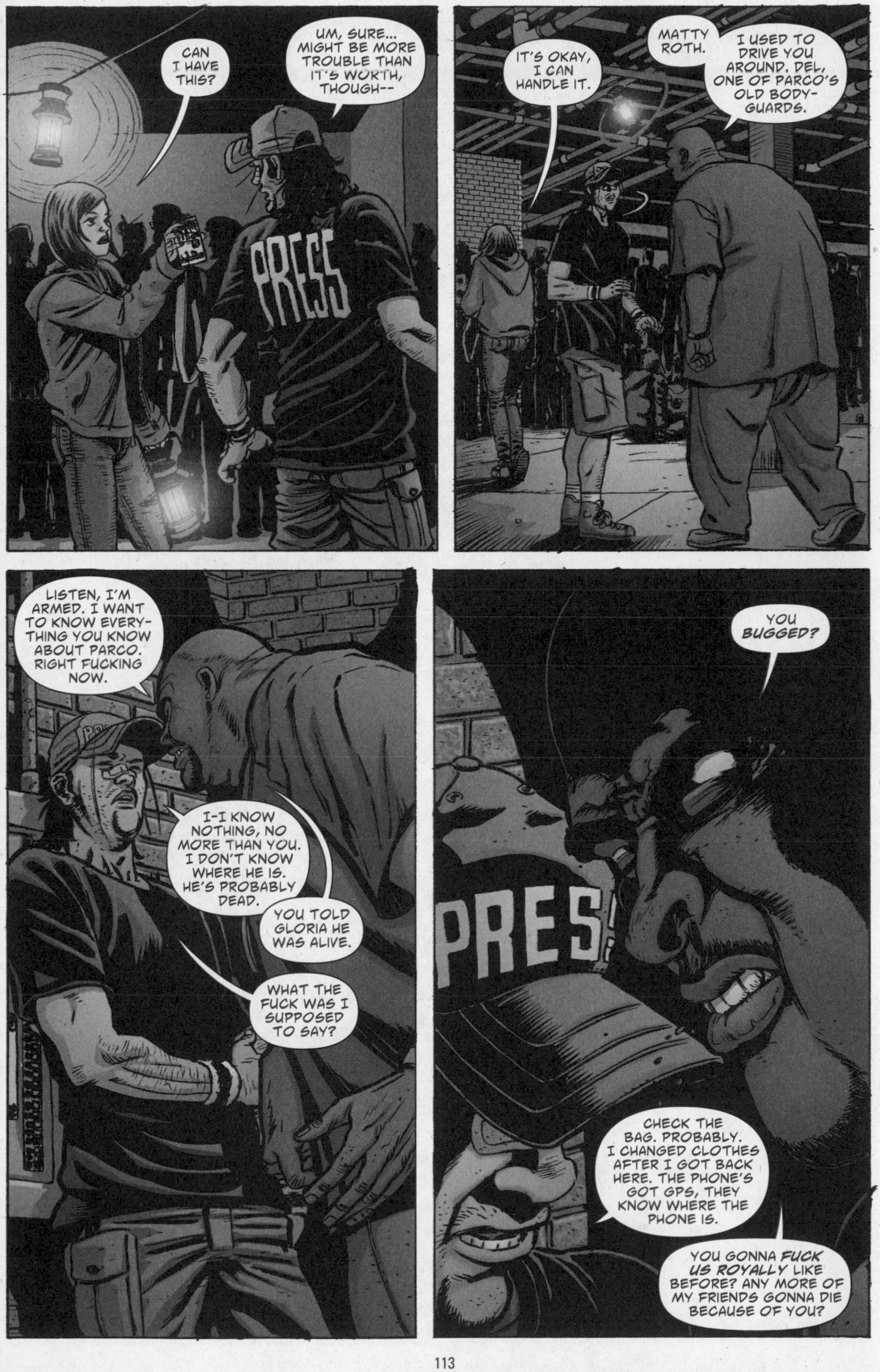
CAN I HAVE THIS?
UM, SURE... MIGHT BE MORE TROUBLE THAN IT'S WORTH, THOUGH--
PRESS
IT'S OKAY, I CAN HANDLE IT.
MATTY ROTH.
I USED TO DRIVE YOU AROUND. DEL, ONE OF PARCO'S OLD BODY-GUARDS.
LISTEN, I'M ARMED. I WANT TO KNOW EVERY-THING YOU KNOW ABOUT PARCO. RIGHT FUCKING NOW.
I-I KNOW NOTHING, NO MORE THAN YOU. I DON'T KNOW WHERE HE IS. HE'S PROBABLY DEAD.
YOU TOLD GLORIA HE WAS ALIVE.
WHAT THE FUCK WAS I SUPPOSED TO SAY?
YOU *BUGGED?*
PRES
CHECK THE BAG. PROBABLY. I CHANGED CLOTHES AFTER I GOT BACK HERE. THE PHONE'S GOT GPS, THEY KNOW WHERE THE PHONE IS.
YOU GONNA *FUCK US ROYALLY* LIKE BEFORE? ANY MORE OF MY FRIENDS GONNA DIE BECAUSE OF YOU?

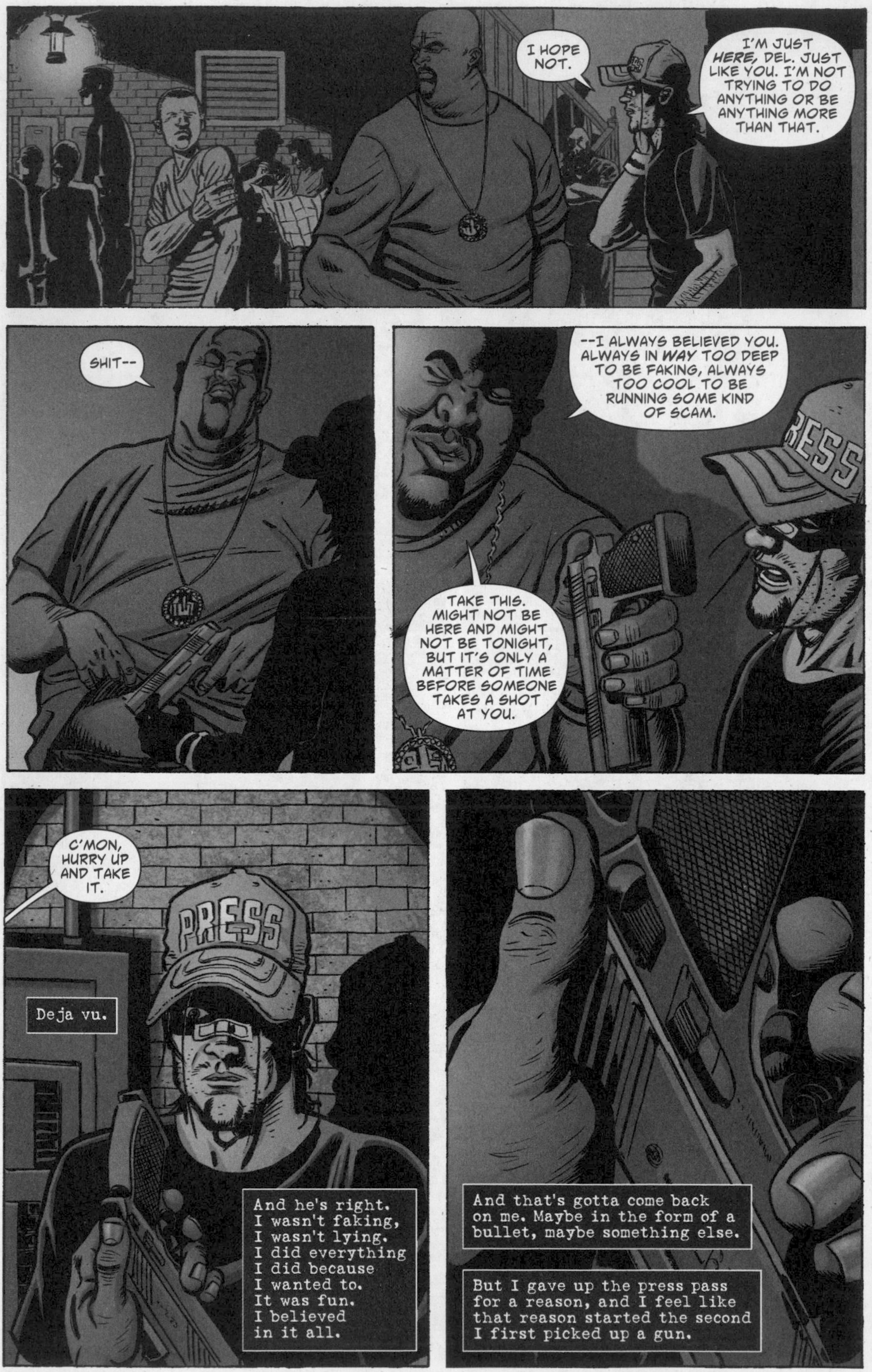

I HOPE NOT.
I'M JUST HERE, DEL. JUST LIKE YOU. I'M NOT TRYING TO DO ANYTHING OR BE ANYTHING MORE THAN THAT.
SHIT--
--I ALWAYS BELIEVED YOU. ALWAYS IN WAY TOO DEEP TO BE FAKING, ALWAYS TOO COOL TO BE RUNNING SOME KIND OF SCAM.
PRESS
TAKE THIS. MIGHT NOT BE HERE AND MIGHT NOT BE TONIGHT, BUT IT'S ONLY A MATTER OF TIME BEFORE SOMEONE TAKES A SHOT AT YOU.
C'MON, HURRY UP AND TAKE IT.
PRESS
Deja vu.
And he's right. I wasn't faking, I wasn't lying. I did everything I did because I wanted to. It was fun. I believed in it all.
And that's gotta come back on me. Maybe in the form of a bullet, maybe something else.
But I gave up the press pass for a reason, and I feel like that reason started the second I first picked up a gun.

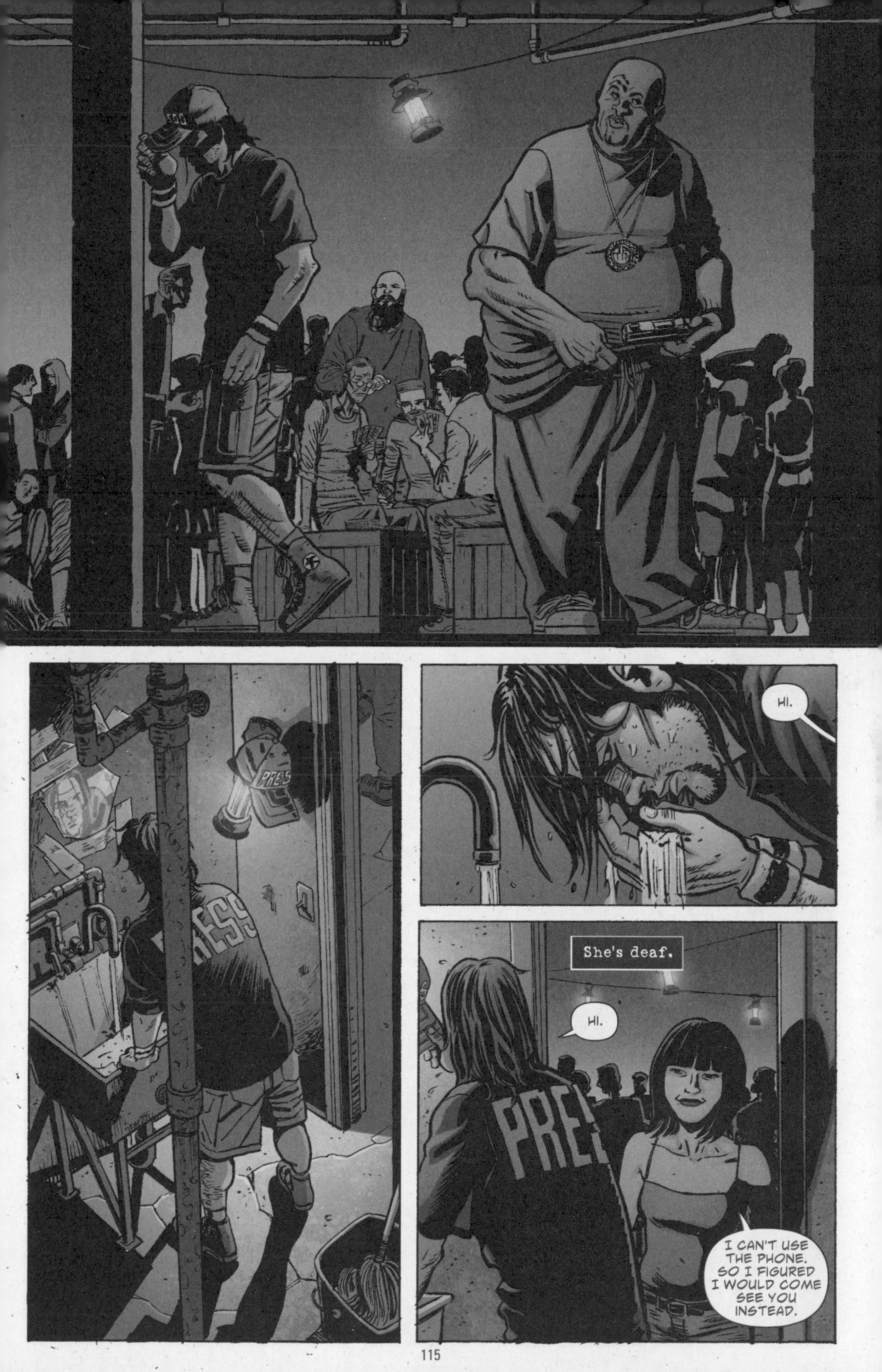
HI.
She's deaf.
HI.
I CAN'T USE THE PHONE. SO I FIGURED I WOULD COME SEE YOU INSTEAD.

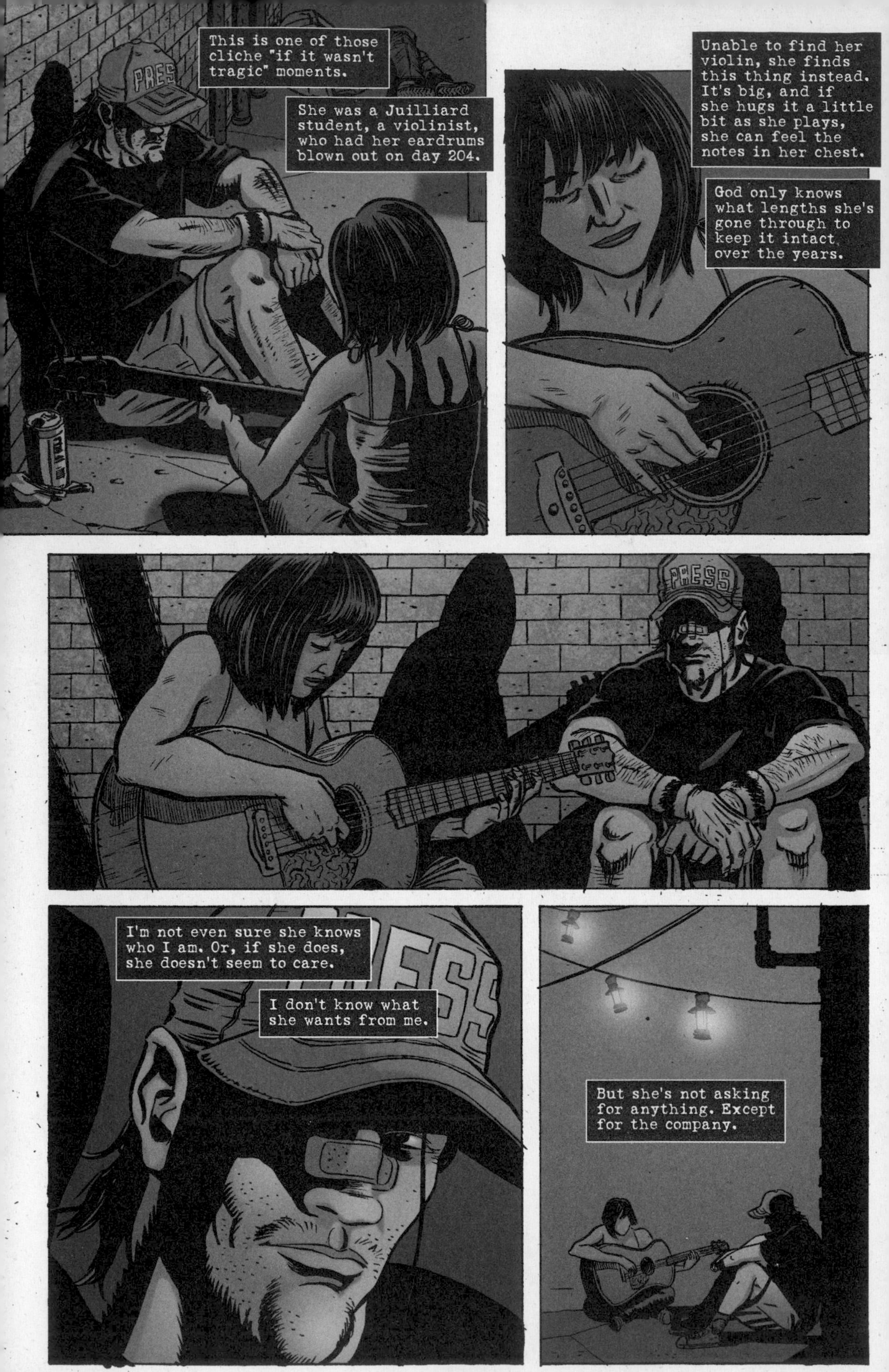
This is one of those cliche "if it wasn't tragic" moments.
She was a Juilliard student, a violinist, who had her eardrums blown out on day 204.
PRES
Unable to find her violin, she finds this thing instead. It's big, and if she hugs it a little bit as she plays, she can feel the notes in her chest.
God only knows what lengths she's gone through to keep it intact over the years.
PRESS
I'm not even sure she knows who I am. Or, if she does, she doesn't seem to care.
I don't know what she wants from me.
But she's not asking for anything. Except for the company.

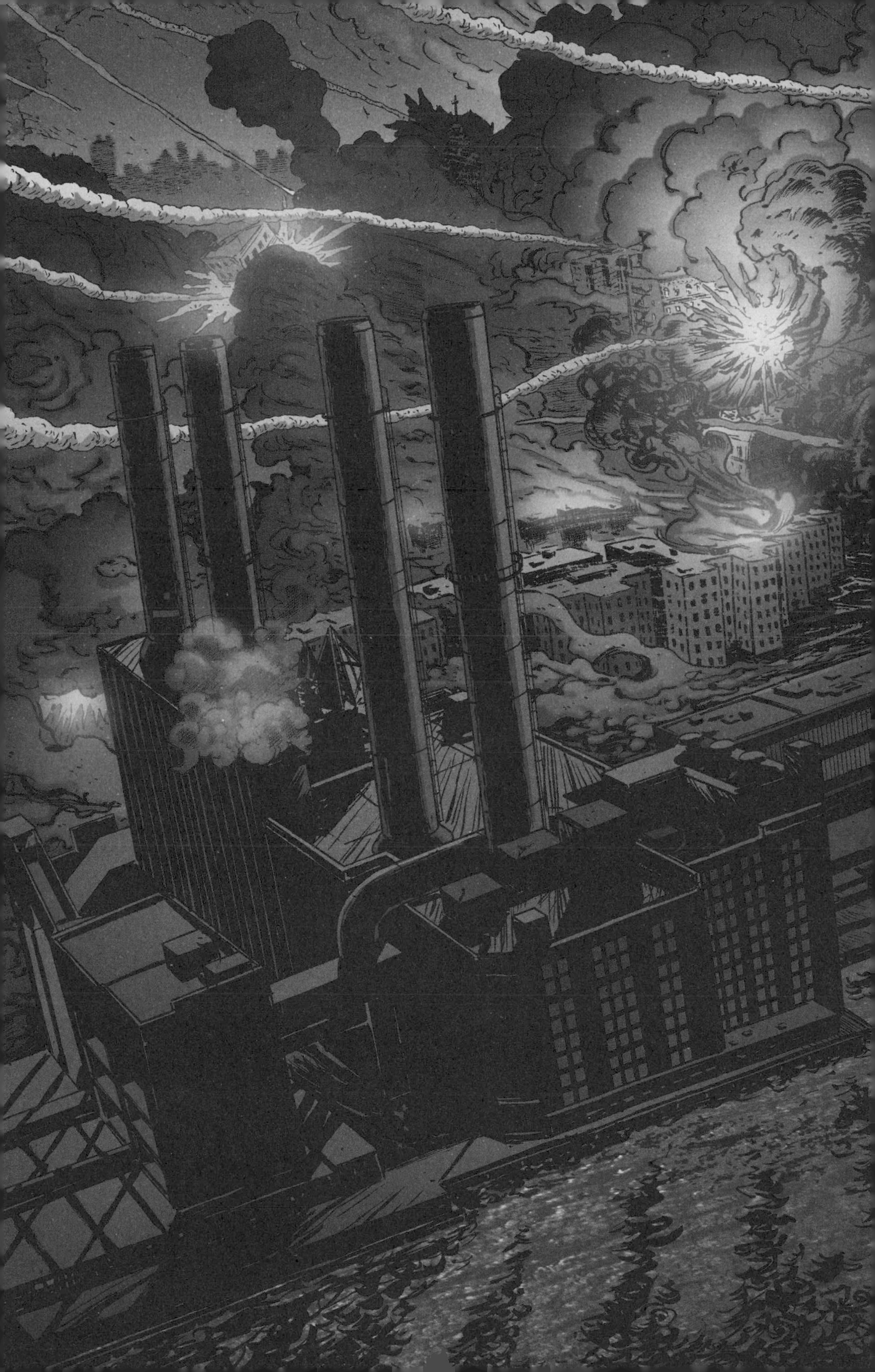

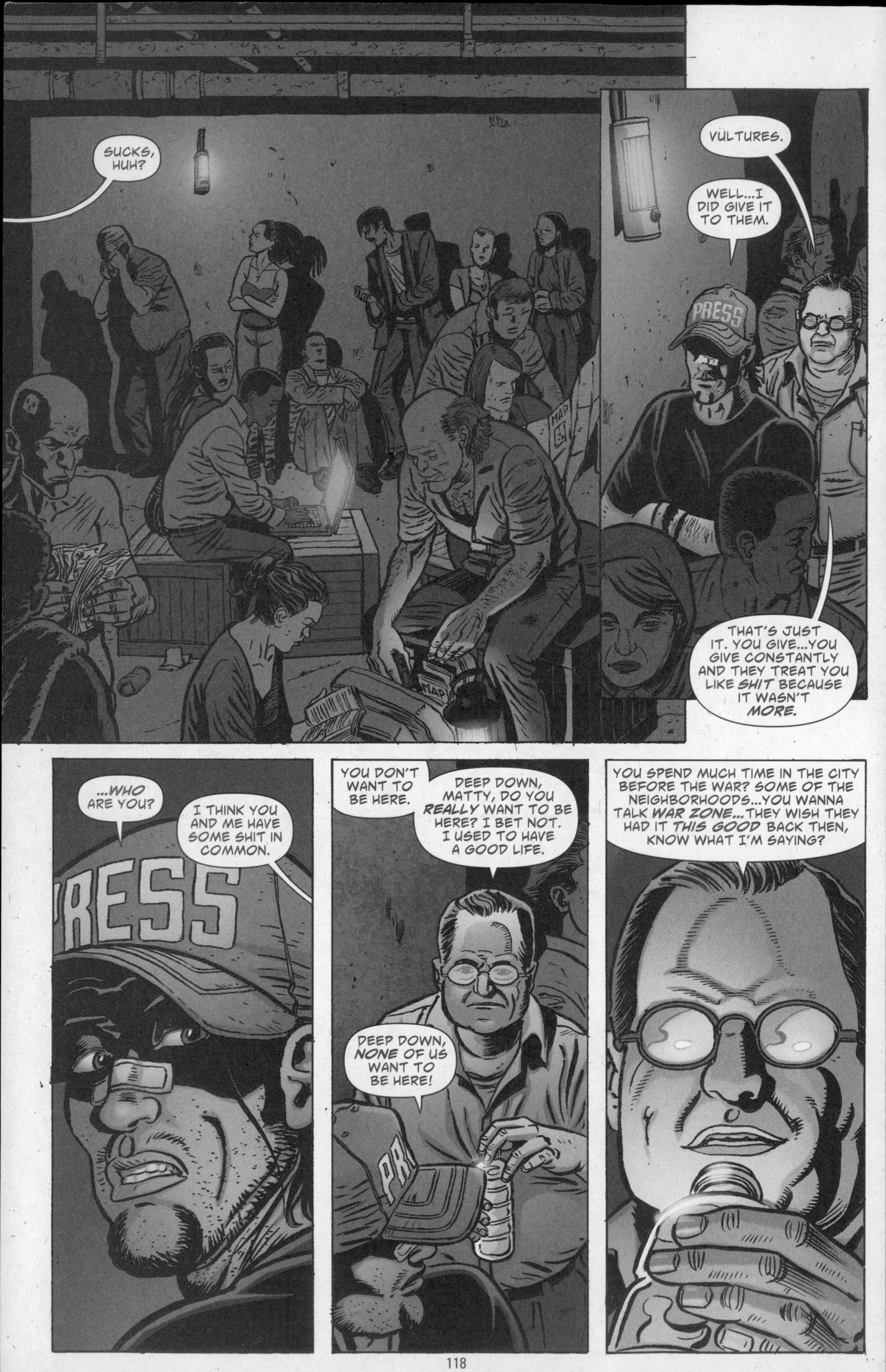
SUCKS, HUH?
VULTURES.
WELL...I DID GIVE IT TO THEM.
THAT'S JUST IT. YOU GIVE...YOU GIVE CONSTANTLY AND THEY TREAT YOU LIKE SHIT BECAUSE IT WASN'T MORE.
...WHO ARE YOU?
I THINK YOU AND ME HAVE SOME SHIT IN COMMON.
YOU DON'T WANT TO BE HERE.
DEEP DOWN, MATTY, DO YOU REALLY WANT TO BE HERE? I BET NOT. I USED TO HAVE A GOOD LIFE.
DEEP DOWN, NONE OF US WANT TO BE HERE!
YOU SPEND MUCH TIME IN THE CITY BEFORE THE WAR? SOME OF THE NEIGHBORHOODS...YOU WANNA TALK WAR ZONE...THEY WISH THEY HAD IT THIS GOOD BACK THEN, KNOW WHAT I'M SAYING?

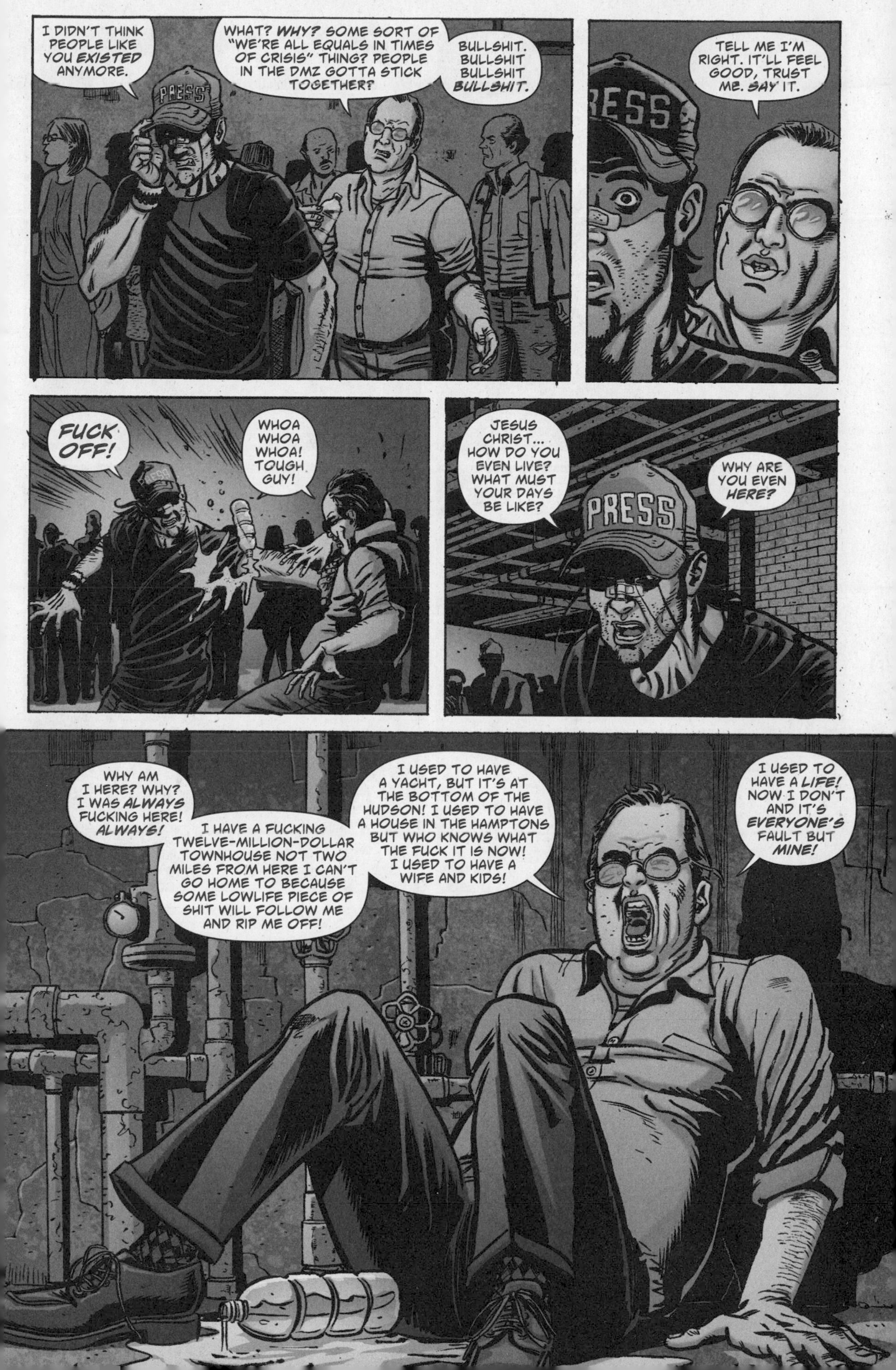
I DIDN'T THINK PEOPLE LIKE YOU EXISTED ANYMORE.
WHAT? WHY? SOME SORT OF "WE'RE ALL EQUALS IN TIMES OF CRISIS" THING? PEOPLE IN THE DMZ GOTTA STICK TOGETHER?
BULLSHIT. BULLSHIT BULLSHIT BULLSHIT.
PRESS
TELL ME I'M RIGHT. IT'LL FEEL GOOD, TRUST ME. SAY IT.
FUCK OFF!
WHOA WHOA WHOA! TOUGH GUY!
JESUS CHRIST... HOW DO YOU EVEN LIVE? WHAT MUST YOUR DAYS BE LIKE?
WHY ARE YOU EVEN HERE?
PRESS
WHY AM I HERE? WHY? I WAS ALWAYS FUCKING HERE! ALWAYS!
I HAVE A FUCKING TWELVE-MILLION-DOLLAR TOWNHOUSE NOT TWO MILES FROM HERE I CAN'T GO HOME TO BECAUSE SOME LOWLIFE PIECE OF SHIT WILL FOLLOW ME AND RIP ME OFF!
I USED TO HAVE A YACHT, BUT IT'S AT THE BOTTOM OF THE HUDSON! I USED TO HAVE A HOUSE IN THE HAMPTONS BUT WHO KNOWS WHAT THE FUCK IT IS NOW! I USED TO HAVE A WIFE AND KIDS!
I USED TO HAVE A LIFE! NOW I DON'T AND IT'S EVERYONE'S FAULT BUT MINE!

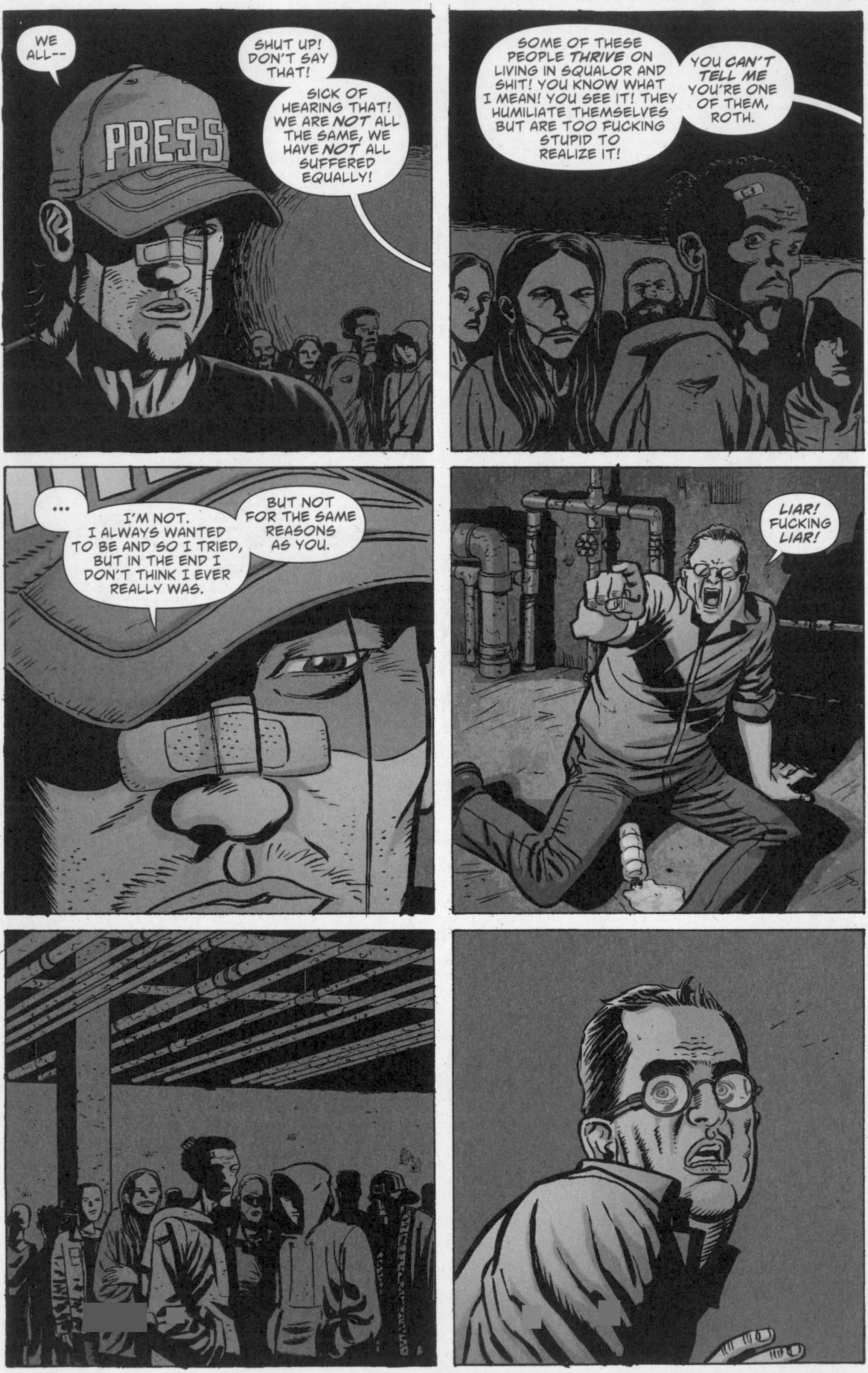
WE ALL--
SHUT UP! DON'T SAY THAT!
SICK OF HEARING THAT! WE ARE NOT ALL THE SAME, WE HAVE NOT ALL SUFFERED EQUALLY!
PRESS
SOME OF THESE PEOPLE THRIVE ON LIVING IN SQUALOR AND SHIT! YOU KNOW WHAT I MEAN! YOU SEE IT! THEY HUMILIATE THEMSELVES BUT ARE TOO FUCKING STUPID TO REALIZE IT!
YOU CAN'T TELL ME YOU'RE ONE OF THEM, ROTH.
...
I'M NOT. I ALWAYS WANTED TO BE AND SO I TRIED, BUT IN THE END I DON'T THINK I EVER REALLY WAS.
BUT NOT FOR THE SAME REASONS AS YOU.
LIAR! FUCKING LIAR!

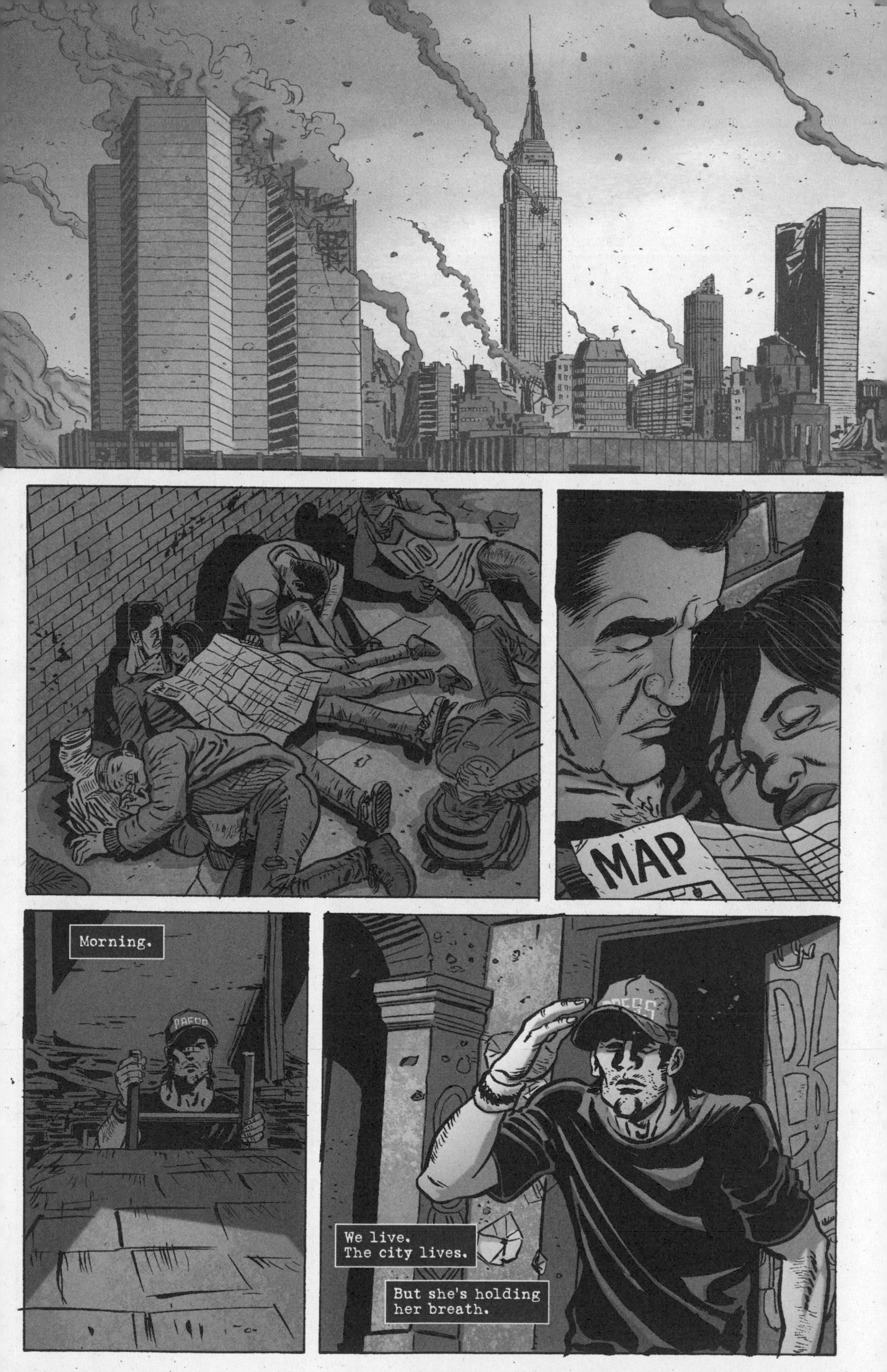
MAP
Morning.
PRESS
We live.
The city lives.
But she's holding
her breath.

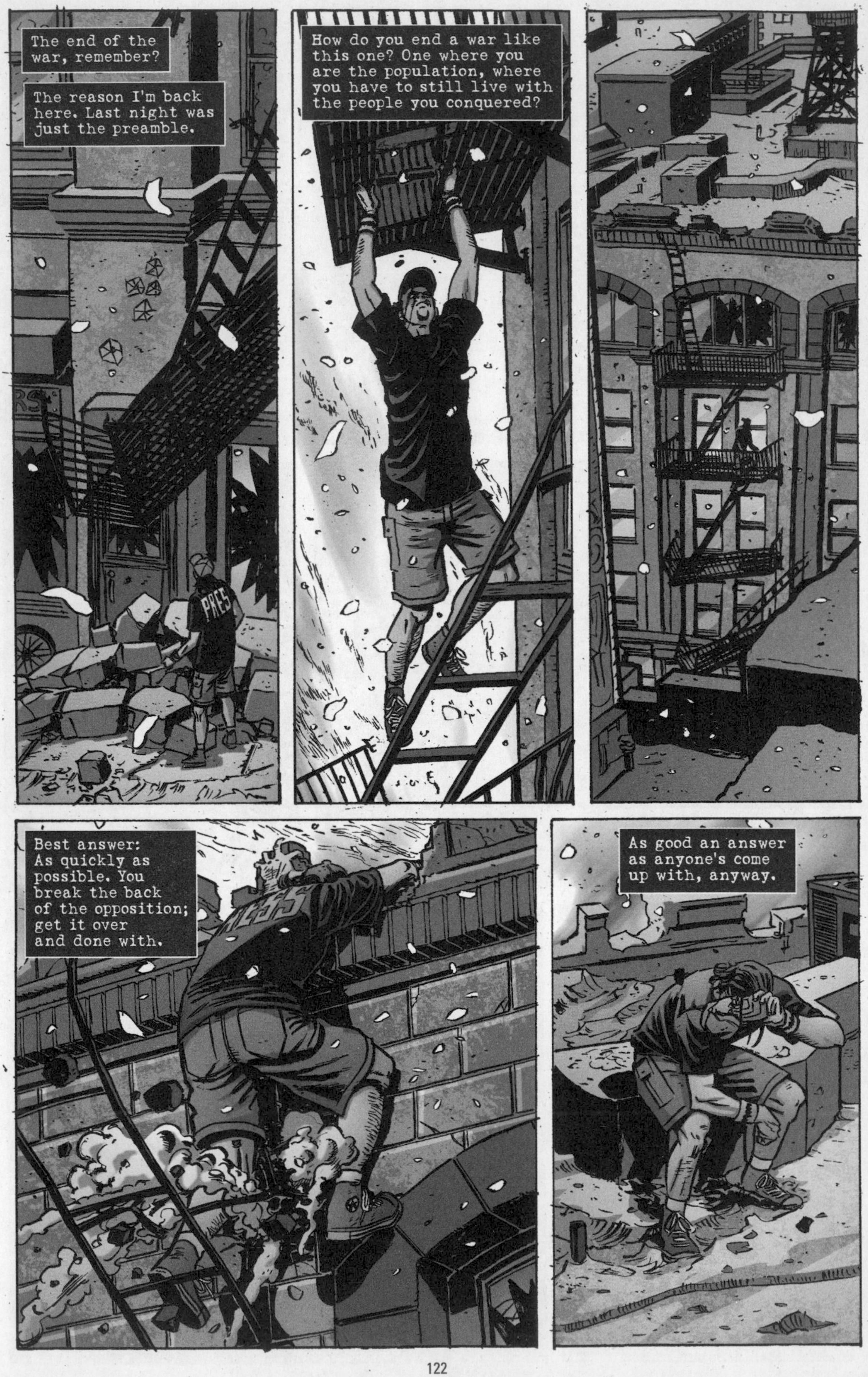

The end of the war, remember?
The reason I'm back here. Last night was just the preamble.
PRES
How do you end a war like this one? One where you are the population, where you have to still live with the people you conquered?
Best answer: As quickly as possible. You break the back of the opposition; get it over and done with.
As good an answer as anyone's come up with, anyway.

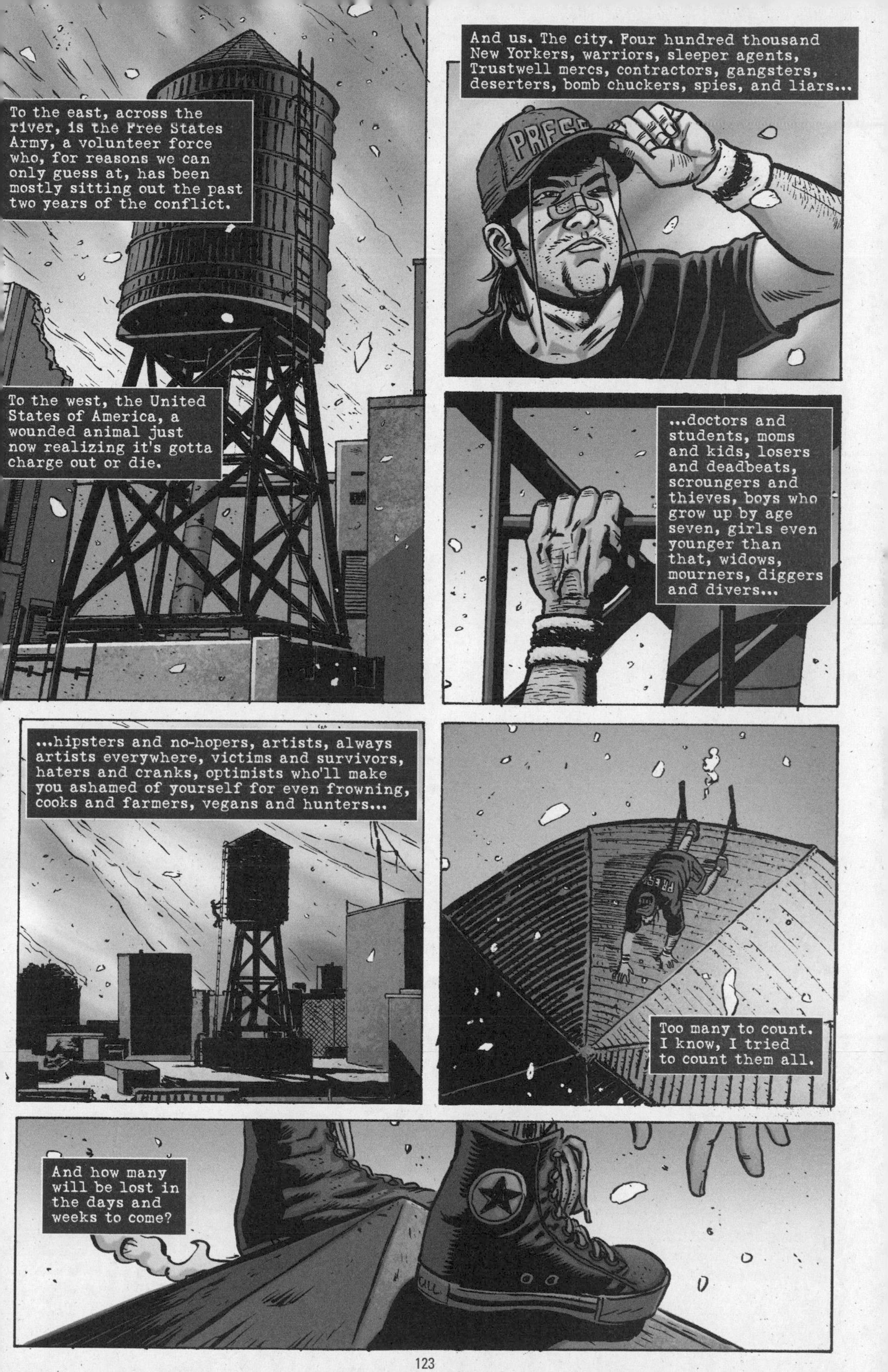
To the east, across the river, is the Free States Army, a volunteer force who, for reasons we can only guess at, has been mostly sitting out the past two years of the conflict.
To the west, the United States of America, a wounded animal just now realizing it's gotta charge out or die.
And us. The city. Four hundred thousand New Yorkers, warriors, sleeper agents, Trustwell mercs, contractors, gangsters, deserters, bomb chuckers, spies, and liars...
PRESS
...doctors and students, moms and kids, losers and deadbeats, scroungers and thieves, boys who grow up by age seven, girls even younger than that, widows, mourners, diggers and divers...
...hipsters and no-hopers, artists, always artists everywhere, victims and survivors, haters and cranks, optimists who'll make you ashamed of yourself for even frowning, cooks and farmers, vegans and hunters...
Too many to count. I know, I tried to count them all.
And how many will be lost in the days and weeks to come?

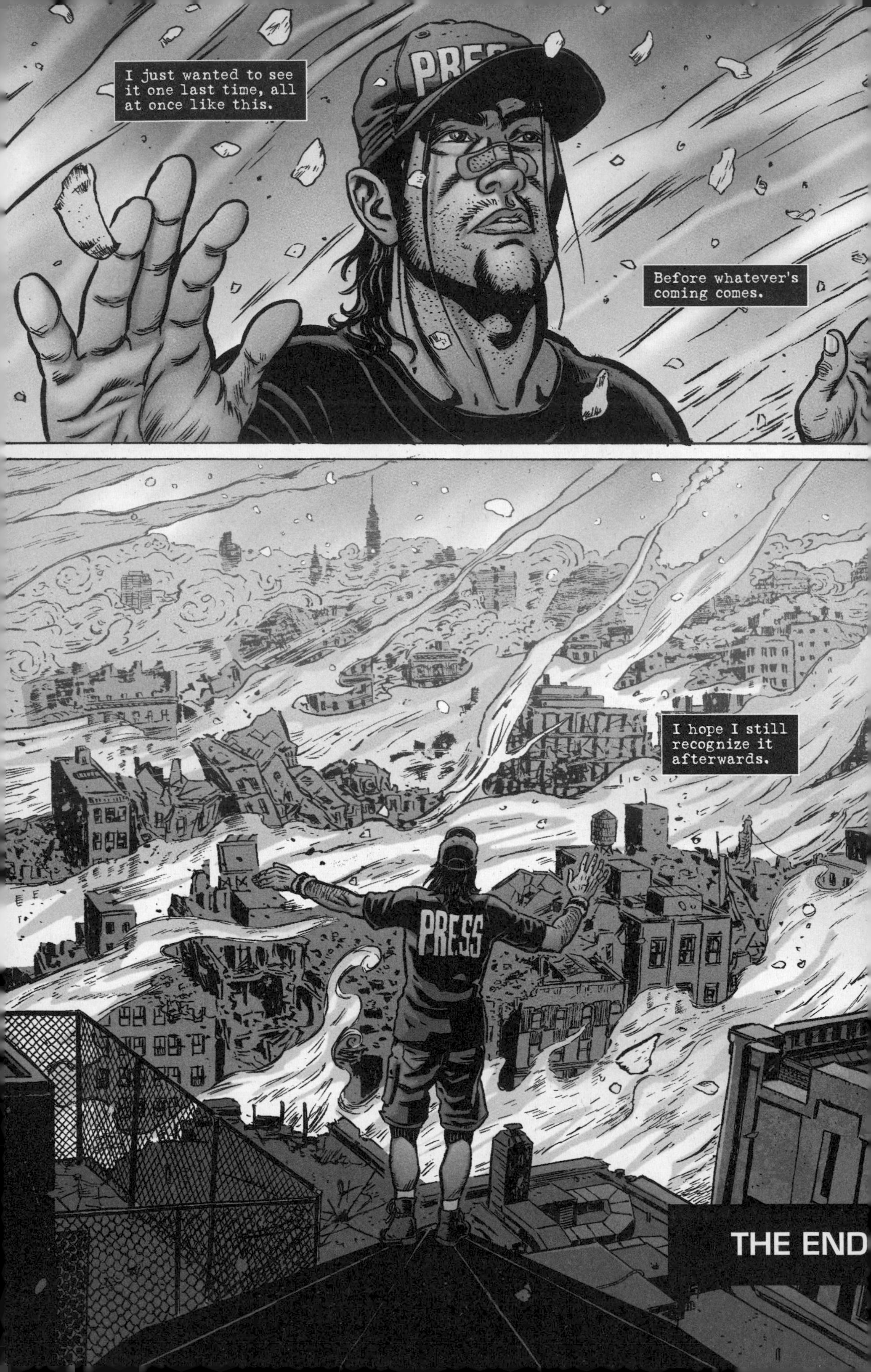
PRESS
I just wanted to see it one last time, all at once like this.
Before whatever's coming comes.
I hope I still recognize it afterwards.
PRESS
THE END

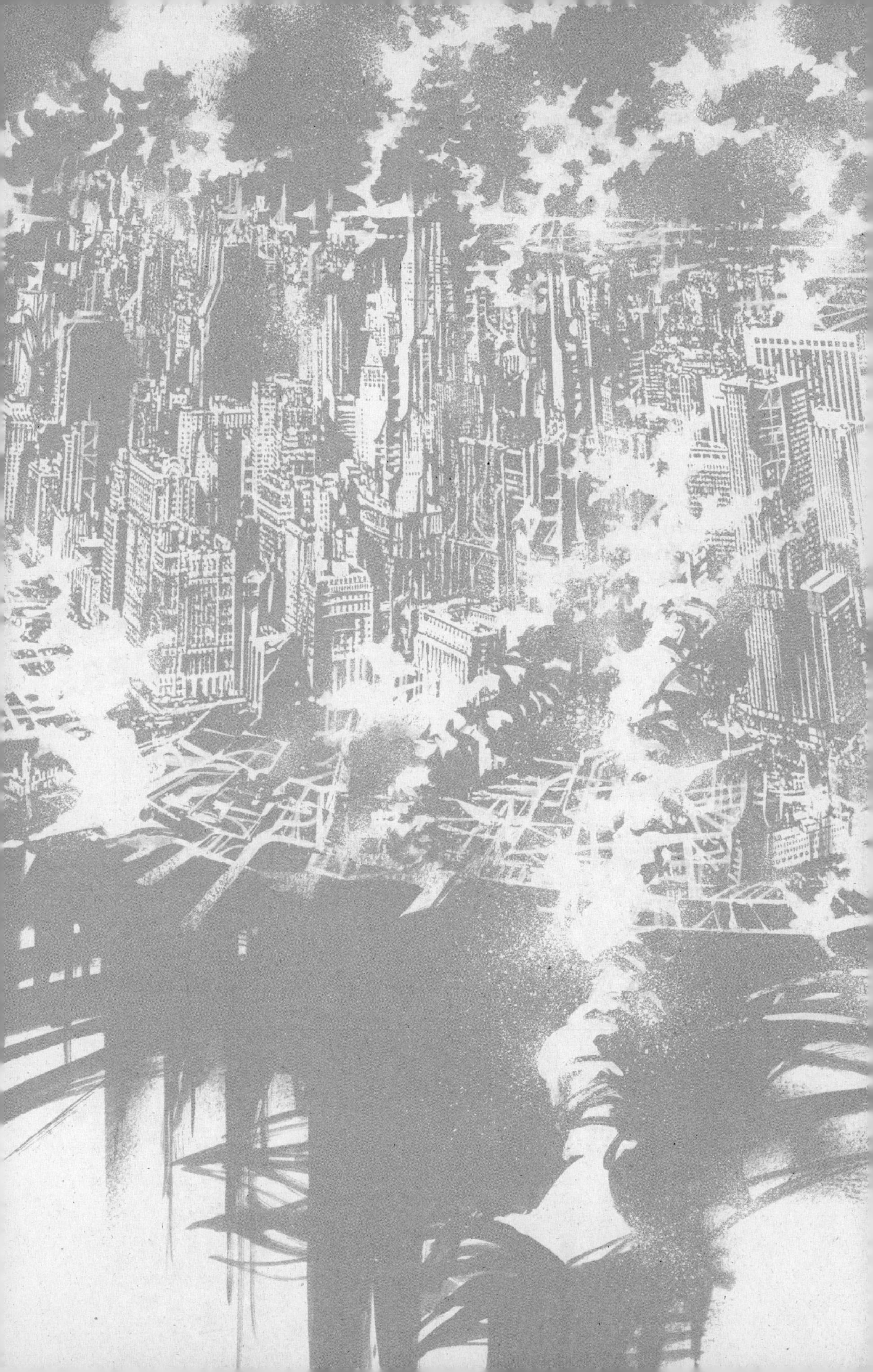

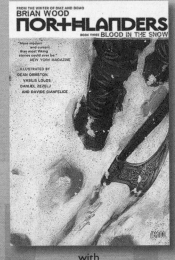
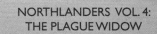

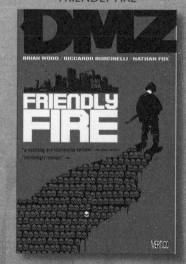

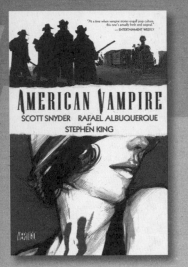
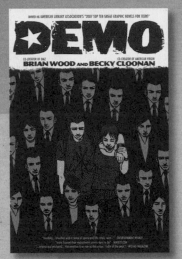
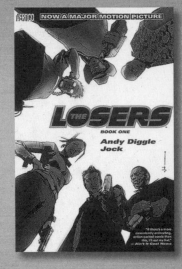
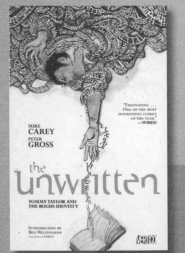